Lecture Notes in Artificial Intel

Subseries of Lecture Notes in Computer Scie
Edited by J. G. Carbonell and J. Siekmann

Lecture Notes in Computer Science
Edited by G. Goos, J. Hartmanis and J. van Leeuwen

Springer

Berlin
Heidelberg
New York
Barcelona
Hong Kong
London
Milan
Paris
Singapore
Tokyo

Anca L. Ralescu   James G. Shanahan (Eds.)

Fuzzy Logic in Artificial Intelligence

IJCAI'97 Workshop
Nagoya, Japan, August 23-24, 1997
Selected and Invited Papers

 Springer

Series Editors

Jaime G. Carbonell, Carnegie Mellon University, Pittsburgh, PA, USA
Jörg Siekmann, University of Saarland, Saarbrücken, Germany

Volume Editors

Anca L. Ralescu
University of Cincinnati, ML 0030, ECECS Department
Cincinnati, Ohio 45221-0030, USA
E-mail: Anca.Ralescu@uc.edu
and
Laboratory for Information Synthesis, Brain Science Institute, RIKEN
2-1 Hirosawa, Wako-shi, Saitama, 351-0198, Japan
E-mail: anca@islab.brain.riken.go.jp

James G. Shanahan
Xerox Research Centre Europe (XRCE)
6, Chemin de Maupertuis, F-38240 Meylan, France
E-mail: James.Shanahan@xrce.xerox.com

Cataloging-in-Publication data applied for

Die Deutsche Bibliothek - CIP-Einheitsaufnahme

Fuzzy logic in artificial intelligence : selected papers / IJCAI '97 workshop,
Nagoya, Japan, August, 1997. Anca L. Ralescu ; Jasmes G. Shanahan (ed.). -
Berlin ; Heidelberg ; New York ; Barcelona ; Hong Kong ; London ; Milan ; Paris ;
Singapore ; Tokyo : Springer, 1999
  (Lecture notes in computer science ; Vol. 1566 : Lecture notes in artificial
  intelligence)
  ISBN 3-540-66374-6

CR Subject Classification (1998): I.2, F.4.1, I.5.1, J.2

ISBN 3-540-66374-6 Springer-Verlag Berlin Heidelberg New York

© Springer-Verlag Berlin Heidelberg 1999
Printed in Germany

Typesetting: Camera-ready by author
SPIN 10702971   06/3142 – 5 4 3 2 1 0   Printed on acid-free paper

We dedicate our work for this volume to
Professor Toshiro Terano

Anca. L. Ralescu
James G. Shanahan

Preface

The present volume is the fourth in Springer-Verlag's Lecture Notes in Artificial Intelligence series dedicated to the subject of Fuzzy Logic in AI. Like the preceding volumes, it is designed around an IJCAI event, this time the Fuzzy Logic in AI Workshop held in conjunction with IJCAI'97, in Nagoya, Japan, in the last week of August 1997. As for the preceding volumes, the participants of the workshops have been encouraged to submit significantly enhanced and revised versions of their workshop contributions. Furthermore, we are including a few invited contributions of work not presented at the workshop, as we did in the previous volumes.

As it happens, this volume is the last one of the 90's. As this is the last decade of a century and millennium, people all over the world have felt the need to ponder about various aspects of their lives, of the state of mankind, etc. On a much smaller scale we too thought that it would be interesting to include in this volume several opinions about the relevance of fuzzy logic to AI. Thus the first three contributions, by Lotfi Zadeh, Didier Dubois and Henri Prade, and James F. Baldwin address directly the relevance of fuzzy sets and fuzzy logic to AI. Each of these contributions reflects, as expected, the rich experience that their authors have in the field. To begin with, Lotfi Zadeh, the founder of fuzzy sets theory and fuzzy logic, presents a compelling argument as to why fuzzy logic is relevant and indeed indispensable to AI. Didier Dubois and Henri Prade present a well documented and formal argument which reflects their very important contribution to the field. It should be mentioned here that by their contributions to each of the IJCAI workshops on fuzzy logic, since the first one in 1991, they have been the most loyal supporters of these events. Finally, Jim Baldwin's contribution presents the relevance of fuzzy sets, as treated in the mass assignment theory, to the concept of computing with words. It too reflects his experience accumulated over a long period of work in this field. We believe that many more longtime researchers in fuzzy logic could have contributed their wisdom to this very important question of the relevance of fuzzy sets and fuzzy logic to AI. Perhaps a future book project could indeed collect many more views on the subject.

The remaining thirteen contributions range from theoretical to applied. They encompass subjects such as knowledge representation and induction, based on ID3 (H. Narazaki and I. Shigaki), or on cartesian fuzzy granules (J. F. Baldwin, T. P. Martin, and James G. Shanahan), case-based reasoning (D. Dubois, F. Esteva, P. Garcia, L. Godo, R. López de Màntaras, and H. Prade), object-oriented logic programming with uncertainty (J. F. Baldwin, T. P. Martin, and M. Vargas-Vera), fusion of symbolic and computational processing for user interfaces (S. Tano), treatment of generalized quantifiers (A. L. Ralescu, D. A. Ralescu, and K. Hirota), neuro-fuzzy methods - an algorithm (V. Niskanen), and applications to air traffic management (L. Zerrouki, B. Bouchon-Meunier,

R. Fondacci, S. Selam), and applications to robotics (J. Zhang and A. Knoll). Several contributions concern problems in image understanding, ranging from reasoning with words about geographic information (Hans W. Guesgen), fuzzy morphology and fuzzy distances (Isabelle Bloch), possibility theory for classification of satellite images (Ludovic Roux), pattern recognition based on possibilistic c-means (L. Wendling and J. Desachy).

We hope that the present volume, in its variety, will be of use to its readers regardless of their involvement with the field of fuzzy logic. Indeed, we hope that it offers once again, a window into the fascinating and challenging world of intelligent systems built on and with fuzzy sets and fuzzy logic.

We thank the contributing authors, some of whom must forgive us for frequent reminders, and Alfred Hofmann of Springer-Verlag for his support and encouragement for this project. Last but certainly not least, we thank Ruth Abraham from Springer-Verlag for her patience and invaluable help in producing this volume.

April 1999

Anca L. Ralescu, Wako-shi, Japan
James G. Shanahan, Meylan, France

Contents

Some Reflections on the Relationship between AI and   1
Fuzzy Logic (FL) - A Heretical View -
Lotfi A. Zadeh

The Place of Fuzzy Logic in AI   9
Didier Dubois and Henri Prade

Mass Assignment Fundamentals for Computing with Words   22
James F. Baldwin

A Method to Use Uncertain Domain Knowledge in the   45
Induction of Classification Knowledge Based on ID3
Hiroshi Narazaki and Ichiro Shigaki

FRIL++ a Language for Object-Oriented Programming with Uncertainty   62
J. F. Baldwin, T. P. Martin, and M. Vargas-Vera

Case-Based Reasoning: A Fuzzy Approach   79
Didier Dubois, Francesc Esteva, Pere Garcia, Lluís Godo,
Ramon López de M àntaras, and Henri Prade

System Identification of Fuzzy Cartesian Granules   91
Feature Models Using Genetic Programming
James F. Baldwin, Trevor P. Martin, and James G. Shanahan

Deep Fusion of Symbolic and Computational Processing   117
for Next Generation User Interface
Shun'ichi Tano

Reasoning with Words about Geographic Information   133
Hans W. Guesgen

Fuzzy Morphology and Fuzzy Distances: New Definitions and   149
Links in both Euclidean and Geodesic Cases
Isabelle Bloch

An Application of Possibility Theory Information Fusion to   166
Satellite Image Classification
Ludovic Roux

Pattern Recognition of Strong Graphs Based on Possibilistic   180
c-means and k-formulae Matching
L. Wendling and J. Desachy

A Fuzzy-Neural Model for Co-ordination in Air Traffic Flow Management   190
Leïla Zerrouki, Bernadette Bouchon-Meunier, and Rémy Fondacci

From Numerical Interpolation to Constructing Intelligent Behaviors   205
Jianwei Zhang and Alois Knoll

A Brief Logopedics for the Data Used in a Neuro-Fuzzy Milieu   222
Vesa A. Niskanen

Evaluation of Fuzzy Quantified Expressions   234
Anca L. Ralescu, Dan A. Ralescu, and Kaoru Hirota

Author Index   245

Some Reflections on the Relationship Between AI and Fuzzy Logic (FL)
- A Heretical View -

Lotfi A. Zadeh[*]

Basically, fuzzy logic is aimed at a formalization of modes of reasoning that are approximate rather than exact. Much of - perhaps most - human reasoning is approximate in nature. From this, one would surmise that fuzzy logic should be welcomed with open arms by AI. This has not been the case. If anything, the AI community has, for the most part, viewed fuzzy logic with skepticism - and sometimes with hostility.

In the AI literature and in programs of AI conferences, the number of papers dealing with fuzzy logic is minuscule. By contrast, the INSPEC database lists close to 20,000 papers with the word "fuzzy" in title, while the more specialized Mathematical Reviews database lists close to 6,500. Furthermore, applications of fuzzy logic are growing rapidly in number, variety and visibility. Why, then, the AI community and fuzzy logic remain so far apart?

In my view, there are two principal reasons. To begin with, the founders of AI built AI on two-valued predicate logic because it was the *only logic* that was available at the time. Built as it was on symbolic logic, symbol manipulation became the principal stock in trade of AI. Numerical computations were not - and still are not - in the mainstream of AI. In particular, the use of probability-based techniques was slow in gaining acceptance. The exclusivity of the commitment of AI to predicate logic and symbol manipulation has exacted a price. Application-areas in which numerical computations play an important role have largely left the fold of AI. Computer vision, robotics and speech recognition are cases in point.

---

[*] Professor in the Graduate School and Director, Berkeley Initiative in Soft Computing (BISC), Computer Science Division and the Electronics research Laboratory, Department of EECS, University of California, Berkeley, CA 994720-1776; Telephone: 5110-642-4959; Fax: 510-642-1111712; E-mail: zadeh@cs.berkeley.edu. Research supported in part by NASA Grant NAC2-1177, ONR Grant N00014-96-0556, ARO Grant DAAH 04-961-0341 and the BISC Program of UC Berkeley.

AI is changing and its commitment to predicate logic and symbol manipulation is not as dominant as it was in the past. In classical Aristotelian logic, the *principle of the excluded middle* asserts that every proposition is either true or false, with no shades of gray allowed. But in the real world, as perceived by humans, it is *partiality* rather than *categoricity* that is ubiquitous. Generally, we have partial knowledge, partial certainty, partial belief, partial understanding and deal with partial causality and partial truth. The concept of partiality, and especially that of *partiality of truth*, plays a central role in fuzzy logic. The essential nature of the role of partiality in human cognition has not as yet gained recognition in AI. It will, eventually.

In the past, what were called intelligent systems were for the most part symbol-manipulation-oriented, e.g., machine translation systems, text understanding systems and game playing systems, among others. Today, what we see is the rapidly growing visibility of systems which are sensor-based and have embedded intelligence, e.g., smart washing machines, smart air conditioners, smart rice cookers and smart automobile transmissions. The counterpart of the concept of IQ in such systems is what might be called Machine IQ, or simply MIQ. However, what is important to recognize is that MIQ is product-specific and does not necessarily involve the same dimensions as human IQ.

Viewed in this perspective, the focus of activity in applications of AI is shifting from writing computer programs that can prove difficult theorems, understand text, provide expert advice and beat a chess champion, to more mundane tasks devolving on the conception, design and construction of products and systems that have a high MIQ, making them reliable, capable, affordable and user-friendly. Among recent examples of systems of this kind are programs which can detect the presence of known or new viruses in computer programs; checkout scanners which can identify fruit and vegetables through the use of scent sensors; car navigation systems which can guide a driver to a desired destination; password authentication systems employing biometric typing information; ATM eye-print machines for identity verification; and molecular breath analyzers which are capable of diagnosing lung cancer, stomach ulcers and other diseases.

The second and more important reason for AI's skepticism reflects a lack of understanding of what fuzzy logic is and what is has to offer. Many of the misconceptions about fuzzy logic stem from the fact that fuzzy logic (FL) is much more than a logical system. More specifically, FL has many distinct facets of which there are four that stand out in importance. These facets and the underlying basic concepts are the following (Fig. 1).

1. the logical facet, FL/L;
2. the set-theoretic facet, FL/S;
3. the relational facet, FL/R;
4. the epistemic facet, FL/E.

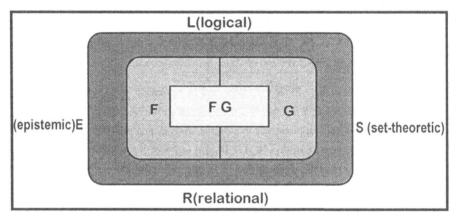

Figure 1. Conceptual structure of fuzzy logic

The logical facet of FL, FL/L, is a logical system or, more accurately, a collection of logical systems that include as a special case both two-valued and multiple-valued systems. As in any logical system, at the core of the logical facet of FL lies a system of rules of inference. In FL/L, however, the rules of inference play the role of rules that govern propagation of various types of fuzzy constraints. Concomitantly, a proposition, p, is viewed as a fuzzy constraint on an explicitly or implicitly defined variable. For example, the proposition *"Mary is young"* may be viewed as a fuzzy constraint on the variable *Age(Mary)*, with "young" playing the role of a constraining fuzzy relation. Similarly, the proposition "Most students are young" may be viewed as a fuzzy constraint on the proportion of young students among students, with the fuzzy quantifier "most" playing the role of a fuzzy constraint on the proportion in question. The logical facet of FL plays a pivotal role in the applications of FL to knowledge representation and to inference from information that is imprecise, incomplete, uncertain or partially true.

The set-theoretic facet of FL, FL/S, is concerned with fuzzy sets, that is, classes or sets whose boundaries are not sharply defined. The initial development of FL was focused on this facet. Most of the applications of FL in mathematics have been and continue to be related to the set-theoretic facet. Among the examples of such applications are: fuzzy topology, fuzzy groups, fuzzy differential equations and fuzzy arithmetic. Actually, any concept, method or theory, T, can be generalized by fuzzification, that is, by replacing the concept of a set with that of a fuzzy set. Fuzzification serves an important purpose: it provides a way of constructing theories that are more general and more reflective of the imprecision of the real world than theories ·in which the sets are assumed to be crisp. It is convenient to denote a fuzzified version of T as T+. For example, if PT denotes standard probability theory then PT+ denotes a fuzzified version of PT.

The relational facet of FL, FL/R, is concerned in the main with representation and manipulation of imprecisely defined functions and relations. It is this facet of FL that plays a pivotal role in its applications to systems analysis and control. The three basic concepts that lie at the core of this facet of FL are those of a linguistic variable, fuzzy if-then rule and fuzzy graph. The relational facet of FL provides a foundation for the fuzzy-logic-based methodology of computing with words (CW) - a methodology in which the concept of a linguistic variable plays a pivotal role [Zadeh 1996].

Basically, a linguistic variable is a variable whose values are words drawn from a natural or synthetic language, with words playing the role of labels of fuzzy sets. For example, Height is a linguistic variable if its values are assumed to be: tall, very tall, quite tall, short, not very short, and so on. The use of words instead of - or in addition to - numbers serves two major purposes: (1) exploitation of the tolerance for imprecision; and (2) reflection of the finite ability of the human mind to resolve detail and store precise information.

The epistemic facet of FL, FL/E, is linked to its logical facet and is focused on the applications of FL to knowledge representation, information systems, fuzzy databases and the theories of possibility and probability. A particularly important application area for the epistemic facet of FL relates to the conception and design of information/intelligent systems.

At the core of FL lie two basic concepts:
   (a) fuzziness/fuzzification;
   (b) granularity/granulation.

As was alluded to already, fuzziness is a condition that relates to classes whose boundaries are not sharply defined, whereas fuzzification refers to replacing a crisp set, that is, a set with sharply defined boundaries, with a set whose boundaries are fuzzy. For example, the number 5 is fuzzified when it is transformed into approximately 5.

In a similar spirit, granularity relates to clumpiness of structure, whereas granulation refers to partitioning an object into a collection of granules, with a granule being a clump of objects (points) drawn together by indistinguishability, similarity, proximity or functionality. For example, the granules of an article might be the introduction, section 1, section 2, and so forth. Similarly, the granules of a human body might be the head, neck, chest, stomach, legs, and so on. Granulation may be crisp or fuzzy; dense or sparse; physical or mental.

A concept which plays a pivotal role in fuzzy logic is that of fuzzy information granulation, or fuzzy IG, for short. In crisp IG, the granules are crisp while in fuzzy IG the granules are fuzzy. For example, when the variable Age is granulated into the time intervals $\{0,1\}$, $\{1,2\}$, $\{2,3\}$, ..., the granules $\{0,1\}$, $\{1,2\}$, $\{2,3\}$, ... are crisp; when Age is treated as a linguistic variable, the fuzzy sets labeled young, middle-aged, old are fuzzy granules that play the role of linguistic values of Age. The importance of fuzzy logic - especially in the realm of applications - derives in large measure from the fact that FL is the only methodology that provides a machinery for fuzzy information granulation. In Fig. 1, the core concept of fuzzy granulation is represented as the conjunction F•G If T is a concept, method or theory, then T generalized through fuzzy granulation is denoted as T++.

By itself, understanding of fuzzy logic is not sufficient to persuade the AI community to put its stamp of approval on FL. What is needed is a demonstration that fuzzy logic is capable of addressing important problems which AI cannot handle. In this context, a key capability which FL offers - and no other methodology does - is the capability to reason with perceptions - perceptions of time, distance, force, weight, direction, speed, likelihood and truth, among others.

Humans possess a remarkable ability to perform a wide variety of physical and mental tasks without any measurements and any computations. Everyday examples of such tasks are parking a car, playing golf, riding a bicycle and driving in heavy traffic.

Underlying this capability is the ability to manipulate perceptions. A basic difference between measurements and perceptions is that in general measurements are crisp whereas perceptions are fuzzy. This explains why non-fuzzy logical systems provide no tools for dealing with perceptions and why fuzzy logic is the only logical system that does so.

My recently initiated computational theory of perceptions (CTP) [Zadeh 1999] is based on the fuzzy-logic-based methodology of computing with words (CW). The point of departure in CTP is description of perceptions as propositions expressed in a natural language. For example:

> The sky is cloudy.
> Cindy is slim.
> Robert is very honest.
> Berkeley is more diverse than Palo Alto.
> Most young men are healthy.
> It is very unlikely that there will be a significant increase
> in the price of oil in the near future.

A key part of CTP is a computational semantics of natural language (CSNL). In CSNL, the meaning of a proposition, p, is expressed as a so-called generalized constraint or a variable. Thus

p -------> X is R

where X is the constrained variable, R is the constraining relation and isr is a copula in which r is a variable whose value defines the way in which R constrains X. Thus, if r=blank, the constraint is possibilistic; if r=v, the constraint is varistic; if r=p, the constraint is probabilistic; and if r=rs, the constraint is of random set type. Many more types of constraints are allowed and, furthermore, the constraints can operate in combination.

As a simple example, the meaning of the proposition "Mary is young" is expressed as

Mary is young -------> Age(Mary) is young

when X=Age(Mary) is the constraining relation R in the fuzzy set young.

Similarly, the meaning of the proposition "Most young men are healthy" is expressed as

ΣCount(healthy/young) is most

where X=ΣCount(healthy/young) is the proportion of healthy men among young men and the constraining relation is the fuzzy quantifier most.

Expressions of the form X isr R are elements of what is called the Generalized Constraint Language (GCL). Thus, the computational semantics of natural language serves as a system for translating from a natural language into GCL. An important part of GCL is a system for constraint propagation from antecedent constraints to consequent constraints. The rules for constraint propagation in GCL coincide with the rules of inference in fuzzy logic.

A simple example suffices to show why predicate logic cannot deal with perceptions. Consider the classical example: all men are mortal; Socrates is a man; therefore Socrates is mortal. There are seven distinct perceptions which can be derived from this example by fuzzification of "all," "men" and "mortal." For example: most young men are healthy; Robert is a young man. What, then, can be said about Robert's health? Neither predicate logic nor probability theory can provide an answer to this question.

A similar example is the following. Assume that a box contains balls of various sizes; most are large and a few are small. What is the probability that a ball drawn at random is neither large nor small? Again, neither probability theory nor predicate logic can answer this question. In this case, as in other cases involving perceptions, computational semantics of natural languages is needed to define the meaning of the perceptions "most balls are large," "a few are small" and "neither large nor small."

In relation to AI, the most important tools provided by fuzzy logic are the methodology of computing with words and the computational theory of perceptions. Without these tools, many real-world problems which lie within the domain of AI cannot be solved. It is this conclusion that forms the basis for my heretical - in AI's perspective - belief that it is only a matter of time before fuzzy logic is added to the armamentarium of AI and is accorded recognition as an important tool for the conception, design, construction and utilization of information/intelligent systems.

References

L. A. Zadeh, Probability Theory and Fuzzy Logic are Complementary rather than Competitive, Technometrics, vol. 37, pp. 271-276, 1995.

L.A. Zadeh, Fuzzy Logic = Computing with Words, IEEE Transactions on Fuzzy Systems, vol. 4, pp. 103-111, 1996.

L.A. Zadeh, From Computing with Numbers to Computing with Words - From Manipulation of Measurements to Manipulation of Perceptions, (in press), IEEE Transactions on Circuits and Systems, January, 1999.

The Place of Fuzzy Logic in AI

Didier DUBOIS – Henri PRADE

Institut de Recherche en Informatique de Toulouse (IRIT), Université Paul Sabatier, 118 route de Narbonne, 31062 Toulouse Cédex 4, France

Abstract: Fuzzy logic is more than thirty years old and has a long-lasting misunderstanding with Artificial Intelligence (A.I.), although the formalization of some forms of commonsense reasoning has motivated the development of fuzzy logic. What fuzzy sets typically brings to AI is a mathematical framework for capturing gradedness in reasoning devices. Moveover gradedness can take various forms: similarity between propositions, levels of uncertainty, and degrees of preference. The paper provides a brief survey of the fuzzy set contribution to the modelling of various types of commonsense reasoning, and advocates the complementarity of fuzzy set methods, and more generally of soft computing techniques, with symbolic A.I.

1 Introduction

To-date, the term "fuzzy logic" often refers to a particular control engineering methodology, that exploits a numerical representation of commonsense control rules, in order to synthetize, via interpolation, a control law. This approach has many common features with neural networks. It is now mainly concerned with the efficient encoding and approximation of numerical functions, and has currently less and less relationships to knowledge representation issues. This is however a very narrow view of fuzzy logic that has little to do with AI. Scanning the fuzzy set literature, one realizes that fuzzy logic may also refer to two other AI-related topics: multiple-valued logics, and approximate reasoning. While the multiple-valued logic stream is very mathematically oriented, the notion of approximate reasoning as imagined by Zadeh is much more related to the mainstream program of AI research: he wrote in 1979 that "the theory of approximate reasoning is concerned with the deduction of possibly imprecise conclusions from a set of imprecise premises". In the following, we shall use the term "fuzzy logic" to refer to any kind of fuzzy set-based method intended to be used in reasoning machineries.

Fuzzy logic methods have not been considered as belonging to mainstream AI tools until now, although an important part of fuzzy logic research concentrates on approximate reasoning and reasoning under uncertainty issues (e.g., Ralescu, 1994; Martin and Ralescu, 1997). Some reasons for this situation may be found in the antagonism which had existed for a long time between purely symbolic methods advocated by AI and numerically-oriented approaches that were involved in fuzzy rule-based systems. Besides, fuzzy sets were a new emerging approach not yet firmly settled, but apparently challenging the monopoly of probability theory as being the unique proper framework for handling uncertainty. In spite of the fact that fuzzy sets have received a better recognition recently, there still exists a lack of appreciation of what fuzzy logic really is by AI researchers, as for instance recently exemplified by Elkan (1994).

In the mid-seventies, at a time when MYCIN was becoming a landmark among rule-based expert systems dealing with uncertainty, the first fuzzy rule-based system was designed by Mamdani's group at Queen Mary College in London following an idea suggested by Zadeh shortly before. This system is the direct ancestor of the most of the fuzzy control systems which have become so largely used in the early nineties. What is at work in rule-based fuzzy control is a simple device for interpolating between numerically-valued conclusions of parallel rules. This interpolation is made on the basis of degrees of matching of the current situation with respect to the fuzzy condition parts of the rules. These degrees estimate the similarity between the current situation and prototypical values which constitute the core of the fuzzy sets describing the firing conditions of the rules. Such coefficients obtained through a matching procedure were quite different from the certainty factors attached to facts and rules in MYCIN-like expert system. However, AI expert systems and fuzzy rule-based controllers did share the idea that the rules were encoding expert knowledge. This view has more or less disappeared in the recent neuro-fuzzy based methods where fuzzy rules are just a convenient format for synthesizing control laws from sets of inputs/outputs pairs and thus for approximating functions and tuning them locally. Then the knowledge representation and approximate reasoning aspects are no longer the main features of the approach in its present development. However, the basic notions of similarity and interpolation might be useful in other, more AI-oriented, applications such as case-based reasoning, for retrieving cases and extrapolating from them by means of gradual rules of the type "the more x is A, the more y is B" (Dubois and Prade, 1996a). Similarity reasoning should encode commonsense inferences of the form if "p is close to p' ", and "p implies q" then "q is not far from being true". Fuzzy set theory is a natural framework for modelling such inference patterns.

Apart from similarity, two other basic semantics can be addressed by fuzzy set-based methods, namely uncertainty and preference: uncertainty pervading available information in reasoning problems, preference among more or less acceptable values in a decision-oriented perspective (Dubois and Prade, 1997). Possibility theory (Zadeh, 1978) offers a framework for dealing with uncertainty when the available information is no longer precise and certain, but represented by means of fuzzy sets. Using fuzzy sets, uncertainty is estimated by means of two dual measures of possibility and necessity. This framework has merits for the representation of states of partial or total ignorance. Another interesting feature of possibility theory is that it only requires purely ordinal scales for the assessing of uncertainty. It provides a very qualitative approach and facilitates the elicitation of the uncertainty levels. Based on possibility theory, a possibilistic logic (which should not be confused with the fully compositional calculus of fuzzy set membership degrees) has been developed, both at the syntactic and semantic level. In this logic, classical logic formulas are associated with lower bounds of necessity measures expressing the level of certainty, or equivalently of epistemic entrenchment of the formulas. It has been established that rational nonmonotonic inference relation (in the sense of Lehmann) can be represented in possibilistic logic, where a default rule "if p then q generally" is understood as the constraint that the possibility measure of "p and q" is strictly greater than the possibility of "p and not q". Connections with other approaches to nonmonotonic reasoning including the one based on infinitesimal probabilities have been laid bare. Possibilistic logic is a genuine extension of classical logic that encodes an uncertainty calculus. Possibilistic assumption-based truth maintenance systems provides simple implementations of nonmonotonic reasoning. Possibilistic logic can be used as well for reasoning from multiple sources of information having different reliability levels. The corresponding data fusion tools have been developed.

When fuzzy sets model preference among values according to flexible constraints, rather than imprecise and uncertain information, possibility theory offers a natural framework for extending the constraint satisfaction problem paradigm to soft and prioritized constraints. Scheduling provides a good example of application of these techniques where, for instance, due dates are often somewhat elastic. Moreover, some parameters like the duration of operations (which are not under our control) may be pervaded with uncertainty. In this situation a trade-off has to be achieved between a high level of satisfaction of constraints and the necessity to cope with unlikely but potentially dangerous states of the world. Possibility theory can be used as the basis for a qualitative utility theory (Dubois and Prade, 1995a) that tackles such a decision problem (including computation with ill-known numerical quantities).

Finally, an important feature of fuzzy sets is to provide a framework for interfacing in a non-rigid way classes with numerical values. In classification problems the use of fuzzy classes obviates the need for arbitrarily classifying borderline cases at the beginning of a reasoning stage. Numerical data can be summarized by means of linguistically labelled fuzzy sets, so as to feed a symbolic reasoning machinery. These issues come close to learning, another subfield of AI where this aspect of fuzzy sets might be particularly interesting.

The contents of this paper largely borrow to the ones of three previous articles by the authors (Dubois and Prade, 1995b, 1996b, 1998). See Yager (1995, 1997) for a complementary point of view.

2 Fuzzy logic in commonsense and approximate reasoning

Fuzzy sets offer a powerful tool for the modelling of various kinds of commonsense reasoning, where membership functions are used for expressing graded notions such as uncertainty, preference and similarity, interfere. Such a theory of gradedness is not necessarily numerical, contrary to what many people tend to believe to-date, but can be purely ordinal (lattice-based). Let us review some of them, after a brief recall of some formal background.

2.1 Logical Embeddings

Very different extensions of classical logic that exploit the notion of a fuzzy set have been proposed. Some are truth-functional, while others are not. We may distinguish between:

- *many-valued logics* that were proposed before fuzzy set theory came to light. They are exclusively devoted to the handling of "vague" propositions `p, i.e., propositions which may be partially true (e.g., propositions involving properties whose satisfaction is a matter of degree). The underlying algebraic structure is then weaker than a Boolean algebra. Such logics can handle truth-values t(`p) that lie in the unit interval and remain truth-functional. There are two families of "fuzzy logics that cope with graded truth. A first family relies on residuated lattice-like structures, and their extensions such as MV-algebras. The syntax is based on related conjunction and implication connectives, and deduction is based on modus ponens in the settting of a Hilbert-like axiomatization. See, e.g., (Hajek, 1995) for an introduction and (Novak, 1996) for a discussion. A very different family of fuzzy logics uses only a clausal language based on a De Morgan algebra, typically the (max, min, 1 − .) triple for modeling disjunction, conjunction and negation. This trend, initiated by Lee (1972), has blossomed in the framework of logic programming. There are to-date a lot of such fuzzy programming language proposals (for instance Mukaidono et al., 1989; Li and Liu, 1990).

- *possibilistic logic* that is built on top of classical logic, and where each crisp proposition is attached a lower bound of a degree of necessity $N(p)$ expressing the certainty of p given the available information. $N(p) = 1$ iff p is surely true and $N(p) = 0$ expresses the complete lack of certainty that p is true (either p is false when $N(\neg p) = 1$, or it is unknown if p is true or false and then $N(\neg p) = 0$). The degree $N(p)$ is compositional *for conjunction only* $(N(p \wedge q) = \min (N(p),N(q))$, and $N(p \vee q) \geq \max (N(p),N(q))$ generally. For instance, if $q = \neg p$, $p \vee q$ is tautological, hence surely true $(N(p \vee q) = 1)$, but p may be unknown $(N(p) = N(\neg p) = 0)$. Moreover $N(\neg p) = 1 − \prod (p)$ where $\prod(p)$ is the degree of possibility of proposition p. Functions N and $\prod$ stem from the existence of a fuzzy set of more or less possible worlds, one of which is the actual one. It is described by means of a possibility distribution π on the interpretations of the language, and $N(p) = 1 − \sup \{\pi(\omega), \omega . \neg p\} = 1 − \prod(\neg p)$, i.e., $N(p)$ is computed as the degree of impossibility of the proposition $\neg p$. A possibilistic logic formula (p,α) understood as $N(p) \geq \alpha$, is represented by a fuzzy set such that interpretations which makes p false have degree $1 − \alpha \geq \prod(\neg p)$ (i.e., the possibility that p is false is upper bounded by $1 − \alpha$), while the interpretations which makes p true have degree 1. Then, the possibility distribution π representing a set of possibilistic formulas is obtained by the min-conjunction of the fuzzy sets representing the formulas (Dubois, Lang and Prade , 1994).

In possibilistic logic a fuzzy set describes incomplete knowledge about where the actual world is, and a weighted formula has a fuzzy set of models. In many-valued logics, fuzzy sets describe the extensions of vague predicates, and a weighted formula has a crisp extension (corresponding to a level cut). The truth-functionality is not compulsory however when dealing with vagueness. In *similarity logics* it is supposed that the vagueness of predicates stems from a closeness relation (Ruspini, 1991) that equips the set of interpretations of the language. Then a Boolean proposition p is actually understood as a fuzzy proposition `p whose models are *close* to models of p. Let [p] be the set of models of p and R(p) = [p] ô R the fuzzy set of models close (in the sense of fuzzy relation R) to models of p. Then generally, $R(p \wedge q) \subseteq R(p) \cap R(q)$, without equality, so that truth-values are not truth-functional with respect to conjunction.

In classical logic, a proposition p entails another proposition q whenever each situation where p is true is a situation where q is true. Entailment is denoted ., and p . q means $[p] \subseteq [q]$ where [p] is the set of models of p. In possiblitistic logic, the type of inference which is at work is plausible inference. The possibility distribution π on the set of interpretations encodes an ordering relation that ranks possible worlds ω in terms of plausibility. Then p plausibly entails q if and only if q is true in the most plausible situations where p is true, i.e., $\max[p] \subseteq [q]$, where $\max[p] = \{\omega \in [p], \pi(\omega)$ maximal$\}$. This type of inference is also called "preferential inference" in nonmonotonic reasoning. In contrast, inference in similarity logics is dual to preferential inference. The set of interpretations of the language is equipped with a similarity relation R. Then p entails approximately q in similarity logic if all the situations where p is true are close to situations where q is true, i.e., $[p] \subseteq$ support[R(q)]. More generally, a degree of strength of the entailment can be computed as $I(q \mid p) = \inf_{\omega \in [p]} \sup_{\omega' \in [q]} \mu_R(\omega,\omega')$. It plays in similarity logic the same role as a degree of confirmation in inductive logic. In possibilistic logic the counterpart of $I(q \mid p)$ is the conditional necessity $N(q \mid p)$ computed from π, i.e., $N(q \mid p) = N (\neg p \vee q) > 0$ if $\prod(q \wedge p) > \prod (\neg q \wedge p)$, and $N(q \mid p) = 0$ otherwise.

These newly emerged notions of fuzzy set-based inference certainly deserve further developments, and lead to very different types of logic. Of interest is the study of their links to the usual entailment principle of Zadeh (defined as a fuzzy set inclusion), and various extensions of consequence relations in multiple-valued logic, as studied by Chakraborty (1988), Castro et al. (1994).

2.2 Fuzzy deductive inference

This type of approximate reasoning has been advocated by Zadeh in the mid-seventies, as a calculus of fuzzy restrictions (Zadeh, 1979; Dubois and Prade, 1991). The principles of this approach rely on the conjunctive combination of possibility distributions and their projection on suitable subspaces. A particular case of the combination/projection procedure, named "generalized modus ponens", has been emphasized, where from a fact of the form "X is A' " and a rule "if X is A then Y is B" (where X and Y are variables, A', A and B are fuzzy sets), a conclusion Y is B' is computed. The generalized modus ponens can be also understood in terms of fuzzy truth-values (Zadeh, 1979; Baldwin, 1979), where the truth-value of a proposition "X is A" is viewed as its compatibility with respect to what is actually known, say, "X is A' " (this compatibility is computed as the fuzzy set of possible values of the membership $\mu_A(u)$ when the fuzzy range of u is A').This conjunction/projection method is at work in the POSSINFER system of Kruse et al. (1994). This type of inference is also a generalization of constraint propagation to flexible constraints, provided that one interprets each statement as a requirement that some controllable variable must satisfy. Then the possibility distributions model preference, and inference come down to consistency analysis (such as arc-consistency, path-consistency, etc.) in the terminology of constraint-directed reasoning. The advantage of fuzzy deductive inference is to directly account for flexible constraints and prioritized constraints, where the priorities are modelled by means of necessity functions (see Dubois, Fargier and Prade, 1994).

2.3 Reasoning under uncertainty and inconsistency

A possibilistic knowledge base K is a set of pairs (p, s) where p is a classical logic formula and s is a lower bound of a degree of necessity ($N(p) \geq s$). It can be viewed as a stratified deductive data base where the higher s, the safer the piece of knowledge p. Reasoning from K means using the safest part of K to make inference, whenever possible. Denoting $K_\alpha = \{p, (p,s) \in K, s \geq \alpha\}$, the entailment K ; (p,$\alpha$) means that K_α ; p. K can be inconsistent and its inconsistency degree is inc(K) = sup$\{\alpha$, K ; ($\perp,\alpha$)$\}$ where $\perp$ denotes the contradiction. In contrast with classical logic, inference in the presence of inconsistency becomes non-trivial. This is the case when K ; (p,α) where $\alpha > $ inc(K). Then it means that p follows from a consistent and safe part of K (at least at level α). This kind of syntactic non-trivial inference is sound and complete with respect to the above defined preferential entailment. Moreover adding p to K and nontrivially entailing q from K $\cup$ {p} corresponds to revising K upon learning p, and having q as a consequence of the revised knowledge base. This notion of revision is exactly the one studied by Gärdenfors (1988) at the axiomatic level.

2.4 Nonmonotonic plausible inference using generic knowledge

Possibilistic logic does not allow for a direct encoding of pieces of generic knowledge such as "birds fly". However, it provides a target language in which plausible inference from generic knowledge can be achieved in the face of incomplete evidence. In possibility theory "p generally entails q" is understood as "p $\wedge$ q is a more plausible situation than p $\wedge \neg$q". It defines a constraint of the form $\Pi(p \wedge q) > \Pi(p \wedge \neg q)$ that restricts a set of possibility distributions. Given a set S of generic knowledge statements of the form "p_i generally entails q_i", a possibilistic base can be computed as follows. For each interpretation ω of the language, the maximal possibility degree π(ω) is computed, that obeys the set of contraints in S. This is done by virtue of the principle of minimal specificity (or commitment) that assumes each situation as a possible one insofar as it has not been ruled out. Then each generic statement is turned into a material implication $\neg p_i \vee q_i$, to which $N(\neg p_i \vee q_i)$ is attached. It comes down, as shown in Benferhat et al. (1992) to rank-order the generic rules giving priority to the most specific ones, as done in Pearl (1990)'s system Z. A very important property of this approach is that it is exception-tolerant. It offers a convenient framework for implementing a basic form of nonmonotonic system called "rational closure" (Lehmann and Magidor, 1992), and addresses a basic problem in the expert system literature, that is, handling exceptions in uncertain rules.

2.5 Hypothetical reasoning

The idea is to cope with incomplete information by explicitly handling assumptions under which conclusions can be derived. To this end some literals in the language are distinguished as being asssumptions. Possibilistic logic offers a tool for reasoning with assumptions. It is based on the fact that in possibilistic logic a clause ($\neg h \vee q$, α) is semantically equivalent to the formula with a symbolic weight (q, min (α, t(h)) where t(h) is the (possibly unknown) truth value of h. The set of environments in which a proposition p is true can thus be calculated by putting all assumptions in the weight slots, carrying out possibilistic inference so as to derive p. The subsets of assumptions under which p is true with more or less certainty can be retrieved from the weight attached to p. This technique can be used to detect minimal inconsistent subsets of a propositional knowledge base (see Benferhat et al., 1994).

2.6 Interpolative Reasoning

This type of reasoning is at work in fuzzy control applications, albeit without clear logical foundations. Klawonn and Kruse (1993) have shown that a set of fuzzy rules can be viewed as a set of crisp rules along with a set of similarity relations. Moreover an interpolation-dedicated fuzzy rule 'if is A then Y is B" can be understood as "the more x is A the more Y is B" and the corresponding inference means that if X = x and $\alpha = \mu_A(x)$ then Y lies in the level cut B_α. When two rules are at work, such that $\alpha_1 = \mu_{A_1}(x)$, $\alpha_2 = \mu_{A_2}(x)$, then the conclusion $Y \in (B_1)_{\alpha_1} \cap (B_2)_{\alpha_2}$ lies between the cores of B_1 and B_2, i.e., on ordered universes, an interpolation effect is obtained. It can be proved that Sugeno's fuzzy reasoning method for control can be cast in this framework (Dubois, Grabisch, Prade, 1994). More generally interpolation is clearly a kind of reasoning based on similarity (rather than uncertainty) and it should be related to current research on similarity logics (Dubois et al., 1997). More generally similarity relations and fuzzy interpolation methods should impact on current research in case-based reasoning.

2.7 Abductive reasoning

Abductive reasoning is viewed as the task of retrieving plausible explanations of available observations on the basis of causal knowledge. In fuzzy set theory causal knowledge has often been represented by means of fuzzy relations relating a set of causes C to a set of observations S. However the problem of the semantics of this relation has often been overlooked. $\mu_R(c,s)$ may be viewed either as a degree of intensity or a degree of uncertainty. Namely, when observations are not binary, $\mu_R(c,s)$ can be understood as the intensity of presence of observed symptom s when the cause c is present. This is the traditional view in fuzzy set theory. It leads to Sanchez (1977) approach to abduction, based on fuzzy relational equations. Another view has been recently proposed by the authors, where by $\mu_R(c,s)$ is understood as the degree of certainty that a binary symptom s is present when c is present. A dual causal matrix R' must be used where $\mu_{R'}(c,s)$ is the degree of certainty that a binary symptom s is absent when c is present. On such a basis the theory of parsimonious covering for causal diagnosis by Peng and Reggia (1990) can be extended to the case of uncertain causal knowledge and incomplete observations. This method is currently applied to satellite failure diagnosis (Cayrac et al., 1994).

3 Soft Computing should not be antagonistic to symbolic AI

Perhaps due to the intermediary, bridging position of fuzzy logic between symbolic and numerical processing, a significant deviation from original motivations and practice of fuzzy logic has been observed in the fuzzy set community in the last five years. Namely, fuzzy rule-based systems are more and more considered as standard, very powerful universal approximators of functions, and less and less as a means of building numerical function from heuristic knowledge, nor of linguistic summarization of data. This trend raises several questions for fuzzy logic. First, if fuzzy logic is to compete alternative methods in approximation theory, it faces a big challenge because approximation theory is a well-established field in which many results exist. Approximate representation of functions should be general enough to capture a large class of functions, should be simple enough (especially the primitive objects, here the fuzzy rules) to achieve efficient computation and economical storage, and should be amenable to capabilities of exploiting data. Are fuzzy rules capable of competing on its own with standard approximation methods on such grounds? the answer is far from clear. On the one hand the universal approximation results for fuzzy rule-based systems presuppose a large number of rules. This is good neither for the economy of representation nor for linguistic relevance. On the other hand the identification between fuzzy rule-based systems with neural nets or variants thereof (radial basis functions and the like, see Mendel, 1995) has created a lot of confusion as to the actual contribution of fuzzy logic. To some extent it is not clear that fuzzy logic-based approximations methods for modeling and control needs fuzzy set theory any longer (Bersini and Bontempi, 1997). Moreover the connection to knowledge representation, part of which relies on the "readability" of fuzzy rules as knowledge chunks, is lost. Actually, from the point of view of approximation capabilities, the good performance of a fuzzy rule-based system seems to be incompatible with the linguistic relevance of the rules. This incompatibility leads systems engineers into cutting off the links between fuzzy logic and Artificial Intelligence, hence with fuzzy set theory itself. This is very surprizing a posteriori since the incompatibility between high precision and linguistic meaningfulness in the description of complex systems behavior is exactly what prompted Zadeh (1973) into introducing fuzzy sets as a tool for exploiting human knowledge in controlling such systems.

It is questionable whether the present trend in fuzzy engineering, that immerses fuzzy logic inside the jungle of function approximation methods will produce path breaking results that puts fuzzy rule-based systems well over already existing tools. It is not clear either that it will accelerate the recognition of fuzzy set theory, since there is a clear trend to keep the name "fuzzy" and forget the contents of the theory.

The reason for this overfocus on fuzzy rules as numerical approximation methods is because control engineers are more concerned with modeling than explaining. Yet, it seems that system engineering practice and soft computing at large can benefit from the readability of fuzzy rule-based systems. Fuzzy rules are easier to modify, they can serve as tools for integrating heuristic, symbolic knowledge about systems, and numerical functions issued from mathematical modeling. Interestingly, the original motivation of fuzzy logic in control engineering (Mamdani and Assilian, 1975) was to represent expert knowledge in a rule-based style and to build a standard control law that faithfully reflects this knowledge. Fuzzy logic control was thus put from the start in the perspective of Artificial Intelligence (Assilian, 1994) because it did not use the classical control engineering paradigm of modeling a physical system and deriving the control law from the model. As such fuzzy logic control is viewed as an application of the approximate reasoning methodology proposed by Zadeh (1973), that exploits formal models of commonsense reasoning. Following this path might have sounded promising, even for control engineers, since they do employ heuristic knowledge in practice, be it when they specify objectives to attain. Supervision also involves a lot of know-how, despite the existing sophisticated control theory, and some interesting works have also been done in fuzzy rule-based tuning of PID controllers. More generally the ranges of applicability of fuzzy controllers and classical control theory are complementary (Verbruggen and Bruijn, 1997). Whenever mathematical modeling is possible, control theory offers a safer approach, although a lot of work is sometimes necessary to bridge the gap with practical problems. Fuzzy logic sounds reasonable when modeling is difficult or costly, but knowledge is available in order to derive fuzzy rules. This philosophy, which has led to successful applications in Europe before fuzzy logic become worldwide popular (for instance the cement kilns controllers of Holmblad and Østergaard (1997)), tends to disappear from the literature of fuzzy control, when one looks at the recent literature.

It must be noticed that while in the beginning of fuzzy control, fuzzy rule-based systems were construed as part of Artificial Intelligence, Artificial Intelligence had rejected fuzzy control as a non-orthodox approach that was not purely symbolic processing. To-date, some fuzzy logic advocates tend to reject symbolic Artificial Intelligence as not capable of dealing with real complex systems analysis tasks. Doing so there is a danger of cutting fuzzy logic from its roots and making fuzzy set theory obsolete as well. Zadeh (1996) himself recently advocated the idea of computing with words as being the ultimate purpose of fuzzy logic and he also insists on the role of fuzzy logic for information granulation (Zadeh, 1997a). In order to achieve this program that repositions fuzzy logic in the perspective of automated explanation tasks, it seems that part of fuzzy logic research should go back to Artificial Intelligence problems, and that fuzzy logic should again serve as a bridge between Systems Engineering and Artificial Intelligence research. Needless to say that in that perspective, control engineers should receive some education in logic, and Artificial Intelligence researchers interested in systems engineering should be aware of control theory. Such a shift in education and concerns would open the road to addressing, in a less ad hoc way, issues in the supervision of complex systems, a problem whose solution requires a blending between knowledge and control engineering, namely computerized tools for automatically explaining the current situation to human operators, and not only tools for approximating real functions, be they non-linear.

4 Conclusion

Reducing soft computing to the simultaneous use of neural nets, genetic algorithms and fuzzy rule-based systems seems to propose a very narrow and heterogeneous view of intelligent computers that may endanger the future of fuzzy set and Artificial Intelligence research. The merits of fuzzy set theory is to offer a bridge between symbolic and numerical processing, while neural nets, as of to-date, fully belong to the numerical processing area, and genetic algorithms are just one among other families of meta-heuristics for combinatorial approximation. What we propose is rather to consider soft computing as a field dedicated to problem-solving methods capable of simultaneously exploiting numerical data and human knowledge, using mathematical modelling and symbolic reasoning systems. A soft computing package is then one that could at the same time learn to solve a problem accurately (such as classification, control, diagnosis and the like) possibly via modeling and optimization techniques, and supply explanations about how it can be solved by moving up to a symbolic level. A fusion of methodologies, why not, but then, of symbolic AI and numerical methods at large, letting fuzzy set theory, neural nets and other fields develop their own paradigms, occasionally helping one another in specific applications where their complementarity is needed.

References

Assilian S. (1974) Artificial Intelligence in the Control of Real Dynamic Systems. PhD Thesis, Queen Mary College, University of London.

Benferhat S., Dubois D., Prade H. (1992) Representing default rules in possibilistic logic. Proc. of the 3rd Inter. Conf. on Principles of Knowledge Representation and Reasoning (KR'92), Cambridge, MA, Oct. 26-29, 673-684.

Benferhat S., Dubois D., Lang J., Prade H. (1994) Hypothetical reasoning in possibilistic logic: basic notions, applications and implementation issues. In: Between Mind and Computer, Fuzzy Science and Engineering, Vol. I (P.Z. Wang, K.F. Loe, eds.), World Scientific Publ., Singapore, 1-29.

Bersini H., Bontempi G. (1997) Now comes the time to defuzzify neuro-fuzzy models. Fuzzy Sets and Systems, 90, 161-169.Benferhat S., Dubois D., Prade H. (1992) Representing default rules in possibilistic logic. Proc. of the 3rd Inter. Conf. on Principles of Knowledge Representation and Reasoning (KR'92), Cambridge, MA, Oct. 26-29, 673-684.

Castro J.L., Trillas S., Cubilla S. (1994) On consequence in approximate reasoning. J. of Applied Non-Classical Logics, 4, 91-103.

Cayrac D., Dubois D., Haziza M., Prade H. (1994) Possibility theory in "fault mode effect analyses" —A satellite fault diagnosis application—. Proc. of the IEEE World Cong. on Computational Intelligence, Orlando, FL, June 26-July 2, 1176-1181.

Chakraborty M. (1988) Use of fuzzy set in introducing graded consequence in multiple-valued logic. In: Fuzzy Logic in Knowledge Based Systems-Decision and Control (M.M. Gupta, T. Yamakawa, eds) North-Holland, 247-257.

Dubois D., Esteva F., Garcia P., Godo L., Prade H. (1997) Similarity-based consequence relations. Int. J. of Approximate Reasoning,

Dubois D., Fargier H., Prade H. (1994) Propagation and satisfaction of flexible constraints. In: Fuzzy Sets, Neural Networks, and Soft Computing (R.R. Yager, L.A. Zadeh, eds.), Van Nostrand Reinhold, New York, 166-187.

Dubois D., Grabisch M., Prade H. (1994) Gradual rules and the approximation of control laws. In: Theoretical Aspects of Fuzzy Control (H.T. Nguyen, M. Sugeno, R. Tong, R. Yager, eds.), Wiley, New York, 147-181.

Dubois D., Lang J., Prade H. (1994) Possibilistic logic. In: Handbook of Logic in Artificial Intelligence and Logic Programming, Vol. 3 (D.M. Gabbay, C.J. Hogger, J.A. Robinson, D. Nute, eds.), Oxford University Press, 439-513.

Dubois D., Prade H. (1991) Fuzzy sets in approximate reasoning — Part 1: Inference with possibility distributions. Fuzzy Sets and Systems, 40, Part 1: 143-202; Part 2 (with Lang J.) Logical approaches: Fuzzy Sets and Systems, 40, 203-244.

Dubois D., Prade H. (1995a) Possibility theory as a basis for qualitative decision theory. Proc. of the 14th Inter. Joint Conf. on Artificial Intelligence (IJCAI'95), Montreal, Canada, Aug. 19-25, 1924-1930

Dubois D., Prade H. (1995b) What does fuzzy logic bring to AI ? ACM Computing Surveys, 27, 328-330.

Dubois D., Prade H. (1996a) What are fuzzy rules and how to use them. Fuzzy Sets and Systems, 84, 169-185.

Dubois D., Prade H. (1997) The three semantics of fuzzy sets. Fuzzy Sets and Systems, 90 141-150.

Dubois D., Prade H. (1996b) New trends and open problems in fuzzy logic and approximate reasoning. Theoria (San Sebastian, Spain), Vol. 11, n° 27, 109-121.

Dubois D., Prade H. (1998) Soft computing, fuzzy logic, and artificial intelligence. Soft Computing, 2 , to appear

Elkan C. (1994) The paradoxical success of fuzzy logic. (with discussions by many scientists and a reply by the author) IEEE Expert, August, 3-46.

Gärdenfors P. (1988) Knowledge in Flux — Modeling the Dynamics of Epistemic States. The MIT Press, Cambridge, MA.

Hájek P. (1995) Fuzzy logic as logic. In: Mathematical Models for Handling Partial Knowledge in Artificial Intelligence (G. Coletti, D. Dubois, R. Scozzafava, eds.), Plenum Press, New York, 21-30.

Holmblad L.P., Østergaard J.J. (1997) The progression of the first fuzzy logic control application. In: Fuzzy Information Engineering: A Guided Tour of Applications (D. Dubois, H. Prade, Yager R.R., eds.), Wiley, New York, 343-356.

Klawonn F., Kruse R. (1993) Equality relations as a basis for fuzzy control. Fuzzy Sets and Systems, 54, 147-156.

Kruse R., Gebhardt J., Klawonn F. (1994) Foundations of Fuzzy Systems. John Wiley, Chichester, West Sussex, UK.

Lehmann D., Magidor M. (1992) What does a conditionnal knowledge base entail? Artificial Intelligence, 55, 1-60.

Li D., Liu D.B (1990) A fuzzy PROLOG database system. Wiley, New York.

Lee R. C. T.(1972) Fuzzy logic and the resolution principle. J. Assoc. Comput. Mach. 19, 109-119

Mukaidono M. Shen Z.L Ding L.(1989) Fundamentals of fuzzy Prolog. Int. J. Approx. Reasoning, 3, 179-193

Mamdani E.H., Assilian S. (1975) An experiment in linguistic synthesis with a fuzzy logic controller. Int. J. of Man-Machine Studies, 7, 1-13.

Martin T.P., Ralescu A.L. (Eds.) Fuzzy Logic in Artificial Intelligence. Towards Intelligent Systems. (Proc. IJCAI'95 Workshop, Montreal, Canada)

Mendel J. (1995) Fuzzy logic systems for engineering: A tutorial. Proc. IEEE, 83, 345-377.

Novak V. (1996) Paradigm, formal properties and limits of fuzzy logic. Int. J. of General Systems, 24, 377-406.

Pearl J. (1990) System Z: a natural ordering of defaults with tractable applications to default reasoning. Proc. of the 3rd Conf. on the Theoretical Aspects of Reasonig About Knowledge (TARK'90), Morgan and Kaufmann, 121-135.

Peng Y., Reggia (1990) Abductive Inference Models for Diagnostic Problem-Solving. Springer Verlag, New York.

Ralescu A. (Ed.) (1994) Fuzzy Logic in Artificial Intelligence (Proc. IJCAI'93 Workshop, Chambery, France). Lecture Notes in Artificial Intelligence, Vol. 847, Springer Verlag, Berlin

Ruspini E. (1991) On the semantics of fuzzy logic. Int. J. of Approximate Reasoning, 5, 45-88.

Verbruggen H.B., Bruijn P.M. 1997) Fuzzy control and conventional control: What is (and can be) the real contribution of fuzzy systems? Fuzzy Sets and Systems, 90, 151-160.

Sanchez E. (1977) Solutions in conposite fuzzy relations equations — Application to medical diagnosis in Brouwerian logic. In: Fuzzy Automated and Decision Processes (M.M. Gupta et al., eds.) North-Holland, 221-234.

Yager R.R. (1995) **Fuzzy sets as a tool for modelling. In:** Computer Science Today. Recent trends and Developments. Lecture Notes in Artificial Intelligence, Vol. 1000, Springer Verlag, Berlin, 536-548.

Yager R.R. (1997) Fuzzy logics and artificial intelligence. Fuzzy Sets and Systems, 90, 193-19!.

Zadeh L.A. (1973) Outline of a new approach to the analysis of complex systems and decision processes. IEEE Trans. Systems, Man and Cybernetics, 3, 28-44.

Zadeh L.A. (1978) Fuzzy sets as a basis for a theory of possibility. Fuzzy Sets and Systems, 1, 3-28.

Zadeh L.A. (1979) A theory of approximate reasoning. In: Machine Intelligence, Vol. 9 (J.E. Hayes, D. Mitchie, L.I. Mikulich, eds.), Wiley, New York, 149-194.

Zadeh L.A. (1996) Fuzzy logic = computing with words. IEEE Trans. on Fuzzy Systems, 4, 103-111.

Zadeh L.A. (1997a) Toward a theory of fuzzy information granulation and its centrality in human reasoning and fuzzy logic. Fuzzy Sets and Systems, 90, 111-127.

Zadeh L.A. (1997b) What is soft computing? Soft Computing, 1(1), p. 1.

Mass Assignment Fundamentals for Computing with Words

James F. BALDWIN
Advanced Computing Research Centre, Dept. of Engineering Mathematics
University of Bristol, Bristol, BS8 1TR, ENGLAND
E-mail: Jim.Baldwin@bristol.ac.uk

Abstract – Various approaches based upon fuzzy and probabilistic methods are presented and discussed as a means to computing with words.

1. Introduction

It is important that we fully understand the contribution that soft computing can make to computing, see clearly the ways in which soft computing can be of use, understand the limits of this contribution and how it relates to other approaches.

Soft Computing is a term which is thrown around and often means very little. We must focus on some definition or at least be aware of what we mean by the term. In a general sense it means a mixture of fuzzy, neural and probabilistic technologies but this is far too vague to be useful. Often the term is used to promote the subject of fuzzy sets without any real attempt to give a precise appraisal of what is meant or how it can aid in real world applications.

I prefer to use the term computing with words and restrict the approach to fuzzy and probabilistic methods. Neural technology can, of course, be used to find optimal or near optimal fuzzy sets but this is just one way of tuning and is not fundamental to the basic approach of soft computing. Neural technology, of course, can play a fundamental part in memory management, perception and language understanding but this is unconnected with fuzzy and probabilistic approaches. This is a distributive network approach while soft computing is concerned with using knowledge bases consisting of rules of some kind. These rules can be logic type rules with uncertainties, causal nets, decision trees while neural nets store knowledge in the weights associated with a net architecture.

We will discuss below in detail what we mean by computing with words. Here we simply define it as using computing methods that compute with words in addition to numbers and symbols. To date computer methods have used only numbers and symbols. Words have some behaviour like symbols and some behaviour like numbers. They can be manipulated like symbols in a purely syntactic manner but we can also use their semantic content to provide different measures of comparison, counting and arithmetic calculations similar to the way we use numbers.

The sort of words which we are talking about are words which can be given to predicate variables. These words represent possibility distributions over the appropriate space and correspond to intervals, regions, or fuzzy sets. Consider the first order logic predicate, height(Name, Ht), which translates as the height of Name is Ht. We can instantiate Ht to a number representing the actual height of Name, an interval which contains this actual height or a fuzzy set which defines a possibility distribution over the Ht space for the actual height. In predicate logic a predicate represents a mapping from an n dimensional space of attribute vectors to {true, false} where the elements of the attribute vectors can be numbers or symbols. We now allow these attribute elements to also be words defined by fuzzy sets.

We can also generalise the mapping by allowing {true, false} to be replaced by [0, 1] and include vague mappings such as intervals on [0, 1] or more generally fuzzy sets on [0, 1]. We call these fuzzy sets truth value restrictions and they define a possibility distribution over [0, 1].

We do not require fuzzy predicates because we can always express the concept of a fuzzy predicate as a true fact in which a binary predicate takes fuzzy sets as arguments. We will explain this more fully with examples.

The statement
      Mary and Pat are friends is fairly true
can be replaced by
      Mary and Pat are quite good friends
so we replace the fuzzy predicate
      friends(Mary, Pat) is fairly true
with the binary predicate
      friendship(Mary, Pat, quite_good)
where quite_good is a fuzzy set on the space good which we can take as [0, 1]

We now discuss a more complicated example requiring compound words. We can make a statement such as 'it is quite true that a given person called Mary has red hair'. This would be written as
      has_red_hair(Mary) is quite_true

We can though, restate this as
      hair_colour(Mary, reddish)
where reddish is the value of the attribute colour. This is a fact which says that it is true that the hair colour of Mary is reddish.

Reddish is a fuzzy concept defined on a multidimensional colour space. In the predicate hair_colour(PERSON, COLOUR) COLOUR is an attribute which can be instantiated to values and these values can be words or a discrete fuzzy set on words. Reddish is a discrete fuzzy set on compound words. The words come from a three dimensional colour space. Each axis of this colour space is partitioned into a mutually exclusive and exhaustive set of fuzzy sets and each fuzzy set is a word. The three dimensional colour space is therefore represented by compound words each being a triple of one word from each of the dimensions.

In a knowledge base system some form of knowledge representation is used and this might be first order logic, logic programming, decision trees, causal nets, probabilistic nets etc. In all cases symbols and numbers are used for instantiation of variables. In first order logic we also have quantifiers. Numbers can be replaced by interval values or fuzzy sets and these are given symbolic names which then become words.

The concept of Quantifier in first order logic can also be generalised from that of existential and universal cases to include others such as most, few etc. This is really equivalent to using intervals or fuzzy sets defined on the [0, 1] space to instantiate probability values.

Thus computing with words is the manipulation of words which are possibility distributions over some numerical valued space which, of course, can be multi-dimensional. The manipulation can be similar to symbolic processing when only the symbol is taken into account or similar to arithmetic with numbers when the semantics of the word, namely, the possibility distribution, is taken into account.

Possibility distributions alone are not enough to make decisions. If a doctor observes certain spots on a child he will first think in terms of what diseases are possible. He then uses his prior knowledge on the probability of diseases occurring to provide him with a posterior or updated probability distribution over the possible diseases. Even though the spots look very much like measles spots he does not decide on this since in the particular region measles are most unlikely since no case of measles has been reported for many years.

Thus we should also take into account the probability distribution associated with the possibility distribution using the prior. We will illustrate this with a simple example.

Consider that you are told that a dice value is even. 'Even' is a word which corresponds to a grouping of dice values, namely, {2, 4, 6}. This defines a possibility distribution, namely

$$\Pi(2) = \Pi(4) = \Pi(6) = 1$$
$$\Pi(1) = \Pi(3) = \Pi(5) = 0$$

In practice we take for granted this possibility distribution and concentrate more on the probability distribution over the dice values. For this purpose we must know the prior, i.e. the distribution before we have this information that the dice value is even. Suppose the dice is known to be fair then we assume a uniform prior $\{Pr(i) = 1/6\}$ and we use the fact that the dice is even to update this prior to a posterior distribution, namely,

$Pr(2) = Pr(4) = Pr(6) = 1/3$
$Pr(1) = Pr(3) = Pr(5) = 0$

we can see this calculation in tabular form as

dice value	prior	dice even {2, 4, 6}	update
1	1/6	$\emptyset$: 0	0
2	1/6	{2} : k 1/6	1/3
3	1/6	$\emptyset$: 0	0
4	1/6	{4} : k 1/6	1/3
5	1/6	$\emptyset$: 0	0
6	1/6	{6} : k 1/6	1/3

normalisation factor
$= 1/2 = 1/k$

This is very obvious for this simple example but in other cases it is useful to understand how we obtain the probability distribution in detail.

Any decision that we wish to take concerning this value for the dice must take account of this updated probability distribution. It is not enough to take account of only the possibility distribution. For example suppose that we know that the dice is weighted and has a prior given in the next table then the update would be as given in that table.

dice value	prior	dice even {2, 4, 6}	update
1	0.1	$\emptyset$: 0	0
2	0.1	{2} : k 0.1 = 0.2	0.2
3	0.2	$\emptyset$: 0	0
4	0.3	{4} : k 0.3 = 0.6	0.6
5	0.2	$\emptyset$: 0	0
6	0.1	{6} : k 0.1 = 0.2	0.2

normalisation factor
$= 0.5 = 1/k$

When we replace the interval by some fuzzy set such as large, the method of calculating the probability distribution must take into account the fact that the possibilities for the possibility distribution are not values from {0, 1} but values in the interval [0, 1]. Otherwise we should be able to do the same as we did for the non- fuzzy case, namely use the prior to determine the probability distribution over the dice values.

We will show later how mass assignment theory can be used to determine this. For now it is enough to realise that we do not add too much additional complexity by using words corresponding to fuzzy sets as opposed to words corresponding to intervals.

Why do we want to use words with fuzzy semantics as opposed to precise definitions?

This is an important question but the answer is at least three fold. Humans use imprecise concepts and therefore if we wish to model users we must model this imprecision. We will also find that the use of fuzzy words as opposed to precisely defined words leads to smoother solutions for problems with continuous outputs and much greater compression of knowledge bases. The greater smoothness comes from the induced interpolation which fuzzy methods automatically provide. The compression comes about because the interaction of neighbouring words reduce the need for higher resolution. We will see the exact reasons for this smoothing and compression later.

The world is not in any way fuzzy. Each tree is different, each leaf is different, each object in the real world is different. No two objects are the same in the real world. It is not useful for humans to take account of every little detail and differentiate between every object from every other object. Humans need to talk about the real world and use concepts that apply to collections of objects with similar properties. We therefore group objects, cluster objects and treat them as belonging to the same class. We can then name this class and talk about the class as a whole using concepts that come about from other groupings of properties and behaviours and functions and causes etc. Thus we can say that Springer Spaniels are very energetic and good with children. Each concept here has a grouping. Springers cover the group of dogs, energetic covers a group of behavioural patterns, good with children also covers a group of moods and behaviours resulting from these moods.

How do we provide these groupings. They do not have precise definitions. We use prototypical cases and new cases are allocated to some groupings by using measures of similarity. Each concept has a fuzzy boundary. Objects can belong to some degree to several groupings of the same space. For example, a mongrel dog may be mostly Springer with some sheep dog characteristics. It belongs to the group of Springers but not completely or uniquely. How we make inferences in these cases which belong to several groupings with varying membership is the basic problem of fuzzy inheritance from multiple cases. It has no general answer and depends on the classes concerned and the inference being made. We can only learn from experience the rules of inference for multiple inheritance with fuzzy classes.

We give the example of multiple inheritance because it motivates the use of a fuzzy object oriented form of knowledge representation which is what we will conclude is necessary for computing with words. Words correspond to classes, fuzzy classes in general and object oriented knowledge bases deal directly with classes and their relationship with one another. This report will conclude that we should use Fril++ because it provides an object-oriented structure in which predicate variables can be instantiated to fuzzy sets and the rules and methods can be probabilistic in nature and the probabilities do not have to be known exactly.

In Fril++ we can instantiate probabilities to intervals which we know to contain the required probability. We could go one step further and allow these instantiations to be fuzzy sets. We will argue against this on the grounds that using fuzzy sets for probabilities lead to computational complexities. We require computational efficiency otherwise our formulation will be theoretical only and of little use. It is an approximation to replace fuzzy probabilities with intervals but we will find that this approximation can be adequate for what we require.

2. Words in the context of computing with words

As we said above, the sort of words that we are talking about are words which can be given to the variables of predicates. For example, the height of a person can be instantiated to a number, an interval containing the actual height, a symbol. Thus we have the cases:

height(X, 70)
height(X, [68. 72])
height(X, Y)

In the case of the interval, we have a possibility distribution over the height space H for the value of height. In this case each value in the interval [68, 72] is possible and all other values are not possible.

But we can also instantiate the height variable to a word such as tall, short etc. which is not just symbolic but has a semantics. The word describes a possibility distribution over the height space but this possibility distribution has possibilities that lie between and include 0 and 1.

height(X, tall)

The symbol tall is defined by a fuzzy set with membership function $\chi_{tall}(h)$ and this defines the possibility distribution over the height space H.

$$\Pi_{tall}(h) = \chi_{tall}(h) \quad \text{for all } h \, \varepsilon \, H$$

We wish to determine the probability distribution over H in a similar way in which we did this for the example in the introduction for the even dice.

How can we modify the prior probability distribution taking into account the new constraint that the height of X is tall?

2.1 Voting model semantics for fuzzy sets

In order to determine this modification we must give some semantics to the membership values which occur in the fuzzy set tall. In the dice case of even value the possibilities were 1 or 0. We knew that those cases of 1 corresponded to cases that could occur and those with value 0 with cases that could not occur. This could be described by a probability distribution over the power set for the dice values. For example, *even* corresponds to $\Pr(\{2, 4, 6\} = 1$ and $\Pr(X) = 0$ for any other $X \varepsilon P$(dice values).

This is why we were able to use $\{2, 4, 6\}$ as the set of values in the top of the tables used in the introduction, namely

"dice value   prior   even dice {2, 4, 6}   update"

How do we represent the possible groupings of values in this table when we have a fuzzy constraint rather than a crisp constraint.

Suppose we are told that the dice value is **large** rather than even where **large** is defined by the fuzzy set

      large = 4 / 0.2 + 5 / 0.8 + 6 / 1

In order to answer this question we introduce the voting model semantics for fuzzy sets.

Suppose we have a representative grouping of people who will take part in the following voting experiment. Each person is shown a dice value and asked to accept this value as large or reject it. They are not allowed to be uncertain but must make a binary decision even though they may be in doubt and have to think hard to come to a decision. There is a constraint on their decision taking - they must be consistent - this is a difficult concept but in this case means that if they vote for x being large then they must also vote for any digit greater than x as being large. This we call the constant threshold constraint.

The membership value of large for a given dice value x will be the proportion of the voters who accept x as being large.

Thus taking the threshold constraint into account the voting pattern could be

persons:

1	2	3	4	5	6	7	8	9	10
voting:

6	6	6	6	6	6	6	6	6	6
5	5	5	5	5	5	5	5		
4	4								

This means that 2 people accept only 6 as possible, 6 people accept the group $\{5, 6\}$ as possible and 2 people accept the grouping $\{4, 5, 6\}$ as possible. This is a representative set for people taken from the population at large. They can only vote the same if the concept is crisp. The reason why the concept is fuzzy is that different people will make different decisions with respect to some of the dice values. If we pick a person at random from the voters and this voter says the dice value is large then there will be a probability of 0.2 that the dice value is 6, a probability of 0.6 that the dice value is 5 or

6 and a probability of 0.2 that the dice value is 4 or 5 or 6. Thus we have a probability distribution over the power set of dice values, namely

$\{6\} : 0.2, \ \{5, 6\} : 0.6, \{4, 5, 6\} : 0.2$

This is what we understand when we are told that the dice value is **large** and we are told that the definition of **large** is that given above.

In the case of even dice we had the probability distribution

$\{2, 4, 6\} : 1$

2.2 Updating prior

We see how to modify the tables in the introduction to update the prior. We use the power set probability distribution at the top of the table. We find the intersections of the sets at the top of the table with those for the prior. How do we allocate the numbers in the table for the updated probabilities. We put a 0 probability for all null sets, as before. An intuitive way is to multiply the row and column probabilities and correct by multiplying by the normalising factor where this is 1 / sum of priors associated with non-null sets in the given column.

We will see later that this is equivalent to the updating method given by mass assignment theory.

Thus using this intuitive idea we obtain

dice value	prior	{6} : 0.2 {5, 6} : 0.6	{4, 5, 6} : 0.2	update
1	1/6	Ø : 0 $\quad$ Ø : 0	Ø : 0	0
2	1/6	Ø : 0 $\quad$ Ø : 0	Ø : 0	0
3	1/6	Ø : 0 $\quad$ Ø : 0	Ø : 0	0
4	1/6	Ø : 0 $\quad$ Ø : 0	{4} : 0.0667	0.0667
5	1/6	Ø : 0 $\quad$ {5} : 0.3	{5} : 0.0667	0.3667
6	1/6	{6} : 0.2 {6} : 0.3	{6} : 0.0667	0.5667

	normalising factor $= 1/(1/6) = 6$	normalising factor $= 1/(2/6) = 3$	normalising factor $= 1/(3/6) = 2$

For the case when we have the other prior used before we obtain

dice value	prior	{6} : 0.2	{5, 6} : 0.6	{4, 5, 6} : 0.2	update
1	0.1	Ø : 0	Ø : 0	Ø : 0	0
2	0.1	Ø : 0	Ø : 0	Ø : 0	0
3	0.2	Ø : 0	Ø : 0	Ø : 0	0
4	0.3	Ø : 0	Ø : 0	{4} : 0.1	0.1
5	0.2	Ø : 0	{5} : 0.4	{5} : 0.0667	0.4667
6	0.1	{6} : 0.2	{6} : 0.2	{6} : 0.0333	0.4333

	normalising factor	normalising factor	normalising factor
	= 10	= 10/3	= 10/6

2.3 Least prejudiced distribution

The updating procedure used above to obtain Pr(x I large) is equivalent to the least prejudiced distribution of the mass assignment theory.

The mass assignment for large is

$$MA_{large} = \{6\} : 0.2, \ \{5, 6\} : 0.6, \{4, 5, 6\} : 0.2$$

This is equivalent to a family of probability distributions over the dice values since to obtain a unique distribution we can allocate the masses associated with a set of points in any way we wish among the elements of the set. If we do this according to the prior we obtain what we have called the least prejudiced distribution.

In the case of the uniform prior this is

$$lpd_{large} = \quad 6 : 0.2 + 0.3 + 0.0667 = 0.5667$$
$$5 : 0.3 + 0.0667 = 0.3667$$
$$4 : 0.0667$$

In the case of the prior

$$1 : 0.1, \ 2 : 0.1, \ 3 : 0.2, \ 4 : 0.3, 5 : 0.2, 6 : 0.1$$

$$lpd_{large} = \quad 6 : 0.2 + 0.2 + 0.0333 = 0.4333$$
$$5 : 0.4 + 0.0667 = 0.4667$$
$$4 : 0.1$$

The calculation done in the table above is, of course, the same as using the prior on the mass assignment to obtain the least prejudiced distribution.

We therefore see that using the mass assignment theory we can obtain a probability distribution for the predicate variable when we are given a fuzzy instantiation of the variable. This computation for the case of an instantiation to a fuzzy set is only a small modification to the case when the instantiation is with a crisp set. This modification arises because the mass assignment in the fuzzy set corresponds to a probability distribution over the nested structure of the power set while in the crisp set it corresponds to a mass of 1 on one set of elements.

Thus whether we use fuzzy sets or crisp sets to define the words used for predicate variable instantiations, we arrive at the same position that the instantiation provides a probability distribution for the predicate variable. Any use of this predicate in making inferences must take this probability distribution into account.

Computing with words thus implies computing with probability distributions and it makes no difference whether these distributions arise because of a fuzzy instantiation of the predicate variables or crisp set instantiations. In both the fuzzy and the crisp cases we have a vagueness of information and this vagueness in both cases is described by a possibility distribution, a multi-valued distribution in the fuzzy case and a binary one in the crisp case. We use the prior to move from the possibility distribution to the probability distribution.

2.4 Example of computing with words

We give here an example of computing with words using the least prejudiced distribution associated with the fuzzy sets. The method of calculation is based on probability theory and we compare the approach with that the more normal way for fuzzy set theory of using the extension principle.

We illustrate the method using a fuzzy arithmetic example.

Consider two fuzzy sets, **large** and **small**, defined on weighted dice with prior
$1 : 0.1, \ 2 : 0.1, \ 3 : 0.2, \ 4 : 0.3, 5 : 0.2, 6 : 0.1$

$\qquad$ **large** $= 4 / 0.2 + 5 / 0.8 + 6 / 1$
$\qquad$ **small** $= 1 / 1 + 2 / 0.8 + 3 / 0.3$

Suppose these are the values of two independent throws of the dice. We will determine the probability distribution for the sum

$\qquad$ **large + small,**

We use the prior to determine the least prejudiced distributions for **small** and **large** and use these to determine the distribution over the sum.

$MA_{large} = \{6\} : 0.2, \ \{5, 6\} : 0.6, \ \{4, 5, 6\} : 0.2$

$lpd_{large} = \qquad 6 : 0.4333, \ 5 : 0.4667, \ 4 : 0.1$

$MA_{small} = \{1\} : 0.2, \ \{1, 2\} : 0.5, \ \{1, 2, 3\} : 0.3$

$lpd_{small} =$ 1 : 0.525, 5 : 0.325, 4 : 0.15

We use the lpd's of large and small to determine the sum of **large** and **small**.

	lpd for large	0.1	0.4667	0.4333
lpd for small	sum	4	5	6
0.525	1	5 : 0.0525	6 : 0.245	7 : 0.2275
0.325	2	6 : 0.0325	7 : 0.1517	8 : 0.1408
0.15	3	7 : 0.015	8 : 0.07 9 : 0.065	

giving
large + small : 5 : 0.0525, 6 : 0.2775, 7 : 0.3942, 8 : 0.2108, 9 : 0.065

Using fuzzy arithmetic with the min / max rule :

         large = 4 / 0.2 + 5 / 0.8 + 6 / 1
         small = 1 / 1 + 2 / 0.8 + 3 / 0.3

	large	0.2	0.8	1
small	sum	4	5	6
1	1	5 : 0.1	6 : 0.8	7 : 0.1
0.8	2	6 : 0.2	7 : 0.8	8 : 0.8
0.3	3	7 : 0.2	8 : 0.3	9 ; 0.3

giving
sum = 5 / 0.1 + 6 / 0.8 + 7 / 1 + 8 / 0.8 + 9 / 0.3

MA_{sum} = {7} : 0.2, {6, 7, 8} : 0.5, {6, 7, 8, 9} : 0.2, { 5, 6 7, 8, 9} : 0.1

We can determine the least prejudiced distribution from this mass assignment and the prior for sum as given by

		0.1	0.1	0.2	0.3 0.2	0.1	
	sum	1	2	3	4	5	6
0.1	1	2 : 0.01	3 ; 0.01	4 : 0.02	5 : 0.03	6 : 0.02	7 : 0.01
0.1	2	3 : 0.01	4 : 0.01	5 : 0.02	6 : 0.03	7 : 0.02	8 : 0.01
0.2	3	4 : 0.02	5 : 0.02	6 : 0.04	7 : 0.06	8 : 0.04	9 : 0.02
0.3	4	5 : 0.03	6 : 0.03	7 : 0.06	8 : 0.09	9 : 0.06	10 : 0.03
0.2	5	6 : 0.02	7 : 0.02	8 : 0.04	9 : 0.06	10 : 0.04	11 : 0.02
0.1	6	7 : 0.01	8 : 0.01	9 : 0.02	10 : 0.03	11 : 0.02	12 : 0.01

i.e the prior

sum : 2 : 0.01, 3 : 0.02, 4 : 0.05, 5 : 0.1, 6 : 0.14, 7 : 0.18, 8 : 0.19, 9 : 0.16
       10 : 0.1, 11 : 0.04, 12 : 0.01

The least prejudiced distribution is

7 : 0.2 + (0.18/0.51)*0.5 + (0.18/0.67)*0.2 + (0.18/0.77)*0.1 = 0.4536
6: (0.14/0.51)*0.5 + (0.14/0.67)*0.2 + (0.14/0.77)*0.1 = 0.1972
8 : (0.19/0.51)*0.5 + (0.19/0.67)*0.2 + (0.19/0.77)*0.1 = 0.2677
9 : (0.16/0.67)*0.2 + (0.16/0.77)*0.1 = 0.0685
5 : (0.1/0.77)*0.1 = 0.013

$lpd_{sum-fuzzy}$ = 5 : 0.013, 6 : 0.1972, 7 : 0.4536, 8 : 0.2677, 9 : 0.0685

While the answers are similar they are by no means the same and gave a slightly different ordering. Which solution should we accept as the more reasonable one. In the first approach we went directly from mass assignments to the least prejudiced distributions and use only these to determine the distribution for the sum. In the fuzzy case we lose information concerning how we obtain a given sum and record only the highest possibility when we can obtain the same sum in more than one way.

In order to decide which is the correct solution we will use the mass assignments directly. By this we mean that we will take into account the mass assignments and the various possible pairings of the scores of the two dice. Even though the pairings (6, 1) and (5, 2) give the same sum we will treat them as different until the end of the computation. In this way no approximation is made in the updating and no assumptions are made.

We use the mass assignments for **large** and **small**, combine the pairings using the fact that the two dice values are independent and use the prior for these pairings to obtain the final least prejudiced distribution for the sum.

MA_{large} = {6} : 0.2, {5, 6} : 0.6, {4, 5, 6} : 0.2

MA_{small} = {1} : 0.2, {1, 2} : 0.5, {1, 2, 3} : 0.3

		0.2 {1}	0.5 {1, 2}	0.3 {1, 2,3 }
0.2	{6}	{(6, 1) = 7} : 0.04	{(6,1)=7, (6,2)=8}} : 0.1	{(6,1)=7, (6,2)=8, (6,3)=9} : 0.06
0.6	{5, 6}	{(5,1)=6, (6,1)=7} : 0.12	{(5,1)=6, (5,2)=7, (6,1)=7, (6,2)=8} : 0.3	{(5,1)=6, (5,2)=7, (5,3)= 8, (6,1)=7, (6,2)=8, (6,3)=9} : 0.18
0.2	{4, 5, 6}	{(4,1)=5, (5,1)=6, (6,1)=7} : 0.04	{(4,1)=5, (4,2)=6, (5,1)=6, (5,2)=7, (6,1)=7, (6,2)=8} : 0.1	{(4,1)=5, (4,2)=6, (4,3)=7, (5,1)=6, (5,2)=7, (5,3)=8, (6,1)=7, (6,2)=8, (6,3)=9} : 0.06

We now use the prior for these pairings, namely,

	sum	0.1 1	0.1 2	0.2 3	0..3 4	0.2 5	0.1 6
0.1	1	2 : 0.01	3 : 0.01	4 : 0.02	5 : 0.03	6 : 0.02	7 : 0.01
0.1	2	3 : 0.01	4 : 0.01	5 : 0.02	6 : 0.03	7 : 0.02	8 : 0.01
0.2	3	4 : 0.02	5 : 0.02	6 : 0.04	7 : 0.06	8 : 0.04	9 : 0.02
0.3	4	5 : 0.03	6 : 0.03	7 : 0.06	8 : 0.09	9 : 0.06	10 : 0.03
0.2	5	6: 0.02	7 : 0.02	8 : 0.04	9 : 0.06	10 : 0.04	11 : 0.02
0.1	6	7 : 0.01	8 : 0.01	9 : 0.02	10 : 0.03	11 : 0.02	12 : 0.01

to obtain the least prejudiced distribution for the pairings in the combined mass assignment as given below.

		0.2 {1}	0.5 {1, 2}	0.3 {1, 2,3 }
0.2	{6}	7 : 0.04	7 : 0.05 8 :0.05	7 : 0.015, 8 : 0.015, 9 : 0.03
0.6	{5, 6}	6 : 0.08, 7 : 0.04	6 : 0.1, 7 : 0.1, 7 : 0.05, 8 : 0.05	6 : 0.03, 7 : 0.03, 8 : 0.06, 7 : 0.015, 8 : 0.015, 9 : 0.03
0.2	{4, 5, 6}	5 : 0.02, 6 : 0.0133, 7 : 0.0067	5 : 0.025, 6 : 0.025, 6 : 0.0167, 7 : 0.0167, 7 : 0.0083 8 : 0.0083 : 0.1	5 : 0.0075 6 : 0.0075 7 : 0.015 6 : 0.005 7, : 0.005 8 : 0.01 7 : 0.0025 8 : 0.0025 9 : 0.005

which gives the least prejudiced distribution for sum as

lpd_{sum} = 5 : 0.0525, 6 : 0.2775, 7 : 0.3942, 8 : 0.2108, 9 : 0.065

which is the same as **large + small** given above.

We therefore see that the use of the least prejudiced distributions for **large** and **small** directly gives the same solution as the mass assignment full method and is much simpler. The use of fuzzy arithmetic only provides an approximate solution.

If we ignore the pairings and simply use the sum then we will only get an approximate solution like we did in the fuzzy case. Information is once again thrown away.

We use the mass assignment approach ignoring the actual pairings and just taking the sum into account. Thus we would get

		0.2 {1}	0.5 {1, 2}	0.3 {1, 2,3 }
0.2	{6}	{7} : 0.04	{7, 8}} : 0.1	{7, 8, 9} : 0.06
0.6	{5, 6}	{6, 7} : 0.12	{6,7, 8} : 0.3	{6,7,8,9} : 0.18
0.2	{4, 5, 6}	{5, 6,7} : 0.04	{5, 6,7, 8} : 0.1	{5, 6, 7, 8, 9} : 0.06

and we can use the prior for sum, namely,

sum : 2 : 0.01, 3 : 0.02, 4 : 0.05, 5 : 0.1, 6 : 0.14, 7 : 0.18, 8 : 0.19, 9 : 0.16
10 : 0.1, 11 : 0.04, 12 : 0.01

to obtain the least prejudiced distribution in this case

		0.2 {1}	0.5 {1, 2}	0.3 {1, 2,3 }
0.2	{6}	7 : 0.04	7 : 0.0486, 8 : 0.0514	7 : 0.0204, 8 : 0.0215, 9 : 0.0181
0.6	{5, 6}	6 : 0.0005, 7 : 0.0675	6 : 0.0824, 7 : 0.1059, 8 : 1118}	6 : 0.0376, 7 : 0.0484, 8 : 0.051, 9 : 0.043
0.2	{4, 5, 6}	5 : 0.0095, 6 : 0.0133, 7 : 0.0171	5 : 00164, 6 : 0.0223, 7 : 0.0295, 8 : 0.0311	5 : 0.0078, 6 : 0.0109, 7 : 0.0140, 8 0.0148, 9 : 0.0125

lpd$_{sum\text{-}ma\text{-}no\text{-}pairings}$ =
5 : 0.0189, 6 : 0.167, 7 : 0.3914, 8 : 0.2816, 9 : 0.0736

which we see as we suggested is only an approximate solution. We note that the solution values are slightly different but the correct ordering is preserved.

3. More general computing with words

When we view computing with words in this way we see that the basic inference mechanisms and any other form of computations must be based on probability theory. We have not strayed from a Bayesian point of view. We have used a modified updating procedure to go from the prior to an updated distribution taking the new constraints into account. When this constraint is a crisp set we use the normal Bayesian updating procedure. When the constraint is fuzzy we use an extended Bayesian updating procedure.

In this section we will discuss the use of computing with words for classification and prediction problems. The basic concept here will be to see further how classical methods of computing using Bayesian techniques need to be modified when using words rather than numbers and symbols. We have illustrated above that probability theory is at the heart of computing with words. Probability computations involve counting. How many objects belong to a certain class is basic to these computations. We have to modify this counting procedure when the classes are fuzzy. The fundamental question of how we do this will be discussed below. The set of words defined over a Universe of discourse will be assumed to form a fuzzy partition. By this we men that for any value of the Universe of discourse, the sum of the membership values of the words will be 1. Any object is assumed to have a feature with value in this Universe of discourse. Let us suppose this value is x in X, the Universe of Discourse. Let us suppose that the fuzzy partition is {fi} where each fi is a word defined by a fuzzy set and further

$$\sum_i \mu_{fi}(x) = 1$$

We think of the Universe of Discourse as composed of classes **fi**. These classes are to be treated in the same way that symbols are treated in probability theory. The object with feature vale x must be allocated to these classes. If the classes are defined by a crisp partition on the Universe of Discourse then the object would belong to one class. The count would be 1 for this class. But, since the classes are defined by fuzzy sets, the object will, in general, belong with varying memberships to more than one class. How do we distribute the count of 1 among these classes? This is the fundamental question. If we can answer this question then this will define the modification to our counting procedure and we can then proceed in the classical way of using probability theory. This single modification is all that is required to use probability theory with words defined by fuzzy sets as opposed to numbers or crisp intervals. Our computational algorithms will not change in nature except in this simple modification of counting. All the classical methods will still be available provided we replace the simple counting of allocating a single object to a single class with our modified counting procedure in which the single object will be distributed among several classes. The sum of the proportions we give to the various classes will, of course, sum to 1 for a single object.

Thus, for example, we can use the Artificial Intelligence ID3 algorithm for forming decision trees with features which can take a fuzzy partition of words as values. The algorithm can be used directly as before but a single tuple in the data base of examples will not travel along a single branch of the decision tree but will be distributed in the correct proportions along varying branches corresponding to the words used as values for the given feature.

Bayesian classifier methods can also be used as before but with the modified counting used instead of the simple counting procedure normally used. Markov chains are applicable but if the branches are defined by words rather than symbols or precise numbers or intervals, we will move from a given node into a distribution of nodes and the probability distribution will depend on the words of the branches form the given node. This is equivalent to the count modification discussed above.

The same is true for causal nets in which the branches form the various nodes are defined by a fuzzy partition of words. This application of using words for causal nets could help reduce the complexity when the variables can take continuous values. The continuous variable would be replaces by a discrete fuzzy partition of words.

The same sort of usage can provided for control problems. The continuous state variables can be replaces with a fuzzy partition of words. This can also apply to control variables. It can also apply to prediction problems in which the output variable which, in general, would be continuous is once again replaced with a discrete fuzzy partition. The prediction problem can then be thought of as a classification problem. We will have an additional problem of how to convert the probability distribution over the output words to a precise value on the original output space. This will be achieved with a defuzzification algorithm which again will depend on probability theory.

The set of possible values of any variable of any computational algorithm can be replaced with a discrete fuzzy partition and this modified counting procedure used to amend the algorithm which otherwise will be the same. There are so many applications which can use this approach to computing with words.

We could use word computational cellular automata which would extend the paradigm of computing with words to many other areas such as physics and evolutionary programming, modelling of life processes and more general systems modelling.

We complicate the counting but simplify the values for the variables. What do we achieve with this? In general, we hope to achieve better generalisation in the case of classification and smoother solutions in the case of prediction, greater compression in the case of induced knowledge bases, simplification of overall computation in the case of causal nets and control problems. In general we can say that we complicate slightly to simplify greatly. We move form a continuous space of feature values into a discrete space of a fuzzy partition and this only complicates the counting procedure. This leads to overall simplification of computation because we need only to take account of a few words treated as symbols rather than continuous variables. We also benefit in induction problems because the fuzzy set interactions provide smoother solutions and better generalisation.

We will now return to the basic issue of how we modify the counting procedure when we use words defined by fuzzy sets rather than words defined by symbols, numbers or intervals.

4. Modified counting procedure

Consider a feature F with continuous range of values R. We divide R into crisp intervals A, B, C, D, E.

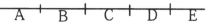

If we take a set of objects of a certain class C with F feature values in R then we can allocate each of these values to their appropriate interval. This will provide an estimate for $Pr(C \mid r)$ for any object with feature value r.

We will now divide R into a set of mutually exclusive fuzzy sets $f_A, ..., f_E$ as shown

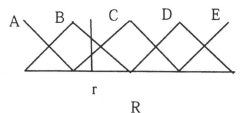

The labels A, ..., E represent words defined by fuzzy sets.

An object with feature value r, as shown must be allocated to the words in the same way as for the crisp case. But in this case we have to modify the procedure because the value r has membership in both the B and C words.

Thus r is represented in the word space as

$r = B / \mu_B(r) + c / \mu_C(r)$

where $\mu_B(r) + \mu_C(r) = 1$

Suppose $\mu_B(r) = 0.7$ and $\mu_C(r) = 0.3$ then we represent this in voting terms as

1	2	3	4	5	6	7	8	9	10
B	B	B	B	B	B	B			
C	C	C							

Because the fuzzy set for r is not normalised we have inconsistency and 3 voters accept neither B or C for r. We will force voters 8, 9 and 10 to accept one of these values - they will accept B and C with equal probability. Therefore the least prejudiced distribution for r in terms of the words is

B : 0.4 + 3(1/2) + 3(1/2) = 0.7
C : 3(1/2) + 3(1/2) = 0.3

These values are the same as the membership of each in r.

This is easily shown to be generally true. We could force the voters who did not accept either B or C to accept these in proportion to the other voters and this would be equivalent to ignoring the voters 8, 9, 10, forming a non normalised least prejudiced distribution and then normalising.

We therefore accept the membership values for each of the words as the probability of the words being chosen by a random voter when told the value of the feature is r.

The object with value r is therefore allocated as
$\mu_B(r)$ to B and $\mu_C(r)$ to C

We can also use trapezoidal fuzzy sets for the words and in this case the least prejudiced distribution is formed in the usual way. In this case the for any value of r, there will only be one fuzzy set with membership 1. With this restriction there can be variable overlapping of the fuzzy sets.

Consider a multi-dimensional feature space. For simplicity we will consider a two dimensional space so we can illustrate graphically the ideas. Let features F1 and F2 take values from continuous ranges R1 and R2. Suppose that we divide R1 and R2 into crisp intervals as illustrated in diagram below.

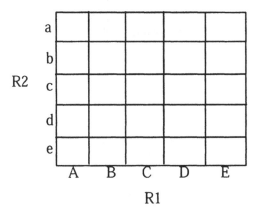

Consider that we wish to determine $Pr(C \mid r1, r2)$ where C is a class of object with features F1 having value r1 and F2 value r2. We use an example set to obtain a relative frequency by counting the number of objects of class C which lie in the cell corresponding to r1, r2 feature values. This number divided by the total number of examples of class C will give an estimate for this probability.

It is this counting procedure which we wish to modify in the case where the intervals are fuzzy rather than crisp. Let the feature spaces R1 and R2 each be divided into a mutually exclusive set of fuzzy sets, f_A, ..., f_E for R1 and f_a, ..., f_e for R2 as shown below. We label these fuzzy sets with word names A, ..., E. a, ..., e respectively.

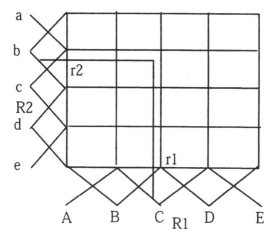

An object with feature value F1 of r1 and F2 of r2 will have membership in more than one fuzzy set for each feature. Consider object with values r1 and r2 shown in diagram above. This object can be represented as (r1, r2) in the original feature space or as

$$(\ B \ / \ \mu_B(r1) + C \ / \ \mu_C(r1), \ b \ / \ \mu_b(r2) + c \ / \ \mu_c(r2) \ )$$

in the new word feature space.

We wish to allocate this object among the cells Bb, Bc, Cb. Cc.

Using the method of allocation described above we will allocate as

$\mu_B(r1) \ \mu_b(r2)$ to Bb, $\mu_B(r1) \ \mu_c(r2)$ to Bc, $\mu_C(r1) \ \mu_b(r2)$ to Cb, $\mu_C(r1) \ \mu_c(r2)$ to Cc

The sum of these allocations is, of course, 1.

With this modified counting procedure, the mass assignment theory shows that we can now ignore the fuzziness and simply use the word cells as if they are crisp. The standard probability theory applies.

5. Computing with words for user modelling

The methods developed in 3 can be used for user modelling - the user model will consist of a knowledge base for the user which will describe the users behaviours and preferences in the form of an appropriate profile for directing actions taken by the computer and answering queries required by the computer for the benefit of the user. Intelligent agents performing specialised tasks can use this knowledge base with sensorial information to provide a better service to the user than would be possible if acting more generally. The use of fuzzy type Fril rules provide both compression of the knowledge base and a smoothness in predictions.

There is an important point that we should discuss here and which we have not previously addressed. The computer will not have a large data base of user behaviours to use to form the rules. The machine learning methods we have discussed to date for automatically forming the rules require representative data bases of positive and negative examples. This is appropriate for some applications. For example, consider that an intelligent filtering agent is used to filter web information so that only useful information for the user is presented to him or her. Suppose the decision made depends on key attribute values and that a history of the users use of information from the past has been recorded. This will provide a suitable data base for the above machine learning methods.

For many applications of intelligent agents and design of improved computer interfaces there will only be sparse data available for deriving a suitable user model. In this case we an make an approximate model and update this model as the user response is recorded and monitored. How do we update the user model when new information of the user response is obtained?

This question of updating Fril type fuzzy rules with ongoing collection of new information is a basic and difficult question. We will not attempt to answer this in this report but leave it for a later report. We can say though that what is required is not just a tuning of the words used in the fuzzy rules but the structure of the rules can change and even new predicates introduced.

Another aspect of importance when using user models and sensorial information from different sources is the need for fusion of solutions. Partial solutions are found from different viewpoints and these must be fused to give a final solution. We have discussed this briefly in earlier reports but we will return to this again later.

6. Conclusions

In this paper we have described what we mean by computing with words and emphasised that using fuzzy words compared with simple intervals should not change greatly the nature of the computations. We have provided a different philosophy to computing with words than is normally assumed. This we believe is more powerful and more accurate and will provide the required sophistication for user modelling.

The paper is self contained but we list below references which illustrate the concepts dealt with here and deal with applications to many different areas.

7. References

Baldwin, J. F. (1986). "Support Logic Programming" in Fuzzy Sets - Theory and Applications, Ed. A. Jones and e. al, D. Reidel. 133-170.

Baldwin, J. F. (1991a). "Evidential Reasoning under Probabilistic and Fuzzy Uncertainties" in An Introduction to Fuzzy Logic and Applications in Intelligent Systems, Ed. R. R. Yager and L. A. Zadeh, Kluwer Academic Publishers. 297-335.

Baldwin, J. F. (1991b). "A New Approach to Inference Under Uncertainty for Knowledge Based systems" in Symbolic and Quantitative Approaches to Uncertainty, Ed. R. Kruse and P. Siegel, Springer-Verlag, Lecture Notes in Computer science 548. 107-115.

Baldwin, J. F. (1992a). "A Calculus For Mass Assignments In Evidential Reasoning" in Advances in the Dempster-Shafer Theory of Evidence, Ed. M. Fedrizzi, J. Kacprzyk and R. R. Yager, John Wiley.

Baldwin, J. F. (1992b). "The Management of Fuzzy and Probabilistic Uncertainties for Knowledge Based Systems" in Encyclopaedia of AI, Ed. S. A. Shapiro, John Wiley. (2nd ed.) 528-537.

Baldwin, J. F. (1993b). "Fuzzy Reasoning in Fril for Fuzzy Control and other Knowledge-based Applications." Asia-Pacific Engineering Journal 3: 59-81.

Baldwin, J. F. (1993a). "Fuzzy , Probabilistic and Evidential Reasoning in Fril", Proc. 2nd IEEE International Conference on Fuzzy Systems, San Francisco, CA, 459-464. (ISBN 0-7803-0614-7).

Baldwin, J. F. (1993). "Fuzzy Sets, Fuzzy Clustering, and Fuzzy Rules in AI" in Fuzzy Logic in AI, Ed. A. L. Ralescu, Springer Verlag. 10-23.

Baldwin, J. F. and Martin, T. P. (1995). "Refining Knowledge from Uncertain Relations – a Fuzzy Data Browser based on Fuzzy Object-Oriented Programming in Fril", Proc. 4th IEEE International , Conference on Fuzzy Systems, Yokohama, Japan, 27-34.

Baldwin, J. F. (1996). "Knowledge from Data using Fril and Fuzzy Methods" in Fuzzy Logic in AI, Ed. J. F. Baldwin, John Wiley. 33-76.

Baldwin, J. F., Lawry, J. and Martin, T. P. (1996). "Efficient Algorithms for Semantic Unification", Proc. Information Processing and the Management of Uncertainty, Spain, 527-532.

Baldwin, J. F. and Martin, T. P. (1991). "An Abstract Mechanism for Handling Uncertainty" in Uncertainty in Knowledge Bases, Ed. B. Bouchon-Meunier, R. R. Yager and L. A. Zadeh, Springer Verlag. 126-135.

Baldwin, J. F. and Martin, T. P. (1992). "Fast Operations on Fuzzy Sets in the Abstract Fril Machine", Proc. First IEEE International Conference on Fuzzy Systems, San Diego, CA, 803-810. (ISBN 0-7803-0236-2).

Baldwin, J. F. and Martin, T. P. (1993). "From Fuzzy Databases to an Intelligent Manual using Fril." J.Intelligent Information Systems 2: 365-395.

Baldwin, J. F. and Martin, T. P. (1994). "Fuzzifying a Target Motion Analysis Model Using Fril and Mathematica", Proc. 3rd IEEE International Conference on Fuzzy Systems, Florida, 1171-1175.

Baldwin, J. F. and Martin, T. P. (1996). "A Fuzzy Data Browser in Fril" in Fuzzy Logic in AI, Ed. J. F. Baldwin, John Wiley. 101-124.

Baldwin, J. F., Gooch, R. M. and Martin, T. P. (1996). "Fuzzy Processing of Hydrophone Sounds." Fuzzy Sets and Systems 77(1): 35-48.

Baldwin, J. F. and Martin, T. P. (1997). "Basic Concepts of a Fuzzy Logic Data Browser with Applications" in Software Agents and Soft Computing: Concepts and Applications, Ed. H. S. Nwana and N. Azarmi, Springer (LNAI 1198). 211-241.

Baldwin, J. F., Martin, T. P. and Pilsworth, B. W. (1987). "The Implementation of FPROLOG - a Fuzzy Prolog Interpreter." Fuzzy Sets and Systems 23: 119-129.

Baldwin, J. F., Martin, T. P. and Pilsworth, B. W. (1988). "FRIL Manual (Version 4.0)". Fril Systems Ltd, Bristol Business Centre, Maggs House, Queens Road, Bristol, BS8 1QX, UK. 1-697.

Baldwin, J. F., Martin, T. P. and Pilsworth, B. W. (1995). "FRIL - Fuzzy and Evidential Reasoning in AI", Research Studies Press (John Wiley).

Baldwin, J. F., Lawry, J. and Martin, T. P. (1997a). "The Application of Generalised Fuzzy Rules to Machine Learning and Automated Knowledge Discovery." International Journal of Uncertainty, Fuzziness, and Knowledge-based Systems (accepted): 1-22.

Baldwin, J. F., Lawry, J. and Martin, T. P. (1997b). "A Mass Assignment Based ID3 Algorithm for Decision Tree Induction." International Journal of Intelligent Systems 12(7): 523-552.

Baldwin, J. F., Lawry, J. and Martin, T. P. (1997c). "Mass Assignment Fuzzy ID3 with Applications", Proc. Fuzzy Logic - Applications and Future Directions, London, 278-294.

Baldwin, J. F., Martin, T. P. and Shanahan J. G. (1997), "Fuzzy logic methods in vision recognition", in Proc. Fuzzy Logic: Applications and Future Directions Workshop, London, UK, pp 300-316.

Baldwin, J. F., Martin, T. P. and Shanahan J. G. (1997), "Modelling with words using Cartesian granule features", in Proc. FUZZ-IEEE, Barcelona, Spain, pp 1295-1300.

A Method to Use Uncertain Domain Knowledge in the Induction of Classification Knowledge Based on ID3

Hiroshi Narazaki 1, Ichiro Shigaki 2

[1] Electronics and Information Technology Research Laboratory, Kobe Steel, Ltd.
5-5, Takatsuka-dai 1-chome, Nishi-ku, Kobe, 651-2271, Japan
[2] Department of Industrial Management, Osaka Institute of Technology
Omiya 5-16-1, Asahi-ku, Osaka, 525-0002, Japan

Abstract. We propose a method to use uncertain and qualitative domain knowledge in inducing a classification tree based on ID3. We introduce a consistency degree between data and domain knowledge such as "*The reduction rate in the latter stage is larger, the quality of a product is usually the better.*" As criteria for inducing a decision tree, we use the consistency degree together with the traditional criterion based on the information-theoretic measure. In this work, the consistency degree is mainly used for pruning the hypotheses whose consistency degree with domain knowledge is below a pre-specified threshold. We demonstrate the effectiveness of our method using the data in a superconducting wire manufacturing domain.

1 Introduction

The progress of computer and network technologies has drastically reduced the cost for collecting, storing, and retrieving data. However, it is often pointed out that what is useful is not the data themselves, but the knowledge that we acquire from those data. Technologies such as *Machine learning* and *data mining* contribute to realizing computerized assistance to make the process of discovering knowledge from data more efficient, where *knowledge discovery* usually refers to finding non-trivial and useful *pattern* in the data, which may be represented in various forms such as a rule and a decision tree.

This paper discusses a method to use uncertain domain knowledge in finding patterns in the data. More specifically, we present a method to use uncertain domain knowledge in induction of a classification tree based on ID3[1].

We describe the motivation of our work.

The straightforward application of a pattern-finding method (such as ID3) often yields patterns which are difficult to explain, or even *conflicting* from the viewpoint of domain knowledge. Though various factors may be considered as the source for such conflict, in this work, we focus our attention on the *data quality* characterized from the viewpoint of consistency between data and existing domain knowledge. In other words, we consider that the data are of poor quality when they are biased and do not reflect the characteristics accepted by domain experts.

Many pattern-finding algorithms employ statistical approaches. In ID3, a decision tree is induced based on the information-theoretic measure on the training data. This approach assumes the training data of *good-quality*: The data should be sufficiently rich in quantity, uniform in distribution, complete, and free of noise.

Unfortunately, in many applications, such assumptions are difficult to be met. The data are often sparse, strongly biased, incomplete, and noisy. Furthermore, collecting data is sometimes costly or even technically difficult. In such a situation, the straightforward application of a pattern-finding method tends to reflect contingencies among the data at hand, rather than the novel finding in the domain.

Valiant's work[2] investigates the effect of data quality on induced knowledge from the statistical viewpoint, in which the problem is to find the condition on the data to induce (almost) correct knowledge. In this work, we pursue a *knowledge approach*, presenting a method to use domain knowledge to reduce the effects caused by the *poor quality* of training data.

The outline of our approach is described as follows:

Domain knowledge is described by fuzzy IF-THEN rules. Then, we define a consistency degree between the data and those fuzzy rules.

We use a *fuzzy* approach because we want to deal with uncertain domain knowledge such as "*the higher temperature in the early stages of the process usually contributes to the improvement of product quality.*" It should be noted that, in the domain where we consider the use of a pattern-finding algorithm, domain knowledge is usually partial, qualitative, and uncertain. (If complete and accurate domain knowledge is available, there is no need to use a patter-finding algorithm.)

Fuzzy logic enables us to represent and use uncertain knowledge in computation as described in [3]. Zadeh interprets a fuzzy rule such as "*A is usually B*" in the following manner: Zadeh defines a *sigma-count*, which is, roughly speaking, a generalized conditional probability $Prob(B|A)$, and the sigma-count follows the *possibility distribution* determined by a membership function of "*usually.*" Our method is based on Zadeh's approach.

We treat the induction problem as a two-criteria decision-making problem where, in addition to the traditional criterion based on statistical characteristics, we use the consistency of the training data with domain knowledge represented by fuzzy rules. As is always the case in multi-criteria decision-making problems, the candidates are only partially ordered, and we need a method to aggregate multiple criteria to rank the candidates. Various methods may be possible for this aggregation, and the choice depends on individual applications. In this paper, we use the following approach: We use consistency degree for screening purpose, i.e. the hypotheses having the consistency degree lower than a certain threshold are removed. Then, we select the *optimum hypothesis* based on the traditional statistical criterion.

In our previous work[4], a machine learning approach to extract knowledge for improving the operation of a sintering process in a steel-making plant is presented. In that work, a machine learning method is applied to generate *candidates* of the parameters that describe operational conditions. Then, domain scientific knowledge is used to select the best parameter set from the viewpoint of consistency with knowledge and practical usefulness. However, in that work, the latter part, i.e. the selection of the consistent and useful parameter set, is totally left for a human expert. This work provides a method to incorporate uncertain domain knowledge explicitly into the induction process when knowledge is described by fuzzy rules.

2 Domain

We discuss our method using the data in the Nb-Ti superconducting wire domain. We give a brief description of the domain.

The Nb-Ti superconducting wire is mainly used in magnetic applications. It is usually fabricated in a multifilamentary form such that the filaments are dispersed in a normal metal matrix. The fabrication process is composed of two stages; monofilamentary wire working and multifilamentary wire working. The monofilamentary working reduces a Nb-Ti ingot to a rod by hot hydrostatic extrusion and drawing. Then, in the multifilamentary working, after assembling the Nb-Ti monofilaments into a bundle and slipping them into a Cu shell, the iterative rod drawing and heat treatment processes are applied to the multifilamentary wires.

A production schedule of Nb-Ti superconducting wire, denoted by P, is specified by the following parameters:

1. n, the number of the iteration of drawing and heat treatment processes.
2. C_i, the parameters in the i-th operation, i.e.

$$C_i = (R_i, T_i, H_i), i = 1, 2, ..., n$$

where R_i, T_i, and H_i are the reduction rate of the diameter in drawing, the temperature $(^\circ C)$ of the heat treatment, and the duration (hours) of the heat treatment, respectively.

We denote a production schedule P of a wire by

$$P = \{C_i = (R_i, T_i, H_i), i = 1, 2, .., n\}.$$

Six production schedules are shown in Table 1. We describe our method using the data in Table 1.

All of the schedules in Table 1 iterate the drawing and heat treatment operations by six times. Each row of the table shows the parameters of a schedule. In each column titled as "1", "2",...,"6", three parameters of C_i are shown. The reduction rate R_i is defined for the multifilamentary wire by the ratio of the diameter in the i-th operation over that in the previous operation. The first operation produces monofilaments, and the operations from the second to the sixth are applied to the multifilamentary wire. Thus R_i is defined for $i \geq 2$, and R_2 is defined as 1.

As a measure for the quality of a superconducting wire, we use the critical current density J_c, which indicates the density of the current (A/mm^2) at the voltage of $10(\mu V)$ for a $1m$-long wire. The wire having the higher value of J_c is considered as the more desirable. Because the values of J_c vary even under the same production schedule, the column titled as "J_c value under $7T$" in Table 1 shows the average and standard deviation of J_c values under the external magnetic field of $7\ T$ (Tesla).

We use a pattern-finding algorithm to answer the following question:

"How can we improve a production schedule to achieve a higher J_c value?"

We want to find manufacturing knowledge to improve the product quality measured by J_c value.

If we have a model of sufficient accuracy that predicts the values of J_c, then the above problem is easily solved. Unfortunately, such a model is not yet well established in the domain, and we apply a pattern-finding algorithm to this problem.

3   Formulation as an Induction Problem

In order to use ID3, we have to prepare training data represented in the form of attribute-value pairs.

We define a *scoring function* for each production schedule as follows:

$$G(P_i) = \frac{\mu(J_c(P_i)) - J_c^{target}}{\sigma(J_c(P_i))} \qquad (1)$$

where $\mu(J_c(P_i))$ and $\sigma(J_c(P_i))$ are the average and standard deviation of J_c values resulted from the production schedule P_i. J_c^{target} denotes the target value which we want to exceed. It is expected that, if we accumulate sufficient data, the larger value of $G(P_i)$ implies the higher probability of achieving $J_c \geq J_c^{target}$. We regard that the pursuit of the higher J_c values is equivalent to that of the higher $G(P_i)$ value.

In the discussion below, we use the three phrases, "the better product quality," "the larger J_c value," and "the larger $G(P_i)$ value," interchangeably.

We give a brief comment on the selection of J_c^{target}. Though the higher value for J_c^{target} is the more desirable, there is naturally an upper limit that we can achieve. A method is to select the upper limit of J_c^{target} so that there exists at least one production schedule, P_j, where $G(P_j) > 0$. With this strategy, from the data in Table 1, we can determine that J_c^{target} should be less than 1891. In the following discussion, we use $J_c^{target} = 1800$.

Picking up two schedules from $\{P_i, i = 1, 2, ..., 6\}$, P_1 and P_2 for example, and comparing them, we find how the difference between the two schedules affect their scores. More formally, let P_1 and P_2 be

$$P_1 = \{C_{1,i} = (R_{1,i}, T_{1,i}, H_{1,i}), i = 1, 2, ..., n\}$$

$$P_2 = \{C_{2,i} = (R_{2,i}, T_{2,i}, H_{2,i}), i = 1, 2, ..., n\}.$$

Let us denote their scores by $G(P_1)$ and $G(P_2)$, respectively.

Comparing P_1 and P_2, we obtain $\Delta(P_1, P_2)$, the *modification pattern* between P_1 and P_2 as follows:

$$\Delta(P_1, P_2) = \{\Delta C_{12,i} = (\Delta R_{12,i}, \Delta T_{12,i}, \Delta H_{12,i}), i = 1, 2, ..., n\}$$

where

$$\Delta R_{12,i} = R_{1,i} - R_{2,i}$$

$$\Delta T_{12,i} = T_{1,i} - T_{2,i}$$

$$\Delta H_{12,i} = H_{1,i} - H_{2,i},$$

We associate the modification pattern with the following difference of G

$$\Delta G_{12} = G(P_1) - G(P_2).$$

(The suffix "12" means that the difference is calculated from P_1 and P_2.)

We call P_1 and P_2 a *target* and a *base*, respectively. When $\Delta G_{1,2} > 0$, we say "*the modification pattern $\Delta(P_1, P_2)$ improves the score by ΔG_{12}.*"

Let the class of modification patterns that yield a larger score value be denoted by "*Good.*" In the above case, if $G(P_1) > G(P_2)$, then $\Delta G_{12} > 0$ and the modification pattern $\Delta(P_1, P_2)$ is a positive instance of the class "*Good.*" It should be noted that, by reversing the target and the base, we obtain a negative instance. For example, in the above case, a modification pattern $\Delta(P_2, P_1)$ is a negative instance of the class *Good* because $\Delta G_{21} < 0$. For the data in Table 1, we have 15 positive instances ($_6C_2 = 15$) and 15 negative instances. We denote the positive and negative instances of the class *Good* by *Pos* and *Neg*, respectively.

Now our problem is stated as follows:

"*With Pos and Neg, find a generalized modification pattern to be a positive instance of Good.*"

We use ID3 to find a generalized modification pattern.

In order to make ID3 applicable, one more step is necessary: The data in *Pos* and *Neg* have numerical value (e.g. $\Delta T_{12,1} = -40°C$). We need to translate such a numerical value into a categorical value (such as *Negative Small*). Though a method such as C4.5[5] already exists to deal with numerical attribute values, we use the following simple and intuitive approach.

We define fuzzy membership functions as shown in Fig. 1 based on the domain expert's suggestions over the domain of each production schedule parameter; The fuzzy sets are labeled as *Negative, Zero, Positive* which express the degree of the delta value being considered as *sufficiently negative, almost zero*, and *sufficiently positive*, respectively.

For simplicity, we do not use the degree information in generating the training data for ID3. Degree information is used in evaluating the consistency degree later.

We translate the numerical value to a category label which has the largest membership degree. For example, if the reduction rate x is associated with the membership degrees 0.3 and 0.7 in the fuzzy sets *Zero* and *Positive*, respectively, we categorize x into *Positive*. The degree information is used to calculate the matching degree between the data and domain knowledge.

With the above categorization, we are now ready to apply ID3 to *Pos* and *Neg*.

4 Outline of ID3

We briefly review ID3. For convenience of our discussion, we introduce notations which are different from the original in [1].

ID3 generates a decision-tree from the data represented by attribute-value pairs. At each node in a decision tree, a *test* on an attribute value is attached. Starting from the root node, we proceed the tree towards leaf nodes, selecting a branch at each node based on the outcome of the test. A leaf node is associated with a class label, and we find the class that the instance at hand belongs to.

ID3 employs the assumption that the decision tree of the simpler structure is the better and more useful. To obtain a simpler decision tree, ID3 uses the following strategy: At each node, the attribute whose value partitions the data into the least *fuzzy* manner is considered as the best for the test.

More formal description is given below.

Suppose that the data are represented by the attributes

$$A = \{A_i, i = 1, 2, ..., m\}.$$

Let the range of values of an attribute A_i be denoted by

$$Dom(A_i) = \{a_{i,j}\}.$$

(e.g., $Domain(OUTLOOK) = \{OVERCAST, RAINY, SUNNY\}$.) Let the set of class labels be

$$C = \{C_k, k = 1, 2, ..., N\}.$$

In the simplest case, we have a single class problem in which there are only two kinds of instances; the *positive* instances which belong to class C_1, and *negative* instances which do not. Our superconducting wire manufacturing problem is a single class problem; we have only one class "*Good*."

Let us assume that we have the instances The selection of the test attribute from A is done based on the three kinds of frequency measures described below:

1. $F(C_k|A_i = a_{ij}, S) = N(C_k, A_i = a_{ij}, S)/N(S)$ where $N(C_k, A_i = a_{ij}, S)$ is the number of instances in S that belongs to class C_k and $A_i = a_{ij}$, and $N(S)$ is the number of the instances in S.
2. $F(*|A_i = a_{ij}, S) = \sum_{k=1}^{N} F(C_k|A_i = a_{ij}, S)$ which is the frequency of the instances in S having $A_i = a_{ij}$.

3. $F(C_k|*, S) = \sum_{i=1}^{m} \sum_{j=1}^{n_i} F(C_k|A_i = a_{ij}, S)$ which is the frequency of the instances among S belonging to class C_k.

First, for each combination of (A_i, a_{ij})

$$I(A_i = a_{ij}) = -\sum_{k=1}^{N} F(C_k|A_i = a_{ij}, S) log F(C_k|A_i = a_{ij}, S)$$

is calculated, and then averaged as

$$I(A_i) = \sum_{j=1}^{n_i} F(*|A_i = a_{ij}, S) I(A_i = a_{ij}).$$

Next, for each class C_k,

$$I(C) = -\sum_{k=1}^{N} F(C_k|*, S) log F(C_k|*, S).$$

Finally, the gain

$$Gain(A_i) = I(C) - I(A_i)$$

is calculated.

The attribute with the largest gain is selected and a node that tests that attribute is generated.

As described above, ID3 iterates

1. frequency calculation, and
2. selection of the attribute which has the maximum gain.

Starting from the entire training data S_0, ID3 continues to partition the data by selecting the test attribute until no more partitioning is possible.

5 Use of Uncertain Domain Knowledge

5.1 Representation and Interpretation of Domain Knowledge

We assume that domain knowledge is described in the following form:

$$"If\ V,\ then\ usually\ W"$$

where V is a pattern on attribute values (e.g. V="OUTLOOK is SUNNY and TEMPERATURE is LOW"), and W states the belief on classification (e.g. "it is a member of class Pos") with a fuzzy quantifier *usually*.

Let *Rules* be

$$Rules = \{Rule_i = "If\ V_i,\ then\ usually\ W_i", i = 1, 2, ..., k\}.$$

We consider the following two rules in our superconducting wire domain.

*Rule*₁: *If the reduction rate in the latter stages is larger, the quality of a product is usually better.*

*Rule*₂: *If the temperature in the early stages is lower, the quality of a product is usually better.*

The expression "*the quality of a product is better (or worse)*" is interpreted as "*G is sufficiently positive (or negative).*"

The above rules contain *fuzzy terms* such as *latter, larger, better, early, lower,* and *usually.* We use fuzzy logic to incorporate fuzzy information as above into a decision-tree induction algorithm.

In the above rules,

1. the premise V_i refers to the pattern on attribute values (e.g. $V_1 =$ "*the reduction rate in the latter stages are larger*"),
2. the consequent W_i refers to the classification of an instance (e.g. $W_1=$ "*the quality of a product is better*"), and
3. the word "*usually*" refers to the certainty of knowledge "*If V_i then W_i.*"

In the following discussion, the rule $Rule_i$ is written as

$$Usually(V_i \rightarrow W_i).$$

To interpret fuzzy terms, we use the membership functions defined in Fig.1. For the interpretation of V, the membership functions defined over the parameters on production conditions are referred. In our work, three membership functions, labeled as *Positive, Negative,* and *Zero,* are defined over the domains of ΔR_i, ΔT_i and ΔH_i. They express the degree that a change in a parameter value is to be considered as sufficient increase, sufficient decrease, or almost zero, respectively. In addition, three membership functions, labeled as *Early, Middle,* and *Latter,* are defined over the iteration number.

More formally, V is given by a conjunction of

$$V = \wedge_{j=1}^{l} v^j$$

$$v^j = ((< position >^j < parameter\ name >^j) < value >^j)$$

where

$$< position >^j \in \{Early, Middle, Latter\}$$

$$< parameter\ name >^j \in \{\Delta R, \Delta T, \Delta H\}$$

$$< value >^j \in \{Positive, Negative, Zero\}.$$

For the interpretation of W, the membership function defined over *DeltaG* is referred. More formally, W_i is given by

$$(\Delta G\ < value >)$$

where

$$< value > \in \{Positive, Negative, Zero\}.$$

As stated before, by comparing two schedules, we obtain either a positive or negative instance of the class *Good*. We denote the database of those instances by

$$DB = \{(\Delta(P_a, P_b), \Delta G_{ab}), a, b = 1, 2, ..., M, a \neq b\}$$

where $\Delta(P_a, P_b)$ is a modification pattern and the difference of the resulted scores, ΔG_{ab}, calculated from P_a and P_b as a target and a source, respectively. In Table 1, $M = 6$ and hence, the cardinality of DB is 30.

We explain how to interpret a rule using $Rule_1$. In $Rule_1$, we have

1. $V_1 = $"*the reduction rate in the latter stages are larger*" , i.e.

$$V_1 = ((Latter \ \Delta R) \ Positive)$$

2. $W_1 = $"*the quality of a product is better*", i.e.

$$(\Delta G \ Positive),$$

and

3. $Rule_1 = Usually(V_1 \rightarrow W_1)$.

We show how to calculate

1. the matching degree of V_1 against $\Delta(P_1, P_2)$,
2. the matching degree of W_1 against $\Delta(P_1, P_2)$,
3. the piece-level consistency between $Rule_1$ and $\Delta(P_1, P_2)$, and
4. the set-level consistency between $Rule_1$ and DB.

5.2 Matching Degree of a Premise

We explain the matching degree using

$$\Delta(P_1, P_2) = \{(\Delta R_i, \Delta T_i, \Delta H_i), i = 1, 2, ..., 6\}$$

and ΔG_{12} where

$$\Delta R_i = R_{1,i} - R_{2,i}$$

$$\Delta T_i = T_{1,i} - T_{2,i}$$

$$\Delta H_i = H_{1,i} - H_{2,i}$$

$$\Delta G_{12} = G_1 - G_2.$$

Consider $V_1 = ((Latter \ \Delta R) \ Positive)$. Let the membership degree of ΔR_i being *Positive* be denoted by $\mu_{Positive}(\Delta R_i)$. By referring to Fig. 1, we can easily associate $\mu_{Positive}(\Delta R_i)$ for the quantity $\Delta R_i = R_{1,i} - R_{2,i}$ calculated from Table 1. We also need $\mu_{Latter}(i)$, the membership degree of ΔR_i being in the *latter stages*. It is also easily obtained by referring to the membership function of *Latter* defined over the iteration number i in Fig.1. Now we combine the above two membership degrees, $\mu_{Positive}(\Delta R_i)$ and $\mu_{Latter}(i)$, in a conjunctive manner, i.e.

$$\mu_{Positive}(\Delta R_i) \wedge \mu_{Latter}(i)$$

$$= Min(\mu_{Positive}(\Delta R_i), \mu_{Latter}(i))$$

where a standard Min operator is used for conjunctive composition of the two membership degrees. We use this value as the matching degree between ΔR_i and a fuzzy statement "*the reduction rate in the latter stage is positive.*"

Next, we compose the above membership degree in a disjunctive manner over $i = 1, 2, ..., n$:

$$\vee_{i=1}^{n}(\mu_{Positive}(\Delta R_i) \wedge \mu_{Latter}(i))$$

$$= Max_{i=1,2,...,n}\{\mu_{Positive}(\Delta R_i) \wedge \mu_{Latter}(i)\}$$

where a standard Max operator is used for the disjunctive composition. We use this value as the matching degree between $\Delta(P_1, P_2)$ and $V_1 = ((Latter\ \Delta R)\ Positive)$, or a fuzzy statement "*the reduction rate in the latter stage is larger.*"

Thus, the matching degree is denoted by

$$Match(V_1; P_1, P_2)$$

$$= \vee_{i=1}^{l}(\mu_{Positive}(\Delta R_i) \wedge \mu_{Latter}(i)).$$

In a general case where $V = \wedge_{j=1}^{l} v^j$, the matching degree becomes the conjunction or the minimum of those of v^js, i.e.,

$$Match(V; P_1, P_2) = \wedge_{j=1}^{l} Match(v^j; P_1, P_2)$$

$$= Min_{j=1,...,l} Match(v^j; P_1, P_2).$$

5.3 Matching Degree of a Consequent

Consider $W_1 = (\Delta G\ Positive)$. The degree of ΔG_{12} being *Positive*, denoted by $\mu_{Positive}(\Delta G_{12})$, is easily obtained by referring to the membership function definbed over ΔG in Fig. 1. We use this membership degree as a matching degree of a consequent W_1 and $\Delta(P_1, P_2)$, i.e.

$$Match(W_1; P_1, P_2) = \mu_{Positive}(\Delta G_{12}).$$

5.4 Consistency Degree

Using $Match(V_1; P_1, P_2)$ and $Match(W_1; P_1, P_2)$, we define a *piece-level consistency degree* between $Rule_1$ and $\Delta(P_1, P_2)$ as follows:

$$Match(V_1, W_1; P_1, P_2) = Match(V_1; P_1, P_2) \wedge Match(W_1; P_1, P_2)$$

$$= Min\{Match(V_1; P_1, P_2), Match(W_1; P_1, P_2)\}$$

This is called a *piece-level* consistency degree because it is calculated between a rule and a piece of data $\Delta(P_1, P_2)$.

As seen from the above, we interpret a rule "If V then W" as a conjunction $V \wedge W$, and we give the high matching degree only when both premise and consequent are satisfied. By aggregating the piece-level consistency degree mentioned above, we define a measure for *set-level consistency*. We sum and normalize $Match(V_1, W_1; P_a, P_b)$ as follows:

$$\Sigma(Rule_1, DB) = \frac{\sum_{\Delta(P_a, P_b) \in DB} Match(V_1, W_1; P_a, P_b)}{\sum_{\Delta(P_a, P_b) \in DB} Match(V_1; P_a, P_b)}.$$

[3] This is the *sigma count* which is originally introduced by Zadeh[3]. As clearly seen, it is a generalized conditional probability. Following Zadeh's approach, we evaluate the set-level consistency of $Rule_1$ based on a membership function of *Usually* defined over the domain of the sigma count as shown in Fig.2. With this membership function, we obtain a matching degree between the data and the knowledge that $Rule_1$ *usually* holds. We denote this set-level consistency degree by

$$Consist(Rule_1, DB) = \mu_{usually}(\Sigma(Rule_1, DB)).$$

5.5 Steps to Evaluate Consistency between Data and Domain Knowledge

Before going further, we summarize the above discussion on the representation and interpretation of domain knowledge. Given *Rules* and *DB*, for each $Rule_i \in$ *Rules*, the following quantities are calculated:

1. $Match(V_i; P_a, P_b)$ and $Match(W_i; P_a, P_b)$, the matching degrees of V_i and W_i against $\Delta(P_a, P_b) \in DB$, respectively;
2. the piece-level matching degree $Consist(Rule_i; P_a, P_b)$,
3. a sigma count of R_i over DB, $\Sigma(Rule_i, DB)$, and
4. the set-level consistency degree $Consist(Rule_i, DB)$.

---

[3] To avoid the denominator from becoming 0, we need to add a small number ϵ.

6   Use of Domain Knowledge in ID3

6.1   Relevance Degree

We use domain knowledge in the attribute selection as follows:

1. Rules that are relevant to the attribute under information gain calculation are extracted from $Rules = \{Rule_j, j = 1, 2, ..., r\}$.
2. The matching degrees of those relevant rules, $Consist(Rule_j, DB)$, $Rule_j \in Rules$, are calculated based on the data DB.
3. The test attribute is selected considering both the conventional information gain and the consistency degree proposed in this work.

We explain how relevant rules are retrieved.

Suppose that we are now evaluating the information gain of an attribute A_j (e.g. $A_j = \Delta R_4$). For the premise $V = \vee_{k=1}^{l} v^k$ in $Usually(V \to W)$, we calculate the *relevance degree* of V with an attribute A_j by

$$Relevance(A_j, V) = \vee_{k=1}^{l} Rel(A_j, v^k) = Max_{1 \le k \le l} Rel(A_j, v^k)$$

where $Rel(A_j, v^k)$ is determined as described below.

It should be recollected that

$$v^k = ((< Position >^k < Parameter\ name >^k) < value >^k).$$

The value of $Rel(A_j, v^k)$ is determined by combining the following two criteria in a conjunctive manner.

1. whether A_j (e.g. ΔR_4) refers to $< Parameter\ Name >$ (e.g. ΔR) or not, and
2. the matching degree of the stage number in A_j (e.g. 4 in ΔR_4) and $< Position >$ (e.g. *Latter*).

The first is a *crisp* condition while the second is *continuous*. For example, if $A_j = \Delta R_4$ and "v=*the temperature in the early stage is lower*", the first condition is not met, and hence, $Rel(\Delta R_4, v) = 0$. In contrast, when $v =$ "*the reduction rate in the latter stage is larger,*" the first condition is met, and hence, $Rel(A_j, v) = \mu_{Latter}(4)$.

To incorporate the above relevance degree, we slightly modify the definition of the matching degree of a premise, $Match(V_i; P_1, P_2)$ in the previous section by incorporating the above relevance degree in a conjunctive manner as follows:

$$Match(A_i; V_j; P_1, P_2) = Relevance(A_i, V_j) \wedge Match(V_j; P_1, P_2)$$

$$= Min\{Relevance(A_i, V_j), Match(V_j; P_1, P_2)\}$$

Accordingly, we also modify the definition of the sigma count as follows:

$$\Sigma(A_i; Rule_j, DB) = \frac{\sum_{\Delta(P_a, P_b) \in DB} Match(A_i; V_j, W_j; P_a, P_b)}{\sum_{\Delta(P_a, P_b) \in DB} Match(A_i; V_j; P_a, P_b)}$$

where ϵ is a small number (such as 0.001) to prevent the denominator from becoming 0).

The consistency degree is obtained by matching this modified sigma count against the membership function of "*usually.*"

$$Consist(A_i, Rule_j, DB) = \mu_{usually}(\Sigma(A_i, Rule_j, DB)).$$

We explicitly show A_i in the above formula to clarify that this consistency is used for evaluating the attribute A_i.

A low consistency degree occurs either when there is no rule in *Rules* which is relevant to A_i or when the rules are inconsistent with the data DB (in the sense that there are rules whose consequent parts do not hold though their premise parts are satisfied.). It should be remembered that the sigma count is not defined when the denominator is zero. If there are no relevant rules, our consistency degree is not defined. Thus, we introduce the following rule: If the denominator

$$\sum_{\Delta(P_a, P_b)\in DB} Match(A_i; V_j; P_a, P_b)$$

is less than ϵ, the consistency degree is "UNDEFINED."

Finally, the above rule-wise consistency is aggregated over *Rules* by

$$Consist(A_i; Rules, DB) = \vee_{Rule_j \in Rules} Consist(A_i, Rule_j, DB)$$

$$= Max_{Rule_j \in Rules} Consist(A_i, Rule_j, DB)$$

Note that this composition should be done for the rules whose consistency degrees are defined. If the consistency degrees of all rules are "UNDEFINED" then $Consist(A_i; Rules; DB)$ is also treated as "UNDEFINED."

We have two criteria for a test attribute selection: Consistency degree of the data with domain knowledge, and information gain. The next problem is how to aggregate these two criteria. As mentioned in the introduction, the formula for the aggregation may depend on individual application. Here we show only one of the possible approaches.

In general, we prefer a test attribute A_i such that

1. the information gain is large, and
2. $Consist(A_i, Rules, DB)$ is large.

6.2 A Decision-Making Strategy

We employ the following strategy: In our domain, the degree of domain knowledge being incomplete and uncertain is large. Thus, we give the first priority to the information gain to rank the attributes. However, we exclude those attributes which are inconsistent with domain knowledge in spite of the high information gain.

This strategy is realized by using a notion of *gamma* level set, i.e. we exclude the attributes from the candidates whose consistency degree is less than γ specified by a user. In other words, the attributes in

$$A^{consistent} = \{A_j; Consist(A_j, Rules, DB) > \gamma\}$$

are considered as candidates for the test attribute.

It should be noted that there may exist attributes which do not have relevant rule. The attributes whose consistency degrees are "UNDEFINED" are denoted by

$$A^{UNDEFINED} = \{A_j; Consist(A_j, Rules, DB) = UNDEFINED\}.$$

Thus, we select the test attribute from $A^{consistent}$ and $A^{UNDEFINED}$ based on the information gain.

First, we select the attributes in $A^{consistent} \cup A^{UNDEFINED}$ by the information gain. Let $A^{highest}$ be the attributes which have the largest information gain. (In general, there may be multiple attributes which have the same highest information gain.) We select the test attribute arbitrarily from $A^{highest} \cap A^{consistent}$ if it is not empty. If empty, we select the attribute arbitrarily from $A^{highest}$.

In the above strategy, the attributes in $A^{UNDEFINED}$ are treated as if they were completely consistent with domain knowledge. This reflects the strategy that new findings (in the sense that no relevant knowledge exists) are treated in favor. However, if the attributes in $A^{highest}$ include an attribute in $A^{consistent}$, we prefer the one in $A^{consistent}$ to those in $A^{UNDEFINED}$. In other words, if the information gain is the same, we prefer the attribute which is supported by domain knowledge.

The above strategy heavily relies on the decision-maker's choice of γ. In practice, our approach is suitable for the interactive process rather than the automatic generation of a decision tree. For example, suppose that $A^{consistent}$ becomes empty. Two options exist. One is to select a test attribute from $A^{UNDEFINED}$, and the other is to lower γ. Lowering *gamma* means that the generated tree is to lower the confidence on the piece of knowledge in question. The choice should be left for the decision-maker.

7 Demonstration using the Data in Table 1

We show how the method stated above works in our sample database.

We apply the information gain calculation for the total training data. Three attributes, ΔT_2, ΔR_4, and ΔR_3, have the highest information gain 0.33. These three attributes are equally efficient in partitioning the training data. Thus, we prefer the attribute with the higher consistency degree. The consistency degrees of ΔT_2. ΔR_4, and ΔR_3 are 0.85 ($\mu_{usually}(0.67) = 0.85$), 0 ($\mu_{usually}(0.49) = 0$), and "UNDEFINED." Thus, based on the strategy stated above, we select ΔT_2 as a test attribute.

In the training data, there are five negative instances which have $\Delta R_4 > 0$. If we select ΔR_4 as a test attribute solely based on the information gain, it leads

Table 1 Sample Data

No.	Operation	Stage Number						Jc under 7T		
		1	2	3	4	5	6	Av.	σ	G
1	Reduction Rate	-	1.00	0.72	0.69	0.41	0.16	1835.75	143.69	0.25
	Temperature	360	400	370	370	370	270			
	Time(Hours)	12	12	12	12	12	2			
2	Reduction Rate	-	1.00	0.72	0.69	0.41	0.16	1691	45	-2.4
	Temperature	400	400	370	370	370	270			
	Time(Hours)	12	12	12	12	12	2			
3	Reduction Rate	-	1.00	0.54	0.54	0.49	0.16	1840.75	10.25	3.97
	Temperature	400	370	370	370	370	270			
	Time(Hours)	12	12	12	12	12	2			
4	Reduction Rate	-	1.00	0.71	0.69	0.41	0.15	1818	25	0.72
	Temperature	370	400	370	370	370	270			
	Time(Hours)	12	12	12	12	12	2			
5	Reduction Rate	-	1.00	0.71	0.69	0.41	0.14	1749	15	-3.4
	Temperature	400	400	370	370	370	270			
	Time(Hours)	12	12	12	12	12	2			
6	Reduction Rate	-	1.00	0.71	0.69	0.64	0.12	1891	138	0.66
	Temperature	400	400	370	370	370	270			
	Time(Hours)	12	12	12	12	12	2			

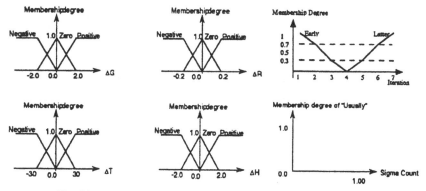

Fig.1 Membership Functions

Fig.2 A membership Function for "Usually"

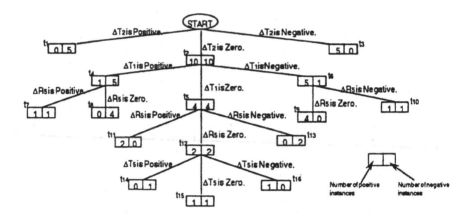

Fig.3 A Decision-tree

to a rule "If $\Delta R_4 < 0$ then it is a negative instance, which is possibly in conflict with our domain knowledge that the larger reduction rate in the latter stages improves the quality of the product."

Based on the above selection, we partition the data based on the attribute value of ΔT_2. Thus, we select this attribute as a test attribute.

Continuing the above steps, we obtain a decision tree as shown in Fig.3

8   Conclusion

We presented a method to incorporate uncertain domain knowledge into the induction of a classification tree. We represent domain knowledge by fuzzy statements, and define consistency degrees between the data and domain knowledge. In this paper, we use a statistical criterion primarily, and domain knowledge is used for screening purposes. This is because, in our domain, the degree of domain knowledge being incomplete and uncertain is large. The incorporation of domain knowledge into a pattern-finding problem makes the problem a multi-criteria decision-making problem, and the aggregation of the two criteria needs more investigation. This is our future work.

Acknowledgement:

This work is partly supported by the international joint research grant of Telecommunications Advancement Organization of Japan (TAO).

References

1. Quinlan J.R.: Induction of decision trees. Machine Learning. **1** (1986) 81–106
2. Valiant L.G.: A theory of learnable. Communications of ACM. **27** (1984) 1134–1142
3. Zadeh L.A.: Syllogistic reasoning in fuzzy logic and its application to usuality and reasoning with dispositions. IEEE Trans. on SMC. **SMC-15** (1985) 754–763
4. Narazaki H., Shigaki I. Watanabe T.: A method for extracting approximate rules from neural networks. Proceedings. of 4th IEEE-FUZZ **4** (Yokohama 1995) 1865–1870
5. Quinlan J. R.: C4.5: Programs for machine learning. CA:Morgan Kafmann (1993)

Fril++ a Language for Object-Oriented Programming with Uncertainty

J. F. Baldwin, T. P. Martin and M. Vargas-Vera * **

A.I. Group,
Department of Engineering Mathematics,
University of Bristol
Bristol BS8 1TR
England, U.K.

Abstract. We present Fril++ an object-oriented extension to Fril. This new programming language supports the modelling of fuzzy applications by integrating a fuzzy logic programming language with the object-oriented paradigm. Fril++ includes the concept of fuzzy objects as an explicit construction in the language. Fuzzy objects are naturally related with multiple inheritance, and so we allow both of these in the language. The multiple inheritance gives us more flexibility, and in any case, the associated ambiguities are not so much of a problem in logic programming as they are in other paradigms. We also exploit the fact that information is expressed by the hierarchy itself. A Fril++ program can explicitly use the hierarchy by means of special constructions integrated into the language. Fril++ provides support for user decisions when there are several answers for a message by having a library of defuzzification methods.

1 Introduction

The programming language Fril is a logic programming style language with the capability of manipulating both probabilistic and fuzzy uncertainty [BMP87, BMP88, BMP93]. The primary difference is that in Prolog all clauses are considered necessarily true, but Fril clauses can be given varying degrees of support. Fril is a logic language, but another major programming paradigm that has been found to be useful is to think in terms of objects rather than logical statements. The object-oriented paradigm has two main uses. Firstly, the real world contains objects and when trying to simulate it on a computer it makes programming rather easier if there is a close correspondence between the real world objects and the software components (e.g. Simula language [DN66]). Secondly, object-oriented languages were also found to support modular software development. The objects make it possible to keep all the important components of a particular entity in one place.

---

* Corresponding author. Email: MARIAV@DAI.ED.AC.UK
** Following A.I. group policy, authors are listed in alphabetical order.

Since our main motivation is modelling real-world systems we decided to incorporate object-oriented features into Fril. The resulting language, Fril++, integrates fuzzy logic programming with an object-oriented paradigm.

In the design of Fril++ we follow a mix of Prolog++ [Mos94], L+O [McC92] and Fril [BMP88]. The object-oriented features allow easier fuzzy modelling of the external world as well as helping the development and maintenance of software. We provide encapsulation of data inside the objects: in an logic system this is not so much to prevent the data from being changed (which is the main concern in an imperative language), but to discourage over-dependence on internal data structures that might change in a later implementation of the class.

The novelty of our approach lies in the introduction of new features in the language such the introduction of the concept of "fuzzy objects". This feature allow us to model real applications in which we have fuzzy objects i.e. objects with a degree of membership in several classes. We allow multiple inheritance and will discuss the reasons for this in the paper. We also point out some ways to explicitly make use of the resulting hierarchy. It turned out that one advantage of the design was that we obtained better ways to handle the defuzzification that is often needed in fuzzy applications.

The paper is organised as follows: Section 2 discusses the basic features of Fril++ such as classes, fuzzy instances, overriding vs. inclusive inheritance, and mutability. Section 3 discusses multiple inheritance in Fril++ and the use of the hierarchy information. Section 4 considers default defuzzification method and a related example. Finally in Section 5 we give some conclusions and further research.

The first prototype of Fril++ has been written in Fril (and so runs under Macintosh, Unix and Windows systems).

2 Basic Design of Fril++

In this section we discuss various basic features of Fril++. We certainly want to have the "standard features" of object-oriented languages. For example, we want protection mechanisms such as public and private methods, and parameterised classes as in L+O [McC92]. Initially, our class instances will not have mutable features, hence we will often not want to be forced to send messages to a particular instance, but instead have the freedom to just send the message to the class itself. Therefore, we support messages both to classes and to instances.

The main difference presented in this section will be the introduction of *fuzzy* instances.

2.1 Classes

A class definition consists of two parts: the heading of the class and the body.

In the heading the programmer has to define: the name/label of the class and its parameters in the case of a parameterised class; a list of super-classes from which it inherits methods; optionally, the access restrictions for the members of a class i.e. public or private; and, a list of components in the case that the object contains sub-objects. Access to the elements of the class is controlled, members can be private (accessible only to class methods) or public (accessible to all). The Fril++ default is that a method is public. In the body the programmer defines a (possibly empty) set of methods. These methods are normal Fril predicates and so can have support pairs associated with them, exactly as in Fril.

As a simple example (modified from the Prolog++ example [Mos94]) let us define three classes a, b and c. Class a inherits all its methods from both classes b and c, but defines no methods of its own. Class b defines methods n/1 and m/1. Class c defines method m/1. Fril++ uses the lisp-like syntax (but prolog-like semantics) of Fril. Comments are C-style, and as usual line-breaks and multiple white-spaces are not significant. We then have

```
(( class (a)        /* class name */
    (b c)           /* list of super-classes */
    ()              /* list of name/arity of private methods */
    ()              /* list of parts */
 )
    /* empty set of method definitions */
)

(( class (b) () () ()
 )
    /* method definitions */
    ((n 3))
    ((m A) (n A)) /* Frils equivalent of  m(A) :- n(A). */
)

(( class (c) () () ()
 )
    ((m 2))
)
```

In Fril++ syntax the symbol "." is used as a separator between the class which is receiving the message and the name of the message itself. The class indicates the context of the evaluation and the message is an expression which might be formed by a set of subgoals. For example, a query to class a can be stated as

```
? ((a . m X ))
```

In this case we are sending a message m to class a, but the class does not contain a local definition of method m so the message is passed up to the superclasses using inheritance. Since class b does have a definition for m we obtain the binding X=3. The successful completion of the proof of m corresponds to the successful handling of the message by the class a.

2.2 Parameterised Classes

In Fril++ we can also write classes with parameters. For example, consider the parameterised train class defined in L+O, but now slightly modified and written in our Fril++ syntax. We also use this example to illustrate the protection mechanism.

```
((class (train SPEED COLOUR COUNTRY)
        (transport vehicle)    /* super-classes */
        (private colour/1)     /* list of private methods */
        ()                     /* parts */
 )
              ((speed SPEED))
              ((colour COLOUR))
              ((country COUNTRY))
              ((get_colour COLOUR) (colour COLOUR))
              ((journey_time DISTANCE T)
                        (speed SPEED)
                        (times T SPEED  DISTANCE))
 )
```

Variables defined in the label, in this case COLOUR, COUNTRY and SPEED, can be used inside the methods defined in the class, and are globally defined over the whole set of definitions.

The declaration (private colour/1) makes colour/1 a private method, and so it is only accessible via the public method get_colour/1. For example, the message
        (((train 100 green albania) . colour CL))
results in an access violation. Whereas
        (((train 100 green albania) . get_colour CL))
will succeed instantiating CL to green. Similarly,
        ((train 100 green albania) . journey_time 1000 X))
is interpreted as "find the value(s) for X for which journey_time(1000,X) is true with respect to the train class with parameters (100 green albania)" and gives the result X=10.

2.3 Instances and Fuzzy Instances

In standard object-oriented programming languages there is no concept of partial membership of an object in a class: an instance is either a member of a class or it is not. However, this is not always the case when we move to a fuzzy environment. Consequently, we introduce the concept of objects having a degree of membership in a class i.e. class membership should be allowed to be fuzzy. We note that there are other approaches: instead of *declaring* an object to be a (fuzzy) member of a class, the strength of the membership is *derived* [GBP93] based on both the attribute values of the object and their relevance to the class definition.

Fril++ has a keyword instance that allows the user to create two types of instances. It allows the definition of instances as in Prolog++ and also instances with a fuzzy membership in a class. The first type of instances can be seen as a particular case of the second type in which the support in the class is equal to 1.

A non-fuzzy instance is created by using the grammar construction

$$(\texttt{instance instance\_name (class\_name } P_1...P_n))$$

where $P_1...P_n$ are the parameters of the class. To create a fuzzy instance we use

$$(\texttt{instance instance\_name (class\_name } P_1...P_n) : (S))$$

where S is a support that describes the degree of membership of the instance in the class. For example, we can create an instance of the train class and with name scotsman by

```
(instance scotsman (train 125 green scotland))
```

and then can send a message to the instance using

```
(scotsman . country X)
```

obtaining X=scotland.

The class has no mutable attributes and in this case sending a message to the instance scotsman is just equivalent to sending the message to the class (train 125 green britain). In such cases the instance names are just mnemonics for a particular class but even then their use can make code a lot easier to read. However, we can make the same instance a member of two different classes, and/or add non-trivial support for the instance, and in this case it is no longer a mnemonic. For example we can simultaneously have the declaration

```
(instance scotsman (train 125 green england) : 0.5 )
```

and now the same query would also yield X=england with 0.5 for its support. Here the name scotsman is not just a mnemonic both because the support for the membership is used by the system to calculate other supports, and also because it has membership in two classes.

We note that the support might be defined by the programmer, or might be computed automatically. We can regard a class as equivalent to a set of instances - in the fuzzy case, we extend the notion of set membership to allow partial membership. The class hierarchy reflects a set inclusion relation, which in the fuzzy case is modelled by fuzzy set inclusion. We therefore make the assumption that if an instance has a membership α in a class, it must have membership of at least α in all the super-classes. Clearly this is reasonable since the class hierarchy becomes increasingly general as one moves upwards.

2.4 Overriding and Inclusive Inheritance

In non-logic programming languages a method can only return one value. Hence, if both a class and a subclass contain definitions for a method the compiler must select just one of these. It is natural that the subclass definition overrides the inherited definition. However, in logic programming there is nothing to prevent a predicate from having multiple definitions (and indeed this is the natural case). Hence it is arguable that in an object-oriented logic programming system the inheritance should be inclusive: all (public) information from the super-class is included into the subclass.

On the other hand, the system is intended for use in modelling and in these cases it is common that the predicates are describing properties of the world and that we really do want exceptions. For example, in the case "a penguin is a bird but it cannot fly" we really do want the non-monotonicity obtained by overriding parts of the bird class. Accordingly, it was decided that Fril++ should offer overriding inheritance as the default. That is a method is automatically inherited if and only if there is no new definition in the subclass. However, it is important to note that we also provide the super keyword which can be used whenever we want to access the definitions that have been overridden. In this way we can always recover the effect of inclusive inheritance by adding clauses which make appropriate calls to the superclasses. We will illustrate this with the following example:

```
((class (a) () () ())
    ((foo 1 ))
    ((foo 2 ))
)

((class (b) (a) () ())     /* class b inherits from class a */
    ((foo 3 ))
)

(instance obj (b))
```

Suppose we make the query

```
? ((obj . foo  X))
```

The message (foo X) is sent to the object obj which is an instance of class b therefore we get the binding X=3, and no other bindings. However, if we had defined class b as

```
((class (b) (a) () ())
    ((foo 3 ))
    ((foo X )  (super . foo X))
)
```

then we will still get the answer X=3, but also, on backtracking, the answers X=1 and X=2 from the calls to super. In this way, inclusive inheritance can be emulated in Fril++. Finally, we note that we could effectively delete foo/1 from class b by defining

```
((class (b) (a) () ())
    ((foo X) (fail))
)
```

In summary, one of the advantages in using logic programming is that program and data are of the same form. Extending the logic programming framework to the object-oriented system Fril++ extends both the programming environment and the expressiveness of the knowledge representation. We would not normally expect to make extensive use of fuzzy classes in a procedural program; however, fuzzy classes can be of considerable use in the data handled by the program, i.e. the knowledge representation.

2.5 Contained Objects

So far we have only considered the generalisation/specialisation (ISA) relation hierarchy as represented by inheritance. However, objects can also be structured by inclusion. That is, there is another important hierarchy: the way that an object is broken down into its component parts, using the HAS-A relation or its inverse the "part-of" relation. Logical theories, and hence logic programs, can be constructed by including references to other theories and also as specialisations of one or more theories.

For example, consider a bicycle which has parts handlebars, 2 wheels, etc. In Prolog++ [Mos94] this is expressed by using a part declaration

```
class bicycle
parts handlebars, wheel*2, ... .
   ...
end bicycle.
```

where the parts are themselves classes.

Note that when there is more than one instance of a part then this is indicated by following it with "*" followed by a numerical expression. On creating an instance of instance of a class which has parts, then each of the component parts is also created automatically. Of course, the parts do not inherit from the whole, otherwise we would be constructing an infinite data structure.

In the methods the parts are referred to by adding a subscript to the class name i.e. we will have `wheel_1` and `wheel_2`, etc. That these are indeed parts of the class are expressed by relations such as

```
(part_of handlebars_1 bicycle)
(part_of wheel_1 bicycle)
(part_of wheel_2 bicycle)
```

which are generated at compile time (from the class definition) and used later in the evaluation of a message. In Fril++ we simply represent this situation by

```
((class (bicycle) () () (handlebars wheel*2))
    ...
)
```

2.6 Mutability of Objects

Logic programming has been very successful in describing static properties of systems, but it lacks facilities for the case in which dynamic changes must be modelled. Several approaches have been proposed in order to include state change into objects, amongst which are: non-logical predicates to simulate assignment [HM90]; "intensional" variables to trace state changes [CW88]; multi-headed clauses [Con88]; identifying objects with proof processes and object's states with arguments occurring in the goals of a given process [AP90].

The solution that we allow (so far) in Fril++ is that of "passing of object labels" as taken in L+O [McC92]. Since we allow parameterised classes we can make the parameters cover all the different states that we desire. Then, instead of changing an existing object, we generate a label that points to a new object with the desired parameters. This is not exactly the same of having mutable objects since we are not changing an existing object, we are creating a new one. The new label will have to be transmitted to all the relevant code in which the object is used, and this provides a slight inconvenience, however, it does have the advantage that we we retain declarativeness. This method does not have the semantic problems associated with a true mutability such as would be obtained with the use of assert/retract on objects, or parts of objects. We are not altering the set of axioms of a theory (an object is viewed as logic theory). Messages to a specific object will always give the same results.

For example, the train program of section 2.1 can be extended as follows

```
(( class   (train SPEED COLOUR COUNTRY) (transport) () () )
        ...    /* as before */

    ((change_speed NEWSPEED NEWLABEL)
            (instance NEWLABEL (train NEWSPEED COLOUR COUNTRY)))
)
```

If we already have

```
(instance scotsman1   (train 125 green britain))
```

then the basic idea is to use this to return a new label to a new object. In the Fril++ code above we made the return of a label explicit, and write

```
?( (scotsman1 . change_speed 200 scotsman2)
   (scotsman2 . journey_time  1000  X)
  )
```

The first message is sent to scotsman1 which returns a pointer to the object scotman2 which has a speed of 200. This new object receives the second message which is to compute the journey_time, and so we will obtain X=5.

Clearly, whilst this approach gives a logically "clean" solution to the problem of mutability, it has considerable performance overheads. For instance, a complicated object such as the "bicycle" class described above would require re-creation of all its sub-parts on creation of a new instance. In order to avoid this performance overhead, we intend to use more efficient techniques to declare and manage the dynamic data. An example of such a technique is that used for the implementation of Prolog++ (see [Mos94] for further discussion).

2.7 Remarks

Fril++ does not deal explicitly with overloading as we have not defined types in our language. However, the user can explicitly add type-tags as a part of terms. In this case the pattern matching handles the overloading naturally.

We also intend to support the broadcast of messages to a list of objects, rather than restricting the user to work with one object at a time. This is under current investigation.

3 Multiple Inheritance

In designing an object-oriented language one of the major decisions is whether or not to allow multiple inheritance. By multiple inheritance we mean the ability of a class to inherit methods from more than one other class. Here we shall argue that the combination of fuzziness and class instances strongly encourage one to allow multiple inheritance. However, we also argue that multiple inheritance is relatively natural in a logic programming language, and moreover that we can make good use of the hierarchy. In particular, we will show how to use the hierarchy as a whole in order to pick out specialised methods. In section 4 we give an example of one of the main applications we envisage for such a use of hierarchy information viz. selecting defuzzification algorithms.

3.1 Why have Multiple Inheritance?

One of the goals in designing Fril++ was that it be suitable for modelling "the world", and in many worlds the hierarchies are not simple trees but need multiple inheritance. However, an equally important goal was that Fril++ be suitable as a general programming language, and it is well-known that multiple inheritance can lead to problems when built into a procedural or functional language. The main problem is that ambiguities arise when a method is defined in two classes, and some subclass inherits from both of them. For example, we might want a class of people that inherit both from a `research_assistant` class and from a `research_student` class: but is natural that both such classes might have a method for `SalaryLevel` in which case we have an ambiguity.

Conventionally there are a number of solutions, such as

- Simply forbid cases in which there is any conflict. This can be softened somewhat by encouraging the programmer to rename methods in order to resolve the ambiguities. Eiffel forces derived classes to rename superclass methods that conflict [Mey88].
- We can impose a search order: The ancestors of a class are searched in some predetermined order (e.g. using a class precedence list) and the first class which contains the method is used. However, this strategy is rather ad hoc (hence confusing), might not be sufficient, and can introduce problems. Other languages allow the programmer to specify the search strategy, but this just increases programming complexity.

– In languages such as C++ qualifiers or roles can be used to explicitly state which method should be inherited when multiple inheritance is presented [ES90].

None of these solutions is particularly compelling. Note that we are referring to the inheritance of "implementations" of methods, and not just method declarations. For example, Java takes the rather nice option (for a non-logic language) of allowing method implementations to be inherited from at most one class, but allowing "inheritance" of method declarations from any number of interfaces.

The problem above arose because, outside of logic programming languages, it is almost always the case that a method would return at most one answer. If we allow multiple inheritance in such languages then we have to be prepared to decide which answer we want. It would be conceivable in a non-logic language to collect the answers together into a list. This would have the problem that if any of the methods have side-effects then the order of invocation will be important. In logic languages we have neither problem, instead it is natural to collect a bag of answers, and (assuming termination and no use of non-logical features) the order of collection is unimportant. That is, there is no need to select a single definition from the hierarchy and instead we can allow the language to use backtracking to handle multiple methods just as if it had multiple clauses defining a single predicate.

However, in a fuzzy environment the situation becomes even more biased towards allowing multiple inheritance. If we allowed fuzzy instances then it is almost inevitable that some instances will be (partial) members of more than one class. Such an instance behaves as if it were an instance of a class that had multiple inheritance, so if we are to allow such instances then we essentially have to allow multiple inheritance for the classes as well. Requiring single inheritance would go with requiring single memberships for instances, and this would be against fuzzy logic concepts.

Also, a standard alternative to use of multiple inheritance is simply to use containment instead. Instead of class A inheriting from both B and C, it can inherit from one, and contain an object from the other. In many cases this if fine. However, even in these cases we had to make a decision as to which to inherit, B or C. The decision might be difficult, or even ad hoc, but at least the two cases are discrete, i.e. cleanly separable. We could do the same in Fril, but the existence of the support pairs allows for interpolations between the two choices. Or, in the fuzzy instance case we can smoothly go from an instance being entirely in B over to being entirely in C. In this case it becomes much more reasonable that we should either inherit both, or contain both. But we do not want to give up on inheritance entirely, hence again we seem to be forced to allow multiple inheritance.

Therefore we decided to allow and support multiple inheritance in Fril++. An instance can have partial membership in more than one class. We do not insist that the memberships be numbers, nor even that they be explicitly stored or evaluated for any particular instance. An instance may be a close match to one class when one subset of its properties is considered; it may be close to another when another subset is considered. The programmer has a set of properties in mind when deciding on the class hierarchy, but it is by no means obvious that every inheritance must take into account the class memberships. An instance must be declared as a member of various classes when it is created; however, the membership is not used by methods unless this is explicitly programmed.

3.2 Using the Hierarchy Information

Multiple answers might be natural, but in certain circumstances we really do want just one answer and so need to combine a set of answers. For example, plain Fril supplies a defuzzification method that can combine multiple fuzzy answers to provide a meaningful single answer. This has the drawback that there is no one best defuzzification method, instead the appropriate method depends on the semantics of the set of answers. The code might well have to include several methods, and then the programmer has to pick the right one, because the lack of structure in a plain Fril program would make it difficult to do this automatically.

In Fril++ the hierarchy itself tells us a great deal about the origin of the multiple answers to some query, and by judicious use of the hierarchy the programmer can obtain *some automatic* selection of the appropriate defuzzification method. That is, when the hierarchy represents generalisation/specialisation then it is natural that we allow this to also be reflected in the method selection process, picking more specialised or more general methods according to the set of data on which they are to operate. For example, the user might want to use the following scheme for selecting a method:

If an instance definitely has a membership in classes $C_1...C_n$ then take the class C_{lcs}, defined as the smallest common super-class of $C_1, ..., C_n$, and use the method from there.

This makes sense in that C_{lcs} is the most specific class (lowest in the hierarchy) that still covers all of the explicit memberships of the instance. If there are no specific class calls in the methods, then all routes for a message from the instance will pass through this class or a descendent of this class. Our system supports this by providing the predicate least_common_superclass/2 which will find the least common superclass of an object based on the classes in which it *explicitly* is given a membership via the instance/2 predicate. Note that if an instance has a membership α in a class, it must have membership of at least α in all of its super-classes. In particular, all declared instances are always implicit members of the very top class: if the predicate accounted for such implicit membership as well as explicit membership then it would always return the top class, and so be rather useless.

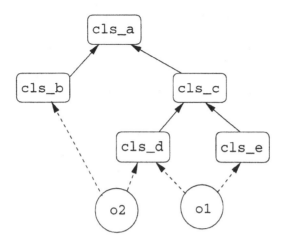

Fig. 1. *A simple hierarchy. Squares represent classes; circles represent instances; normal lines denote an "isa" relation between class and superclass; and dashed lines represent membership in a class.*

As an example, consider a system of five classes and two instances (as illustrated in Fig. 1) with class definitions

```
((class (cls_a) () () ())
      ((foo X) ...definition... )
)

((class (cls_b) (cls_a) () ())   ... )

((class (cls_c) (cls_a) () ())
      ((foo X) ...definition... )
)

((class (cls_d) (cls_c) () ())   ... )

((class (cls_e) (cls_c) () ())   ... )
```

and (explicit) instance definitions

```
(instance o1 cls_d)          (instance o2 cls_d)
(instance o1 cls_e)          (instance o2 cls_b)
```

Object o1 is a member of both classes `cls_d` and `cls_e`, and so has lowest common superclass `cls_c`. In Fril++ this is obtained by

```
?(least_common_superclass o1 LCS_o1)
```

giving the result

```
LCS_o1 = cls_c
```

Similarly, for object o2 the the closest common superclass is `cls_a`. Hence, the goal (`least_common_superclass o2 LCS_o2`) binds LCS_o2 to `cls_a`.

By having the hierarchy we can provide language support for the user's decisions about what to do regarding method selection. In selecting methods for object o1 we might want to use the fact that it is entirely a member of sub-classes of `cls_c`, and so can use a specialised method stored in that class. In contrast, object o2 might require a rather more general, and perhaps less accurate, method stored in `cls_a`. In the above example this is achieved by

```
(least_common_superclass OBJECT CLASS)
(CLASS . foo X)
```

When OBJECT=o1 we get `cls_c . foo`, and when OBJECT=o2 we get `cls_a . foo`.

In the next section we shall see an example of such a structure, and discuss its usage when `foo` is to be a defuzzification method.

Finally, we note that we intend to make the entire class/subclass hierarchy accessible to the user (but in a "read-only" form). The user can then write extensions of `least_common_superclass` as they desire.

4 Defuzzification

We describe a default defuzzification algorithm suitable for Fril++ , and give an example of its use.

4.1 Default Defuzzification

Fril already contains a built-in predicate `supp_value` that can perform the defuzzification process. It combines fuzzy sets into an expected fuzzy set (which is a generalisation of the expected value [Bal94a, Bal94b]), and then extracts a single non-fuzzy answer. The approximation method is based on the mass assignment theory, and was proposed in [Bal94a, Bal94b]. Hence, in Fril++ we supply a predicate `default_defuzz`, that collects all the answers, sets up appropriate data structures, and then feeds them into `supp_value`. That is, to defuzzify a query such as (`object . query A`) the first step collects all solutions for A from classes in which `object` has a membership, and the second step feeds the answers into `default_defuzz`.

In general, no method of combining values can be universally applicable. It is rather naive to assume that a single membership value can be given to an instance in a class, and then all properties of the class apply to the instance with exactly that membership value. More realistically, the inheritance of any particular property depends on how well the instance matches the class with respect to that property. For example, if an instance of a shape is judged to have partial membership in the classes of squares and circles because it has rounded corners, the inheritance of the "number of corners" property should come purely from the "square" class. Calculation of area, on the other hand, could come from the "circle" class based on some fuzzy estimate of the "radius" - this calculation incorporates uncertainty in the parameter value and is inherited completely, not partially.

Thus although a default mechanism for combining multiply inherited values is provided, the expectation is that it will be overridden in almost all applications.

4.2 Example

The definition of fuzzy sets and their use as parameters in predicates is one of the most important properties in Fril and hence also in Fril++. This example shows that the defuzzification still works with continuous fuzzy sets. The set of answers are already defined as a fuzzy sets so the algorithm given in the previous subsection only needs to get the expected fuzzy set.

Let us consider a class publication in which we define a fuzzy measure of circulation count by means of the fuzzy sets low, medium and high.

```
((class (publication) () () ()
 )
        set( uni1 0 10000 )
        (low     [    0:1    500:1    2000:0 ]  uni1)
        (medium [ 500:0   2000:1   10000:0 ]  uni1)
        (high    [2000:0   5000:1   10000:1 ]  uni1)

        ((defuzz X) (default_defuzz X))
)
```

For example, the circulation is low if the number of prints is between 0 and 500. A circulation of 4000 would be both medium and high to a degree.

We also want to handle various specialist publications in Music and some science publications such as Mathematics and Computer Science. Hence, we define the following sub-classes

```
((class (music_pub) (publication) () ())
        ((circulation medium ))
)

((class (sci_pub) (publication) () ())
        ((circulation low  ))
)

((class (maths_pub) (publication) () ())
)

((class (cs_pub) (publication) () ())
        ((circulation high    ))
)
```

In each sub-class except maths_pub we defined "circulation" which is a measure of the popularity of each sub-field. For example, the programmer has decided science publications are not really popular, so its measure of circulation is generally going to be low unless overridden. So sci_pub is expected as low publication but just the subclass cs_pub overrides this and expects a high circulation.

Suppose we receive the (hypothetical) publication "Musical Computing". We might decide to represent this by an instance mc with partial memberships in each of the two subclasses cs_pub and music_pub.

```
(instance mc (cs_pub   ) : 0.8 )
(instance mc (music_pub ) : 0.6 )
```

Similarly, if we have the publication "Mathematics for Computer Science", then we might use the instance mcs with the partial memberships:

```
(instance mcs (cs_pub   ) : 0.6 )
(instance mcs (math_pub ) : 0.4 )
```

The instance and class structure is then just the same as in Fig. 1. We can then form the query

```
?(( mc . circulation   X ) )
```

obtaining the answers

```
((circulation medium )): 0.6
((circulation high   )): 0.8
```

and the non-fuzzy answer obtained after applying the default defuzzification method is

```
((circulation  5677.98))
```

In a similar fashion by querying instance mcs with

```
?(( mcs . circulation   X ) )
```

we obtain

```
((circulation low   )): 0.4
((circulation high  )): 0.6
```

and the non-fuzzy answer from the defuzzification method is

```
((circulation  6083.33))
```

Of course different defuzzification methods might give different answers. Changing the definition of the class sci_pub to

```
((class (sci_pub) (publication) () ())

    ((circulation low ))
    ((defuzz X ) (sci_defuzz X))  /* new definition */
)
```

changes the answers for instance mcs but not for mc. For example, suppose that sci_defuzz just takes the maximum of the two answers, then we get

```
((circulation high   )): 0.6
```

where high is the fuzzy set defined in the class publications.

5 Conclusions

In this paper we presented Fril++, an object-oriented logic programming language which also has integrated facilities for dealing with uncertainty and fuzziness. As well as many of the standard object-oriented features, Fril++ has new features to handle fuzzy objects and the modelling of fuzzy systems.

We found that introducing fuzzy objects in Fril++ (almost) inevitably forces us to allow *multiple* inheritance. Modern object-oriented extensions to procedural or functional languages tend to avoid providing multiple inheritance because of the problems arising from multiple method definitions. However, in a logic language such multiple definitions are not necessarily so much of a problem, but actually can be rather natural.

We also presented a way to exploit the resulting non-trivial hierarchies. The programmer can use the hierarchy information to obtain some automatic selection of methods based on the fuzzy memberships of the objects. For example, given an object that has (partial) memberships in a number of classes, we can access methods that are in the least common superclass of these classes. One use of this would be as a convenient way to handle multiple defaults for defuzzification, and we presented such an example.

In the future we intend to extend the abilities to manipulating objects and extract information from the hierarchy.

References

[AP90]   J.M. Andreoli and R. Pareschi. Linear Objects: logical processes with built-in inheritance. In D. H. Warren and P. Szeredi, editors, *The Seventh International Conference on Logic Programming*, pages 495–510. MIT press, 1990.

[Bal94a] J.F. Baldwin. Evidential Logic Rules from Examples. In *Proc. EUFIT-94*, Aachen, 1994.

[Bal94b] J.F. Baldwin. Soft Computing in Fril. In *Proc. EUFIT-94*, Aachen, 1994.

[BMP87]   J. F. Baldwin, T.P. Martin, and B. W. Pilsworth. The Implementation of Prolog - a Fuzzy Prolog Interpreter. *Fuzzy Sets and Systems*, 23:119–129, 1987.

[BMP88]   J. F. Baldwin, T.P. Martin, and B. W. Pilsworth. *Fril Reference Manual*. Fril Systems LTD, 1988.

[BMP93]   J.F. Baldwin, T.P. Martin, and B. W. Pilsworth. Fril: A Support Logic Programming System. In *AI and Computer Power: The Impact on Statistics*, pages 129–149. Chapman&Hall, 1993.

[Con88]   J. S. Conery. Logical Objects. In R. A. Kowalski and K. A. Bowen, editors, *The Fifth International Conference and Symposium on Logic Programming*, pages 420–434. MIT press, 1988.

[CW88]   W. Chen and D. S. Warren. Objects as Intentions. In R. A. Kowalski and K. A. Bowen, editors, *The Fifth International Conference and Symposium on Logic Programming*, pages 404–419. MIT press, 1988.

[DN66]   O. Dahl and K. Nygaard. Simula, an Algol-based Simulation Language. *Comm. of ACM*, 9:671–678, 1966.

[ES90]   M. A. Ellis and B. Stroustrup. *The Annotated C++ Reference Manual*. Addison-Wesley, 1990.

[GBP93] R. George, B. P. Buckles, and F. E. Petry. Modelling Class Hierarchies in the Fuzzy Object-oriented Data Model. *Fuzzy Sets and Systems*, 60:259–272, 1993.

[HM90]   J. S. Hodas and D. Miller. Representing Objects in a Logic Programming Language with Scoping Constructs. In D. H. D. Warren and P. Szeredi, editors, *The Seventh International Conference on Logic Programming*, pages 511–526. MIT press, 1990.

[McC92] F. G. McCabe. *Logic and Objects*. Prentice Hall, 1992.

[Mey88] B. Meyer. *Object-Oriented Software Construction*. Prentice Hall, 1988.

[Mos94] C. Moss. *Prolog++*. Addison Wesley, 1994.

Case-Based Reasoning: A Fuzzy Approach

Didier DUBOIS*, Francesc ESTEVA**, Pere GARCIA**, Lluís GODO**,
Ramon LÓPEZ DE MÀNTARAS** and Henri PRADE*

* Institut de Recherche en Informatique de Toulouse (IRIT), Université Paul Sabatier, 118 route de Narbonne, 31062 Toulouse Cédex 4, France

** Institut d'Investigacio en Intel.ligencia Artificial (IIIA), Consell Superior d'Investigacions Cientifiques (CSIC), Campus Universitat Autonoma de Barcelona, 08193 Bellaterra, Spain

Abstract. This paper is an attempt at providing a fuzzy set-based formalization of case-based reasoning. The proposed approach assumes a principle stating that "the more similar are the problem description attributes, the more similar are the outcome attributes". If this principle is accepted it induces constraints on the fuzzy similarity relations which are acceptable with respect to the cases stored in the memory. The idea of having cases in the memory with different levels of typicality is also discussed. A weaker form of this principle concluding only on the graded possibility of the similarity of the outcome attributes, is also considered. These two forms of the case-based reasoning principle are modelled in terms of fuzzy rules. Then an approximate reasoning machinery taking advantage of this principle enables us to apply the information stored in the memory of previous cases to the current problem. Extensions of the proposed approach in order to handle incomplete or fuzzy descriptions is also considered and studied. The paper does not take into account the learning aspects of case-based reasoning.

1. Introduction

Case-based reasoning (CBR) systems (Kolodner, 1993; Aamodt and Plaza, 1994) are a particular type of analogical reasoning systems which nowadays have an increasing number of applications in different fields and specialized software products. As it is known, the goal of CBR is to infer a solution for a current case from solutions of a family of previously solved problems, the memory of precedent cases. Theoretical and empirical works have focused among others on the definition and elicitation of similarity measures, on retrieving the relevant cases, on extrapolating pieces of knowledge from cases in the memory, on the logical modelling of the inference mechanism and on the management of incomplete, imprecise or uncertain description of cases. Although these different steps apparently require some graded notion of similarity and some approximate reasoning capabilities, there have been rather few attempts for introducing fuzzy set-based tools in analogical reasoning until recently, up to some exceptions (Farreny and Prade, 1982; Bouchon-Meunier and Valverde, 1993). However, in case-based reasoning, some works have focused on the handling of fuzzy descriptions in the retrieval step (Salotti, 1989, 1992; Jaczynski and Trousse, 1994), on the learning of fuzzy concepts from fuzzy examples (Plaza and López de Màntaras, 1990), on the integration with rule-based reasoning (Dutta and Bonissone, 1993), and very recently on the logical modelling of the inference mechanisms based on similarity measures (Plaza et al., 1996a), in the use of fuzzy predicates for expressing preferences when computing similarities (Bonissone and Cheetman, 1997) and in the use of fuzzy rules for guiding case-based reasoning (Dubois et al., 1997b). See (Dubois and Prade, 1994) for a general overview on similarity-based approximate reasoning and for an investigation of the potentials of fuzzy logic for modeling the different steps mentioned above.

Following a paper by the same authors (Dubois et al.1997b), this work only deals with problems where cases can be given as n-tuples of completely, incompletely or fuzzily described attribute values, this set of attributes being divided in two non-empty disjoint subsets: the subset of problem description attributes and the subset of solution or outcome attributes, denoted by $\mathcal{S}$ and $\mathcal{T}$ respectively. These subsets are taken according to the problem we deal with. A *case* will be denoted as a tuple (s, t) where s and t stand for complete sets of precise attribute values of $\mathcal{S}$ and $\mathcal{T}$ respectively. In order to perform a case-based reasoning we assume that we have a finite set M of known cases or precedents, called *case base* or *memory* (M is thus a set of pairs (s,t)), and a current problem description, denoted by s_0, for which the precise values of all attributes belonging to $\mathcal{S}$ are known. Then case-based reasoning aims at extrapolating or estimating the value t_0 of the attributes in $\mathcal{T}$, for the current problem.

Case-based reasoning, in general, assumes the following implicit principle: "*similar situations give (or may give) similar outcomes*". Thus, a similarity relation S between problem descriptions and a similarity measure T between outcomes are needed. In this paper we briefly discuss how to get them. In terms of the relations S and T this implicit CBR-principle can be expressed as,

"*the more similar are the problem description attributes in the sense of S,*
the more similar are the outcome attributes in the sense of T"

and will be modelled throughout this paper in the framework of fuzzy rules. A key idea is that each case in M, together with the CBR-principle, induces a fuzzy gradual rule. That is, for each (s,t) in M and a current case s_0, we have the following basic reasoning pattern. From the gradual rule "the closer a problem description to s, the closer its solution to t", and from the observation s_0, we conclude that a value t_0 is possible for the current case if it is at least as close to t as s_0 is close to s.

Throughout this paper we will refer to what we call deterministic case-based problems when the above principle is applicable, otherwise we will refer to non-deterministic problems (where only a weaker form of the principle, concluding only on the *possibility* that the outcome attributes are similar, can be used).

Section 2 provides a refresher on similarities. Section 3 and 4 describe the fuzzy set modelling of deterministic and non-deterministic CBR problems respectively for completely described cases. Section 5 generalizes the two above models to deal with incompletely described cases. We use a running example for illustrative purposes.

2. Background on fuzzy similarity relations

In CBR, the evaluation of the similarity between cases is a crucial matter. In this paper we model the notion of similarity in a general sense by means of fuzzy relations. Given a universe U of possible values for a feature, a fuzzy relation S on U is a mapping S: UxU $\rightarrow$ [0,1][1] and the properties usually required for our purpose of similarity modelling are the following (Zadeh,1971):

(i) $\forall$ u $\in$ U, S(u,u) = 1,   (*reflexivity*)

(ii) $\forall$ u,v $\in$ U, S(u,v) = S(v,u),   (*symmetry*)

(iii) $\forall$ u,v,w $\in$ U, S(u,v) $\otimes$ S(v,w) $\leq$ S(u,w),   ($\otimes$-*transitivity*)

where $\otimes$ is usually a t-norm operation[2]. While *reflexivity* and *symmetry* are minimum properties that are clearly required when evaluating the closeness of cases, *transitivity*, even graded, does not always seem compulsory. Indeed, in case-based reasoning, given a current situation s_0, in order to retrieve the most similar cases from the memory M, we estimate the similarity of s_0 with each of the situations s_i in M pairwisely, and we do not compute the similarity between s_0 and s_j by transitivity from the similarity of s_0 and s_i and that of s_i and s_j. Transitivity may even be thought to be an undesirable property in some settings, since s_0 may be somewhat intermediary between two situations which are not close themselves. Moreover we may also require the *separating* property ((i') $\forall$ u,v $\in$ U, S(u,v) = 1 if and only if u = v). Besides, on ordered universes we shall also require that the similarity be *convex*, namely for all x,y,u,v $\in$ U such that [x,y] $\supseteq$ [u,v], then S(x,y) $\leq$ S(u,v).

Example 1. Many similarity measures which are often used in CBR make a rather neat distinction between those elements which are considered to be similar from those which are considered dissimilar by means of some threshold. As an extreme case consider, on the set of real numbers, the non-fuzzy similarity relation S_ε defined as

$$S_\varepsilon(x, y) = \begin{cases} 1, & \text{if } |x - y| \leq \varepsilon \\ 0, & \text{otherwise} \end{cases}.$$

This type of relation is clearly not transitive. But even if a relation is $\otimes$-transitive for some operation $\otimes$, the corresponding notion of extended transitivity can be very different. For instance, in case $\otimes$ is the Lukasiewicz t-norm, $\otimes$-transitivity does not restrict at all the value of S(x,z) as soon as S(x,y) + S(y,z) $\leq$ 1 for all y. The situation in that sense would be very different if the relation is min-transitive, which is much stronger.

The more general relations we shall consider for CBR-problems are fuzzy relations satisfying (i) and (ii), which are called *proximity* relations. If a proximity relation further satisfies (iii) w.r.t. a t-norm $\otimes$, it is called a $\otimes$-*similarity* relation. In both cases we say that

---

[1] In this paper, we use the notations $S(s_1,s_2)$ and $T(t_1,t_2)$ for denoting the degrees of similarity for simplicity, rather than using the notations $\mu_S(s_1,s_2)$ and $\mu_T(t_1,t_2)$ commonly used in the fuzzy set literature where they distinguish between a fuzzy set F and its membership function μ_F. Thus, in this paper we shall write F(u) instead of $\mu_F(u)$.

[2] A t-norm $\otimes$ is a non-decreasing binary operation on [0,1] satisfying associativity, commutativity, 1 being the neutral element and 0 being an absorvent element. Noticeable t-norms are min, product and Lukasiewicz operation (a $\otimes$ b = max(0, a + b − 1)).

the relation is *separating* if it satisfies (i'). Nevertheless, for the sake of simplicity, from now on we will generally use the term *similarity* to denote both proximity and $\otimes$-similarity relations whenever no further precision is required. See (Ovchinnikov, 1991) for a good overview on similarity relations.

Usually, the global evaluation of the similarity between two multiple-feature descriptions is obtained by aggregating degrees of similarities for each feature. The aggregation has to be done in such a way that the resulting similarity relation should preserve properties, like reflexivity, symmetry (and possibly $\otimes$-transitivity), of the individual similarities. In general min-combination preserves reflexivity and symmetry. With respect to transitivity, it is worth noticing that if S_1 and S_2 are $\otimes$-transitive then both $S_{\otimes}((x_1, x_2), (y_1, y_2)) = S_1(x_1, y_1) \otimes S_2(x_2, y_2)$ and $S_{min}((x_1, x_2), (y_1, y_2)) = \min(S_1(x_1, y_1), S_2(x_2, y_2))$ are still $\otimes$-transitive. It is clear that the min-combination gives the minimum value to the similarity, and thus keeps the most discriminating value as a global value of the similarity, while the max-combination would give as a value the least discriminating one. Other well-known combination operations like averages, take values between min and max (but do not usually preserve transitivity).

Moreover we may think of a weighted aggregation if we consider that we are dealing with a fuzzy set of features having different levels of importance. For instance, if we aggregate the similarity degrees by means of the min operation, a weighted version (e.g., Dubois and Prade, 1988) can be defined by

$$S(x, y) = \min_{i=1,n} \max(S_i(x_i, y_i), 1 - \lambda_i)$$

with $\max_{i=1,n} \lambda_i = 1$, where case x (resp. y) is described by the vector of feature values $(x_1, ..., x_n)$ (resp. $(y_1, ..., y_n)$) and λ_i is the level of importance of the ith feature. Clearly $\lambda_i = 1$ means that the feature is fully important for the assessment of the global similarity, while if $\lambda_i = 0$, the feature is not taken into account. An easy computation shows that reflexivity, symmetry and $\otimes$-transitivity are preserved by this weighted aggregation, as pointed out by Fodor and Roubens(1994) who also suggest other weighted aggregations of fuzzy relations. Moreover separatingness is also preserved if $\lambda_i \neq 0$ for all $i = 1, 2,..., n$.

In the following example, and in the next sections, different proximity and similarity relations are presented and used.

Example 2. Suppose we have a data base about second-hand cars. Suppose also that every car has exactly 6 attributes in our data base and suppose that the problem description attributes are the first five, i.e., $\mathcal{S} = \{year, power, mileage, equipment, shape\}$, and the outcome attribute is the last one, i.e. $\mathcal{C} = \{price\}$. The ranges of *year*, *power*, *mileage* and *price* are numerical and the range of the *equipment* and *shape* attributes consists of 4 qualitative levels, linearly ordered: "bad"< "poor"< "good" < "excellent". The global similarity S will be defined by aggregation of similarities S^i (i = 1, ..., 5) for each description attribute. S^1 and S^3, corresponding to *year* and *mileage*, are defined by,

$$S^i (u,v) = \min(u,v) / \max(u,v).$$

This seems to be a reasonable similarity measure for these attributes because it is not uniform, that is, the greater are two values having the same difference, the more similar they are. Here the similarity relative to the power (S^2) is assumed to be linear w.r.t. the difference of power. For S^2 we use

$$S^2(u,v) = 1 - (|u - v| / 1000).$$

Finally, the similarities S^4 and S^5, between the elements of the qualitative range are taken as,

$$S^i(u,v) = \begin{cases} 1, & \text{if } u = v \\ 2/3, & \text{if } u \text{ and } v \text{ are consecutive w.r.t. the attribute order} \\ 1/3, & \text{if there is exactly one element between } u \text{ and } v \\ 0, & \text{otherwise} \end{cases}$$

Obviously all these S^i are reflexive and symmetric and thus they are proximity relations. Just for the sake of illustration, in Table 1 we present an small memory of cases (second hand cars), together with a car (case $C_0 = (s_0, t_0)$, with $s_0 = (s_0{}^1, s_0{}^2, s_0{}^3, s_0{}^4, s_0{}^5)$) whose market value is to be estimated.

cases (s, t)	years old (s^1)	power (s^2)	mileage (s^3)	equipement (s^4)	shape (s^5)	price (t)
C_1	1	1.300	20.000	poor	good	8.000
C_2	2	1.600	30.000	excellent	poor	7.000
C_3	2	1.600	40.000	good	good	5.000
C_4	3	1.500	60.000	excellent	poor	5.000
C_0	2	1.600	50.000	poor	good	?

Table 1. Cases of the second hand cars example.

An important comment is in order here. The aggregation of the S^i's presupposes that they are commensurate. In practice it means that an expert should define meaningful fuzzy proximity relation, using the same scale, namely [0, 1]. Otherwise, different numerical encodings of the proximity relations on each attribute domain (maintaining the same total orderings) can lead, whatever the chosen aggregation function is, to different global proximity relations. Once the S^i's are defined we can use different conjunctive aggregation functions, such as min and product, for obtaining the global similarity. For simplicity in this example we are not introducing any importance weighting in the aggregation although it may be natural to do it in such an example.

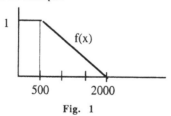

Fig. 1

Besides, only for illustrative purposes, a possible definition for T is $T(u, v) = f(|u-v|)$, $f(x)$ being the function depicted in Figure 1. In the next section, in the deterministic case, we will discuss the problem of coherence of the memory and of the gradual rules obtained from cases through the CBR-principle. We will also discuss which constraints T has to satisfy if we require that coherence be assured when M and S are given.

3. Deterministic CBR Problems

In the deterministic setting, for each case (s_i, t_i) of the memory M, the principle assumed to hold is that "the more similar is s_i to the input s_0, the more similar is t_i to the outcome". We also assume that a similarity S on the set of problem description attribute values U (domain of $\mathcal{S}$), and a similarity T on the set of solution attribute values V (domain of $\mathcal{T}$) are available. In terms of the similarities S and T, the principle can be interpreted as the fuzzy gradual rule:

the more X is $S(s_i)$, the more Y is $T(t_i)$,

where X and Y are variables ranging on $\mathcal{S}$ and $\mathcal{T}$ respectively, $S(s_i): U \rightarrow [0, 1]$ and $T(t_i): V \rightarrow [0, 1]$ are fuzzy sets defined as $S(s_i)(s) = S(s_i, s)$ and $T(t_i)(t) = T(t_i, t)$ respectively. The semantics of such rules is given by the following constraint on the joint possibility distribution $\pi_{X,Y}$ (Dubois and Prade, 1992):

$$\pi_{X,Y}(s, t) = S(s_i, s) \rightarrow T(t_i, t)$$

where $\rightarrow$ denotes the residuated implication such as $x \rightarrow y = 1$ if $x \leq y$, and $x \rightarrow y = y$ otherwise (Gödel implication).

It is worth noticing that the gradual rule "the more X is $S(s_i)$, the more Y is $T(t_i)$" means that the similarity of any s with s_i constrains the similarity of t_i with any t associated with s at a minimum level, i.e., $S(s_i, s)$ is a lower bound of $T(t_i, t)$. Thus, $\forall \alpha \in [0,1]$, we have

$$s \in S(s_i)_\alpha \Rightarrow t \in T(t_i)_\alpha \qquad (1)$$

where $S(s_i)_\alpha = \{(s_i, s') \mid S(s_i, s') \geq \alpha\}$ is the α-cut of $S(s_i)$ and $T(t_i)_\alpha$ is similarly defined. In particular, if $S(s_i, s) = 1$, we should have $T(t_i, t) = 1$. Moreover, if T is such that $T(t_i, t_j) = 1 \Leftrightarrow t_i = t_j$ (separating property of T), then the classical functional dependency

$$s_i = s \Rightarrow t_i = t, \qquad (2)$$

is a consequence of (1) using the reflexivity of S. Constraint (1) is then clearly stronger than (2). Obviously, when $S(s_i, s) = 0$, $T(t_i, t)$ is no longer constrained.

Given an input value $s = s_0$, the solution is a fuzzy set F_i with membership grades $F_i(s_0)(t) = S(s_i, s_0) \rightarrow T(t_i, t)$. In the following we only use the core of this fuzzy set, i.e., the elements t with membership 1. Thus the solution set for Y is:

$$E_i(s_0) = \{t \mid T(t_i, t) \geq S(s_i, s_0)\},$$

i.e. the set of t's such that the implication $S(s_i, s_0) \rightarrow T(t_i, t)$ takes the value 1. This amounts to take the "crisp" implication $x \rightarrow^* y = 1$ if $x \leq y$, $x \rightarrow^* y = 0$ otherwise, instead of $\rightarrow$. If the memory M contains n cases, then we have n fuzzy rules and the core of the fuzzy set solution for an input value s_0 is the intersection of sets $E_i(s_0)$, that is,

$$E(s_0) = \bigcap_{i=1,...,n} \{t \mid T(t_i, t) \geq S(s_i, s_0)\}. \qquad (3)$$

Notice that $E(s_0)$ can be empty if T is not permissive enough. This set is not empty for any input s_0 if the family of gradual rules "the more X is $S(s_i)$, the more Y is $T(t_i)$ " for (s_i, t_i) in M is coherent in the sense of (Dubois et al., 1996). This coherence means that the family of crisp rules of the form (1) for i=1,n and for $\alpha \in [0, 1]$ is coherent, which is equivalent to say that if the condition parts of a subset of rules in this family have a non-empty intersection, then their conclusion parts should also intersect. Formally speaking, it means that for any I contained in $\{1,2,...,n\}$ and any $\alpha_i \in (0,1]$ for $i \in$ I, it holds

$$\bigcap_{i \in I} S(s_i)_{\alpha_i} \neq \emptyset \Rightarrow \bigcap_{i \in I} T(t_i)_{\alpha_i} \neq \emptyset. \qquad (4)$$

In summary, $E(s_0)$ is not empty for any s_0 if and only if condition (4) is satisfied.

Besides, if we want to be coherent with respect to the memory M, the solution $E(s_j)$ for each s_j appearing in M has to contain t_j. This condition is equivalently expressed by the constraint

$$\forall (s_i,t_i),(s_j,t_j) \in M,\ S(s_i,s_j) \leq T(t_i,t_j). \tag{5}$$

So (5) expresses that when s_i and s_j are close, t_i and t_j should be at least as close.

Only if T is separating does (4) imply (5). Indeed if T is separating and (4) is satisfied, $E_i(s_i) = \{t_i\}$ and then from (3) condition (5) follows. But in general (4) does not imply (5) as it is shown in the following example. Let $M = \{(s_1,t_1), (s_2,t_2)\}$ and define two proximity relations S and T as follows: $S(s, s') = 3/4$ for any $s \neq s'$ and $T(t_1,t'') = T(t_2,t'') = 1$ for some t'' different from t_1 and t_2, and $T(t, t') = 1/2$ otherwise. Obviously condition (5) fails but (4) holds (t'' is in all the intersections of $T(t_i)_{\alpha_i}$ for any α_i).

On the other hand (5) does not imply (4) as it is shown in the continuation of example 2 below. Thus, once the "deterministic model" is adopted, and the similarity S is defined, the CBR principle induces constraints on the similarity relation T: both conditions (4) and (5) should be enforced when building T.

It is worth noticing that the constraints (5) are easy to handle. The interesting T is the minimal one (in the sense of fuzzy set inclusion ($T \supseteq T'$ iff $T(t,t') \geq T'(t,t')$)) yielding the most informative gradual rule. Formally speaking, given M and S, the minimal solution for convex T satisfying the constraints (5) is defined by

$$T(t, t') = 1 \text{ if } t = t',\ T(t, t') = \max_{(s_i,\ t_i),(s_j,\ t_j) \in M} \{S(s_i, s_j) \mid t,t' \in [t_i, t_j]\} \text{ otherwise.} \tag{6}$$

Even if S is separating, T may not be so; it happens when M contains two cases (s,t) and (s,t') with $t \neq t'$. Moreover the transitivity of S does not entail the transitivity of T. Transitivity of T can be obtained, if necessary, taking the transitive closure.

Of course the relation T defined by (6) provides only a lower bound of the minimal T satisfying both (5) and (4). In this paper we shall not further discuss the computation of the minimal solution of this optimisation problem.

Example 2 (continued). Let us compute T_{min} and T_{prod} given by (6) with S being obtained using first the minimum and then the product aggregations:

(i) $T_{min}(t, t') = 1$ if $t = t'$, $T_{min}(t, t') = 1/2$ if $t,t' \in$ [5.000, 8.000] and $T_{min}(t, t') = 0$ otherwise.

(ii) $T_{prod}(t, t') = 1$ if $t=t'$, $T_{prod}(t, t') = 3/10$ if $t,t' \in$ [5.000, 7.000], $T_{prod}(t, t') = 7/60$ if $t,t' \in$ [5.000, 8.000] and one of t or t' does not belong to [5.000, 7.000] and $T_{prod}(t, t') = 0$ otherwise.

For an input s_0, it can be checked that the (core of the fuzzy set) solution in case of the minimum aggregation is {5.000} and the empty set in case of the product. The last result shows that (5) can hold while (4) is not satisfied. This is the reason why it is important in practice to use a pair S, T such that both (4) and (5) are satisfied.

Remark.- We may think of the following generalisation of the deterministic model. The idea is to introduce some weighting α_i associated to the cases (s_i,t_i) of M and thus, to weaken the constraints (5) in the following way:

$$\forall (s_1,t_1),(s_2,t_2) \in M, \quad \min(\alpha_1, \alpha_2, S(s_1,s_2)) \leq T(t_1,t_2). \qquad (7)$$

Moreover the gradual rule $S(s_i) \rightarrow T(t_i)$ is changed accordingly into $\min(\alpha_i, S(s_i)) \rightarrow T(t_i)$, which is also equivalent to $S(s_i) \rightarrow (\alpha_i \rightarrow T(t_i))$ if the implication is residuated with respect to the minimum (Gödel implication). This means that the case (s_i, t_i) is changed into the imprecise case $(s_i, T(t_i)_{\alpha_i})$. Indeed $\alpha_i \rightarrow T(t_i)(t) = 1$ if $\alpha_i \leq T(t_i)(t)$. Thus the solution is,

$$E(s_0) = \bigcap_{(s_i,t_i) \in M} E_i^*(s_0),$$

where $E_i^*(s_0) = \{t' \mid \min(\alpha_i, S(s_i,s_0)) \leq T(t_i,t')\}$. Notice that when $\alpha_i = 1$ we have $E_i^*(s_0) = E_i(s_0)$ and when $\alpha_i = 0$, $E_i^*(s_0)$ becomes the whole set of possible values for t and it amounts to delete the case (s_i,t_i) from the memory M.

This extension based on the introduction of degrees α_i is related to the so-called proximity entailment in (Dubois et al., 1997a; Dubois et al., 1997b). From an interpretation point of view we may think of α_i as a kind of typicality weight and the modified gradual rule can be read as

"the more similar is s_0 to a typical case s, the more similar is t_0 to t".

Generally speaking, memories of cases are not usually well structured, and they may contain cases that can be considered as atypical or not coherent with the rest of the cases stored in the memory. These cases could make the finding of a meaningful proximity T satisfying (4) and (5) impossible. Thus the introduction of a measure of *typicality* of the cases of the memory M could be interesting for assessing the relevance of cases.

4. Non-Deterministic Problems

The deterministic principle-based model may be felt too strong in some practical applications where M may for instance simultaneously include cases like (s,t) and (s,t') with $t \neq t'$. Indeed in such a case the enforcing the constraints (4) and (5) may lead to use a similarity relation T which is too permisive. An alternative solution is to use a weaker version of the CBR principle stating that

"the more similar s_1 and s_2, the more *possible* t_1 and t_2 are similar".

In our context, this weak principle becomes a non-deterministic (fuzzy) dependency rule of the form "the more similar is s to s_0 (in the sense of S), the more *possible* is the similarity of t to t_0 (in the sense of T)". It should be pointed out that this rule only concludes on the *possibility* of t_0 being similar to t. This acknowledges the fact that, often in practice, a database may contain cases which are rather similar with respect to the problem description attributes, but which are sensibly distinct with respect to outcome attribute(s). This emphasizes that case-based reasoning can only lead to cautious conclusions.

The formal expression of the above principle requires to clarify the intended meaning of "possible" in it. Rules of the form "the more X is A, the more possible Y is B" correspond to a particular kind of fuzzy rules called "possibility rules" (Dubois and Prade, 1996). They express that "the more X is A, the more possible B is a range for Y", which can be understood as "$\forall u$, if X = u, it is possible at least at the degree A(u) that Y lies in B". When B is an ordinary subset, it clearly expresses that i) if $v \in B$, v is possible for Y at least at the level A(u) if X = u, and ii) if $v \notin B$, nothing is said about the minimum possibility level of value v for Y. It leads to the following constraint on the joint possibility distribution $\pi_{Y|X}$ representing the rule (where $\pi_{Y|X}(v,u)$ estimates to what extent $Y = v$ is possible when $X = u$), namely

$$\begin{cases} \pi_{Y|X}(v) \geq A(u) \text{ if } v \in B \\ \pi_{Y|X}(v) \geq 0 \text{ if } v \notin B \end{cases}.$$

When both A and B are fuzzy sets it generalizes into

$$\forall\, u \in U, \forall\, v \in V, \min(A(u), B(v)) \leq \pi_{Y|X}(v,u). \tag{8}$$

This clearly gives back the above expression when $B(v) \in \{0,1\}$. This model of fuzzy rule is close to Mamdani's (1977) original proposal in fuzzy logic-based control.

Coming back to our CBR problem, since we apply the principle "the more similar are s and s_0 (in the sense of S), the more possible is that t and t_0 are similar (in the sense of T)" then, according to (8), the fuzzy set of possible values t' for t_0 with respect to case (s, t) is given by

$$\pi_{t_0}(t') = \min(S(s, s_0), T(t, t')). \tag{9}$$

As it can be seen, what is obtained is the fuzzy set T(t) of values t' T-similar to t, "truncated" by the global degree $S(s,s_0)$ of similarity of s and s_0. The inequality in (8), which leads to a max-based aggregation of the various contributions obtained from the comparison with each case (s,t) in the memory M of cases, acknowledges the fact that each new comparison may suggest new possible values for t_0. Since (9) applies to all the pairs $(s,t) \in M$, we obtain the following fuzzy set E_{s_0} of possible values t' for t_0 :

$$E_{s_0}(t') = \max_{(s,t) \in M} \min(S(s,s_0), T(t,t')). \tag{10}$$

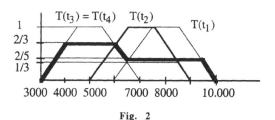

Fig. 2

The representation of this set in the case of our second-hand cars example is given in Figure 2 when S is the min-aggregation of the S^i's and T is the proximity relation given at the end of Example 2. Notice that the resulting set E may be quite uninformative if rather similar cars have very different prices in M, as it is expected. However the maximal height part of the fuzzy set in Fig. 2 is informative enough since it suggest with strength 2/3, a price in the interval [4000, 6000].

5. Dealing with incomplete cases

In this section we extend the fuzzy approach to CBR in order to deal with cases which may be incompletely described. To do this, we propose that each (possibly incompletely described) case $(\underline{s}_i, \underline{t}_i) \in M$ be understood as the generic fuzzy rule:

If X is $\underline{s}_i$-*similar*, then Y is $\underline{t}_i$-*similar*

where $\underline{s}_i$ and $\underline{t}_i$ are fuzzy sets, and s_i-*similar* and t_i-*similar* are also fuzzy sets with membership functions:

$\underline{s}_i$-*similar*$(s) = \max_{s'} \min(S(s', s), \underline{s}_i(s'))$ and

$\underline{t}_i$-*similar*$(t) = \max_{t'} \min(T(t', t), \underline{t}_i(t'))$,

that is, the convex hulls of $\underline{s}_i$ and $\underline{t}_i$ with respect to S and T respectively. Then, taking a particular current (possibly incompletely described) problem as the fuzzy statement "X is $\underline{s}_0$", we apply the traditional fuzzy logic machinery, namely the Generalized Modus Ponens (Zadeh,1979) in order to infer a fuzzy statement "Y is $\underline{t}^i_0$", where $\underline{t}^i_0$ is the fuzzy solution set for $\underline{s}_0$ w.r.t. case $(\underline{s}_i, \underline{t}_i) \in M$. $\underline{t}^i_0$ can be obtained as a sup-min composition of $\underline{s}_0$ with the fuzzy relation $R_i(s, t) = \underline{s}_i$-*similar*$(s) \rightarrow \underline{t}_i$-*similar*$(t)$ (resp. $R_i(s, t) = \min(\underline{s}_i$-*similar*$(s)$, $\underline{t}_i$-*similar*$(t))$) in the deterministic (resp. non-deterministic) approach, namely:

$$\underline{t}^i_0(t) = \sup_s \min(\underline{s}_0(s), R_i(s, t)) \tag{11}$$

Next we briefly show how to proceed for obtaining the general (fuzzy) solution set $\underline{t}_0$ in the two models.

• **Deterministic model.** In the deterministic model, the fuzzy rules are interpreted as gradual rules, and thus the solution from the i-th case is given by

$$\underline{t}^i_0(t) = \sup_s \min(\underline{s}_0(s), \underline{s}_i\text{-}similar(s) \rightarrow \underline{t}_i\text{-}similar(t)),$$

but the general solution is not given by $\bigcap_i \underline{t}^i_0$ since the $\sup_s$ and the $\min_i$ do no commute in the expression (12) below corresponding to the application of the fuzzy set machinery to the whole set of cases:

$$E(\underline{s}_0)(t) = \sup_s \min(\underline{s}_0(s), \min_i R_i(s, t)) \tag{12}$$

$\bigcap_i \underline{t}^i_0$ is only an upper bound of $E(s_0)$. It is easy to check that, when s_0, s_i, t_i, are precisely known, we recover the approach of Section 3.

Example 2 (continued). Suppose that we have a case $(\underline{s}, \underline{t})$ that is only described for the year (2), power (1.600), mileage (30.000), shape (poor) and price (7.000) attributes, and the value for equipment attribute is missing. Then $\underline{s} = \{(2, 1.600, 30.000, x, poor) \mid x \in \{bad, poor, good, excellent\}\}$ and $\underline{t} = \{7.000\}$. If the current case is imprecisely defined by $\underline{s}_0=\{(2, x, 40.000, good, good) \mid x \in [1.300, 2.000]\}$, the core of the solution[3] for $\underline{s}_0$ with respect to the case $(\underline{s}, \underline{t})$ is core$(E(\underline{s}_0)) = \{t' \mid \max\{T(t, t') \mid t \in \underline{t}\} \geq 1/3\} = [5.500, 8.500]$, i.e., the elements of $E(\underline{s}_0)$ with membership 1.

• **Non-deterministic model.** In the non-deterministic model, the fuzzy rules are interpreted as possibility rules, that is, the relation R_i describing the rule is defined as $R_i(s,t) = \min(\underline{s}_i\text{-}similar(s), \underline{t}_i\text{-}similar(t))$,

---

[3]when again S is the min-aggregation of the S^i's and T is the proximity relation given at the end of Example 2

$$t^i_0(t) = \sup_s \min(\underline{s_0}(s), \min(\underline{s_i}\text{-}similar(s), \underline{t_i}\text{-}similar(t))).$$

In this setting, the general solution $E(\underline{s_0})$ is the disjunctive aggregation of the t^i_0's, that is:

$$E(\underline{s_0})(t) = \max_i \ t^i_0(t).$$

Again, it is easy to check that we recover the approach of Section 4 when $\underline{s_0}, \underline{s_i}, \underline{t_i}$, are precisely known.

6 Conclusion and Further Work

In this paper we have been concerned with the modelling of some aspects of CBR using fuzzy set-based techniques, as well as their applicability. The basic tool is the use of fuzzy similarity relations both between problem descriptions and between outcomes of the cases. Each case in the memory is interpreted either as a gradual fuzzy rule (deterministic model) or as a possibility rule (non-deterministic model).

This fuzzy framework gives us the means of defining to what extent a memory M is coherent w.r.t. the use of a pair (S, T) of fuzzy similarity relations in the deterministic approach. Given a CBR-framework (M, S, T) its coherence Coh(M,S,T) is defined as a measure (between 0 and 1), which estimates how much the cases given in the memory are in agreement with our theoretical model, and in some sense the possibility to find a solution for a current case. We have

$$\text{Coh}(M,S,T) = \text{Min}\{S(s_i, s_j) \to T(t_i, t_j) / (s_i, t_i), (s_j, t_j) \in M\}.$$

(M,S,T) is then said to be coherent iff Coh(M, S, T) = 1. In particular, Coh($\{(s_1, t_1), (s_2, t_2)\}$) = 1 iff $S(s_1, s_2) \le T(t_1, t_2)$. Moreover note that Coh(M$\cup\{(s, t)\}$) $\le$ Coh(M), i.e. the introduction of a new case cannot increase the coherence. Then, given a CBR problem (M, S, T, s_0), it can be checked that a value t is a solution for s_0 in the deterministic approach iff Coh(M$\cup\{(s_0,t)\}$) = 1. A more detailed investigation of this notion of coherence is left for further research.

Acknowledgements. The authors acknowledge partial support of the bilateral CSIC - CNRS grant called"Similarity based-reasoning and its applications". The IIIA authors also acknowledge partial support from the CYCIT project SMASH (TIC96-1138-C04-01).

References

Aamodt A., Plaza E. (1994) Case-based reasoning: Foundational issues, methodological varoations and system approaches. Artificial Intelligence Communications, 7(1), 39-59.

Bonissone P., Cheetman W. (1997) Financial Applications of Fuzzy Case-Based Reasoning to Residential Property Valuation. Proc. of the 6th IEEE Inter. Conf. on Fuzzy Systems (FUZZ-IEEE'97), Barcelona, Spain, 37-44.

Bouchon-Meunier B., Valverde L. (1993) Analogy relations and inference. Proc. of the 2nd IEEE Inter. Conf. on Fuzzy Systems (FUZZ-IEEE'93), San Francisco, CA, March 28-April 1st, 1140-1144.

Dubois D., Esteva F., Garcia P., Godo L., Prade H. (1997a) A logical approach to interpolation based on similarity relations. Int. J. of Approximate Reasoning, 17 n°1, pp.1-36

Dubois D., Esteva F., Garcia P., Godo L., López de Mantaras R., Prade H. (1997b) Fuzzy Modelling of Case-based Reasoning and Decision, Proc. Int. Conf. Case-based Reasoning ICCBR'97 (D.Leake and E. Plaza, eds.), Springer Verlag, 599-611.

Dubois D., Prade H. (1988) Possibility Theory, Plenum Press, New York.

Dubois D., Prade H. (1992) Gradual inference rules in approximate reasoning. Information Sciences, 61, 103-122.

Dubois D., Prade H. (1994) Similarity-based approximate reasoning. In: Computational Intelligence Imitating Life (Proc. of the IEEE Symp., Orlando, FL, June 27-July 1st, 1994) (J.M. Zurada, R.J. Marks II, X.C.J. Robinson, eds.), IEEE Press, New York, 69-80.

Dubois D., Prade H. (1996) What are fuzzy rules and how to use them. Fuzzy Sets&Systems, 84, 169-185.

Dubois D., Prade H., Ughetto L. (1996) Coherence of fuzzy knowledge bases. Proc. of the 5th IEEE Inter. Conf. on Fuzzy Systems (FUZZ-IEEE'96), New Orleans, LO, Sept. 8-11, 1996, IEEE Press, 1858-1864.

Dutta S., Bonissone P.P. (1993) Integrating case- and rule-based reasoning. Int. J. of Approximate Reasoning, 8, 163-203.

Farreny H., Prade H. (1982) About flexible matching and its use in analogical reasoning. Proc. of the 1982 Europ. Conf. on Artificial Intelligence (ECAI'82), Orsay, France, July 12-14, 43-47.

Fodor J., Roubens, M. (1994) Fuzzy Preference Modelling and Multicriteria Decision Support. Kluwer Academic, Dordrecht, The Netherlands.

Jaczynski M., Trousse B. (1994) Fuzzy logic for the retrieval step of a case-based reasoner. Proc. of the EWCBR'94, 313-321.

Kolodner J. (1993) Case-Based Reasoning. Morgan Kaufmann, San Mateo, CA.

Mamdani E.H. (1977) Application of fuzzy logic to approximate reasoning using linguistic systems. IEEE Trans. Comput., 26, 1182-1191.

Ovchinnikov S.V. (1991) Similarity relations, fuzzy partitions, and fuzzy orderings. Fuzzy Sets and Systems, 40, 107-126.

Plaza E., Esteva F., Garcia P., Godo L., López de Màntaras R. (1996a) A logical approach to case-based reasoning using fuzzy similarity relations. To appear in Information Sciences.

Plaza E., López de Màntaras R. (1990) A case-based apprentice that learns from fuzzy examples. In: Methodologies for Intelligent Systems, Vol. 5 (Z.W. Ras, M. Zemankova, M.L. Emrich, eds.), Elsevier, 420-427.

Salotti S. (1989) Représentation centrée objet et filtrage flou pour raisonner par analogie: Le système FLORAN. Actes du 7ème Congrés "Reconnaissance des Formes et Intelligence Artificielle" (RFIA'89), Paris, 29 nov.-1er dec., 1695-1707.

Salotti S. (1992) Filtrage flou et représentation centrée objet pour raisonner par analogie: Le système FLORAN. (In French) PhD thesis, University of Paris XI, Orsay, France.

Zadeh L.A. (1971) Similarity relations and fuzzy orderings. Information Sciences, 177-200.

Zadeh L.A. (1979) A theory of approximate reasoning. In: Machine Intelligence, Vol. 9 (J.E. Hayes, D. Michie, L.I. Mikulich, eds.), Elsevier, New York, 149-194.

System Identification of Fuzzy Cartesian Granule Feature Models Using Genetic Programming

James F. BALDWIN, Trevor P. MARTIN, James G. SHANAHAN[1,2]

Advanced Computing Research Centre, Dept. of Engineering Mathematics
University of Bristol, Bristol, BS8 1TR, ENGLAND
e-mail {Jim.Baldwin, Trevor.Martin, Jimi.Shanahan }@bristol.ac.uk

Abstract – A Cartesian granule feature is a multidimensional feature formed over the cross product of words drawn from the linguistic partitions of the constituent input features. Systems can be quite naturally described in terms of Cartesian granule features incorporated into additive models (if-then-rules with weighted antecedents) where each Cartesian granule feature focuses on modelling the interactions of a subset of input variables. This can often lead to models that reduce if not eliminate decomposition error, while enhancing the model's generalisation powers and transparency. Within a machine learning context the system identification of good, parsimonious additive Cartesian granule feature models is an exponential search problem. In this paper we present the G_DACG constructive induction algorithm as a means of automatically identifying additive Cartesian granule feature models from example data. G_DACG combines the powerful optimisation capabilities of genetic programming with a rather novel and cheap fitness function which relies on the semantic separation of concepts expressed in terms of Cartesian granule fuzzy sets in identifying these additive models. G_DACG helps avoid many of the problems of traditional approaches to system identification that arise from feature selection and feature abstraction such as local minima. G_DACG has been applied in the system identification of additive Cartesian granule feature models on a variety of artificial and real world problems. Here we present a sample of those results including those for the benchmark Pima Diabetes problem. A classification accuracy of 79.7% was achieved on this dataset outperforming previous bests of 78% (generally from black box modelling approaches such as neural nets and oblique decision trees).

1. Introduction

The ability to learn is considered the sine qua non of intelligence, which makes it an important concern for both cognitive psychology and artificial intelligence. The field of machine learning (ML), which crosses these disciplines, studies the computational processes that underlie learning in both humans and machines. The field's main objects of study are the artefacts; specifically algorithms that improve their performance with experience [33]. One of the primary goals of the field is to model the mechanisms that underlie human learning referred to as "cognitive simulation" in [44]. In achieving this we can find out how humans work and can perhaps help them to be better in their work.

---

[1] Supported by European Community Marie Curie Fellowship Program.
[2] Address correspondence to this author.

On the other hand from an engineering and system identification perspective, ever since the introduction of the first operational modern computer (Heath Robinson) in 1940 by Alan Turing's team, scientists and engineers have tried, with varying degrees of success, to increase its usefulness to mankind. Machine learning is one of the fields that can potentially make this more of a reality. Machine learning can be viewed as a means of automatically programming computers (or identifying systems) thus alleviating many of the problems facing our cyborg society:

- It can help to model problem domains where domain knowledge is overly difficult to capture (too much, too little, too expensive etc...) for example in intelligent activities such as vision understanding [7], speech understanding [25]. Because machine learning can transform training data into knowledge it holds the potential of overcoming the knowledge acquisition bottleneck.

- As data collection methods and storage technologies improve we face the challenge of a data flood. [18] note that "It has been estimated that the amount of data in the world doubles every 20 months ... earth observation satellites planned for the 1990s are expected to generate one terabyte (10^{15}) of data everyday". It is clearly infeasible for humans to trawl such data in search of patterns or relationships. This task falls within the field of Knowledge Discovery in Databases in which learning plays a key role in pan handling data for nuggets of knowledge (data mining).

- To overcome the programming bottleneck (software lag) that results from deploying computers i.e. to automate the process of automation. This is seen as one of the most important areas of computer science over the next twenty years.

Within the field of ML there have been many fine successes and some serve to fuel other ML goals. For example, [13] presented an empirical study which "provides evidence that machine learning models can provide better classification accuracy than explicit knowledge acquisition". Kononenko [29] references 24 papers where inductive learning systems were actually applied in medical domains, such as oncology, liver pathology, prognosis of patient survival in hepatitis, urology, cardiology, gynaecology amongst many others. He remarks that "typically, automatically generated diagnostic rules slightly outperformed the diagnostic accuracy of physician specialists". In some cases the automatically programmed systems enhance human understanding. [36] provides further examples of success, with lots of fielded examples, in the field of machine learning.

Numerous approaches to system identification through machine learning exist. These can be quite easily categorised based upon two principles: performance accuracy and transparency (human understandability) of the induced model. To date most approaches that have focussed on the transparency of processes (through symbolic representation) have had only mild success in terms of performance accuracies compared to their mathematical counterparts. In this paper we present examples that support this, including a diabetes diagnosis system (see Section 5.2) where a symbolic learning approach such as ID3 [39] was applied to model this diagnosis process. Mathematically-derived approach such as neural networks were also applied, however the mathematically-based approaches outperform (in terms of accuracy) the symbolic approach even though the symbolic approach performs the best in terms of model transparency and understandability. With regard to current approaches to machine learning, these goals seem to be incompatible in that no one approach satisfies them both.

The work presented tries to fulfil both the desires of having accurate and understandable models that arise out of learning. This is enabled through the use of Cartesian granule features; multi-dimensional features built on words, thus enabling the paradigm "modelling with words". Systems can be quite naturally described in terms of Cartesian granule features incorporated into additive models (if-then-rules with weighted antecedents) where each Cartesian granule feature focuses on modelling the interactions of its constituent subset of input variables. Additive Cartesian granule feature models were originally introduced to overcome decomposition error, and also to enhance the model generalisation powers and transparency [6, 8, 41, 42].

In the context of automatically identifying additive Cartesian granule feature models from example data the discovery of good, highly discriminating, parsimonious Cartesian granule features, which adequately model the system at hand, is an exponential search problem. Numerous system identification algorithms exist (see Section 2 for a review), however most algorithms suffer from various problems that arise from poor feature selection and poor feature abstraction techniques. These problems include: inductive bias introduced by filter feature selection techniques; local optimum models that generally arise from the greedy nature of the search algorithms used in the identification process and also from treating feature selection and feature abstraction as two independent processes. Consequently, we propose the G_DACG constructive induction algorithm, which automatically identifies the important variable interactions and their abstractions that should be described using Cartesian granule features. The identified Cartesian granule features are then incorporated into additive models that generally provide good generalisation and transparency. G_DACG combines the powerful optimisation capabilities of genetic programming with a rather novel and cheap fitness function which relies on the semantic separation of concepts expressed in terms of Cartesian granule fuzzy sets in identifying these additive models. Furthermore it avoids some of the pitfalls of other identification algorithms such as local minima and provides a population-based (collective) approach to finding a solution as opposed to individual-based approaches.

The material in this paper is organised as follows: In Section 2 we overview system identification, focussing on the important roles feature selection and feature abstraction play in this process. Various structure identification strategies commonly used in machine learning are also reviewed. Section 3 serves as an introductory section to Cartesian granule features, a corresponding induction algorithm and additive models. In Section 4 we present the G_DACG constructive induction algorithm which automatically identifies additive Cartesian granule feature models. We illustrate this G_DACG algorithm on some problems in Section 5 and compare the results obtained with other standard machine learning approaches. Finally we finish off with some conclusions in Section 6.

2. System Identification through Induction

System identification through inductive learning can be viewed as the non-trivial general process of discovering useful models or knowledge about an application domain from observation data and background knowledge. System identification is a multi-faceted research area, drawing on methods, algorithms, and techniques from diverse umbrella fields such as knowledge representation, machine learning, pattern recognition, cognitive science, artificial intelligence, databases, statistics, probability, knowledge acquisition for expert systems and data visualisation. The unifying goal of these areas is the identification of predictive models from data and background knowledge that can simplify or enhance an application area. In this work, we are mainly concerned with the black box approach to system identification [34], in that we do not use any a priori knowledge in the model construction i.e. the model is constructed directly from the data or observations provided. Although expert or a priori knowledge in various guises can be incorporated into the system identification process, this is not addressed in this paper. Traditional approaches to systems modelling divide the problem of system identification into two sub-problems: those of structure identification and parameter identification.

2.1 Structure Identification

Structure identification is mainly concerned with selecting the language (i.e. the variables and their representations) in terms of which the models will be expressed. This language is defined in terms of the input features (and their derivations) and also for some forms of knowledge representations, in terms of the feature universe abstractions (sometimes linguistic). Feature selection and discovery form integral steps in this process. In fuzzy and other distribution based approaches (such as probability density estimation, radial basis function networks, etc.) a further level of identification is required where the granularity of the input feature universes needs to be determined. When dealing with prediction problems (i.e. output universe is continuous in nature) the granularity of the output universe will also have to be determined. These types of system are not considered here however, [42] gives details and examples of a heuristic approach to output granularity identification in the case of additive Cartesian granule feature modelling.

2.1.1 Feature selection and discovery

Feature selection can be viewed as the process of selecting those features that should be used in the subsequent steps of an induction or modelling process. Feature discovery can be viewed as a process of synthesising features from the base features and consequently involves feature selection. The synthesised features (and possibly the original feature set) can then be used by any induction process for the extraction of concept descriptions. Synthesised features tend to lead to more succinct and more discriminating concept descriptions. Numerous ways of synthesising new features have been proposed in the literature including [5, 11]; a genetic programming approach to the synthesis of compound features as algebraic expressions of base features. These synthesised features are subsequently used in fuzzy modelling. Several examples presented in [31, 32, 48] have incorporated feature synthesis indirectly into model construction through genetic programming. Logical rule induction systems such as

AQ17 [36] generate new features by combining base features using mathematical and logical operators in order to provide adequate concept descriptions. Feature synthesis and selection also forms an important part of neural network construction, where the hidden nodes may be viewed as higher order features that are discovered by the learning algorithm. Features are automatically selected as a result of training. Principal component analysis [23] offers an alternative route in constructing higher-order features from weighted combinations of base features based on variance measures. In the work presented here we construct Cartesian granule features based on the cross product of granules used to partition the base feature universes. In our work and in general one of the most critical steps in feature synthesis is the feature selection process.

There has been substantial work on feature selection in various fields such as pattern recognition, statistics, information theory, machine learning theory and computational learning theory. Numerous feature selection algorithms exist. [14, 28] characterise the various approaches as follows: those that "embed" the selection within the basic induction algorithm, those that use feature selection to "filter" features passed to induction, and those that treat feature selection as a "wrapper" around the induction process. Since feature selection plays a critical role in the discovery of Cartesian granule features we now briefly examine the various approaches to feature selection using these categories.

2.1.1.1 Embedded Approaches to Feature Selection

Embedded feature selection involves selecting features within the induction algorithm (single use/one-pass of induction process), where the general idea is to add or remove features from a concept description in response to an evaluation function e.g. prediction errors on unseen data. The various techniques differ mainly in the search strategies and heuristics used to guide the search. Because the search space can be exponentially large, managing the problem requires strong heuristics. For example, logical description induction techniques such as ID3, C4.5, and CART carry out a hill-climbing search strategy, guided by information-gain heuristics, to search programs (discover good features conjunctions), by working from general to specific. The ASMOD algorithm, which identifies B-spline and neuro-fuzzy models, and its various extensions [15, 24] are examples of an embedded feature selection strategy where the model is iteratively refined by modifying, adding or removing features. MARS [19], a identification algorithm for truncated spline models, is also an example of an embedded feature selection strategy.

These embedded techniques, due to the search mechanisms employed, are very vulnerable to starting points, and local minima [14, 15, 24, 28]. These search techniques work well in domains where there is little interaction amongst the relevant features. However, the presence of attribute interactions, can cause significant problems for these techniques. Parity concepts constitute the most extreme example of this situation, but it also arises in other target concepts. Embedded selection methods that rely on greedy search cannot distinguish between relevant and irrelevant features early in the search. Although combining forward selection and backward elimination to concept construction may help to overcome this problem. A better alternative may be to rely on a more random search such as simulated annealing, or a more random and diverse search technique such as genetic algorithms or genetic programming.

2.1.1.2 Filter Approaches to Feature Selection

A second general approach to feature selection introduces a separate process for this purpose that occurs before the basic induction step. For this reason [28] have termed them filter methods; they filter out irrelevant features before induction occurs. The pre-processing step generally relies on general characteristics of the training set to select some features and exclude others. Thus filtering methods are independent of the induction algorithm that will use their output and they can be combined with any such method. RELIEF [26] and FOCUS [1] and their extensions are amongst the more commonly used approaches to feature selection and have been shown to contribute significant improvements to a variety of induction approaches such as decision trees, nearest neighbours and naïve Bayesian classifiers [14]. RELIEF samples training instances randomly, summing a measure of the relevance of a particular attribute across each of the training instances. The relevance measure used is based upon the difference between the selected instance and k nearest instances of the same class and k nearest instances in the other classes ("near-hit" and "near-miss") [30]. REIGN [12] relies on the use of a feed forward neural networks (using back propagation learning algorithm) combined with a hill climbing search strategy to determine the features set that should subsequently be used by a fuzzy induction algorithm. Principal component analysis [23] is a form of filter that constructs higher-order features, orders them and selects the best such features. These features are then passed on to the induction algorithm. Filter approaches, while interesting and useful, totally ignore the demands and capabilities of the induction algorithm and thus can introduce an entirely different inductive bias to that of the induction algorithm [28]. This leads to the argument that the induction method planned for use with the selected features should provide better estimate of accuracy than a separate measure that has an entirely different inductive bias; this leads to the wrapper technique for feature selection.

2.1.1.3 Wrapper Approaches to Feature Selection

A third generic approach for feature selection is done outside the induction method but uses the induction method as the evaluation function. For this reason [28] refer to these as wrapper approaches. The typical wrapper approach conducts a search in the space of possible parameters. Each state in the parameter space corresponds to a feature subset and various other information depending on the induction algorithm used (for example the granularity of feature universe in the case of Cartesian granule features). Each state is evaluated by running the induction algorithm on the training data and using the estimated accuracy of the resulting model as a metric (other measures can also be used). Typical search techniques use a stepwise approach of adding or deleting features to previous states beginning with a state where all features or no features are present. The G_DACG constructive induction algorithm presented subsequently in Section 4.3 is an example of a wrapper approach to feature selection. The wrapper scheme has a long history within the statistics and pattern recognition communities [17, 22]. The major disadvantage of wrapper methods over filter schemes is the former's computational cost, which results from calling the induction algorithm for each parameter set evaluated. The approach is also susceptible to local minima when used in conjunction with stepwise search strategies.

2.1.2 Feature Abstraction

In the case of some forms of knowledge representation, an extra step in language selection is required; that of feature abstraction. Feature abstraction occurs usually in the form of partitioning. This helps reduce information complexity and in some cases enhances transparency and understandability. In fuzzy set based approaches to learning such as described in [46, 49] fuzzy partitioning is used. The granularity of the partitions in these approaches is determined heuristically. In the case of [49] granularity is determined using a clustering approach. In logical description induction techniques such as ID3, C4.5, and CART feature abstraction is achieved through crisp partitioning of the feature universes. This partitioning is normally accomplished by information-gain or purity heuristics. In general for these fuzzy set and decision tree based approaches the system identification algorithms perform the steps of feature selection and feature abstraction independently of each other. This can lead to models which are sub-optimum in nature. In the case of feedforward neural networks [21] partitioning is achieved through non-linear weighted sum combinations of features. The number of hidden nodes plays an important role in this type of partitioning and generally is determined either manually or automatically through network constructor algorithms [21]. In the case of Cartesian granule features, feature universes are abstracted by words that are characterised by fuzzy sets (linguistic universes). The level of granulation can be determined by expert input or automatically by the G_DACG constructive induction algorithm. G_DACG combines the feature selection and abstraction steps thus alleviating local minima problems. Characterising the granules by fuzzy sets provides the added advantage of smooth continuous behaviour across the universe of discourse. This is contrasted with a less desirable highly non-linear behaviour that typically results from crisp partitioning.

2.2 Parameter Identification

Parameter identification on the other hand can be viewed primarily as an optimisation procedure that fine-tunes the model language. In the case of polynomial curve fitting parameter identification consists of identifying the co-efficients in the polynomial. This is normally achieved by minimising the square of the output error. In most fuzzy set based systems parameter identification corresponds to identifying the location of the fuzzy sets that linguistically partition the variable universes [46, 49]. Once again commonly used procedures such as the mountain method [49] achieve parameter identification by minimising the output error using a back propagation type learning algorithm. In the case of additive Cartesian granule feature modelling parameter identification is concerned with selecting suitable granule characterisations and with setting up the class aggregation rules for the constituent Cartesian granule features: estimating the weights associated with the individual Cartesian granule feature (submodels); and tuning the rule filters. This is achieved by minimising the square of the output error.

3. Additive Cartesian Granule Feature Modelling

Cartesian granule features were originally introduced to overcome decomposition error, a problem which has plagued traditional AI and fuzzy approaches to knowledge based systems, and also to provide the transparency of traditional symbolic AI approaches [6,

8, 41, 42]. Cartesian granule features are a new type of multidimensional feature defined over the Cartesian product of words drawn from the linguistic partitions of the constituent feature universes. Variables defined over Cartesian granule universes can be viewed as multidimensional linguistic variables whose states are Cartesian granules i.e. Cartesian words where each word is characterised by a fuzzy set defined over the corresponding base variable universe.

3.1 Cartesian Granule Features

Here we give a brief overview of Cartesian granule features. A *granule* [50, 51], is a fuzzy set of points, which are labelled by a word. This collection of points is drawn together as result of indistinguishability, similarity, proximity or functionality. A *Cartesian Granule*, is an expression of form $W_1 \times W_2 \times ..... \times W_m$ where each W_i is a word or label associated with a fuzzy set defined over the universe Ω_i and where "$\times$" denotes the Cartesian product. A Cartesian granule can be visualised as a clump of elements in an n-dimensional universe sharing similar properties. A *Cartesian granule universe* is a discrete universe defined over $P_1 \times P_2 \times ..... \times P_m$ where each P_i is a linguistic partition of universe Ω_i and where "$\times$" denotes the Cartesian product. In other words given a set of single attribute features $\{F_1, F_2 ... F_m\}$ defined over $\Omega_1 \times \Omega_2 \times .... \times \Omega_m$ where Ω_I is a universe of discourse over which F_i is defined, we form a linguistic partition P_i over each universe Ω_I. Partition P_i will consist of labelled fuzzy sets as follows :

$$\{A_{i1}, A_{i2}, ..., A_{ic}\}$$

We form the Cartesian granule space $\Omega_{P_1 \times P_2 \times .... \times P_m}$ by taking the cross product of the words associated each fuzzy set across each partition P_i resulting in a discrete universe

$$\Omega_{P_1 \times P_2 \times .... \times P_m} : \{ A_{11}A_{21}...A_{m1}, A_{12}A_{22}...A_{m2}, ..., A_{1c}A_{2c}...A_{mc}\}$$

where each Cartesian granule is merely a string concatenation of the individual fuzzy set labels A_{ij}.

A *Cartesian Granule Feature* is a feature defined over a *Cartesian Granule Space*. A *Cartesian granule fuzzy set* is a discrete fuzzy set defined over a *Cartesian granule universe*. Each *Cartesian granule* is associated with a membership value, which is calculated by combining the membership values, individual feature values have in the fuzzy sets which characterise the granules. For example, the Cartesian granule $w_{11} \times w_{21} \times ..... \times w_{m1}$ where each w_{i1} is the word associated with the first fuzzy subset in each linguistic partition P_i. Here the membership value associated with the Cartesian granule $w_{11} \times w_{21} \times ..... \times w_{m1}$ is calculated as follows:

$$m_{w_{11}}(x_1) \wedge m_{w_{21}}(x_2) .... \wedge m_{w_{m1}}(x_m)$$

where x_i is the feature value associated with the i-th feature within the data vector. Here the aggregation operator $\wedge$ can be interpreted as any T-norm [27, 40] such as product or min. The choice of conjunction operator is considered in [42].

3.1.1 A Cartesian Granule Fuzzy Set Example

The following example illustrates how to form a two dimensional Cartesian granule fuzzy set corresponding to a data vector. Using the single attributes *position* and *size* (attributes associated with objects in a digital image domain) we form a Cartesian granule universe. This is achieved by linguistically partitioning each of the base variable universes. One possible linguistic partition could be:

$$P_{position} = \{left, middle, right\} \quad and \quad P_{size} = \{small, medium, large\}.$$

This is depicted in Figure 1. Next we form the Cartesian granule universe defined over the words associated with the linguistic partitions. Our Cartesian granule space will consist of the following discrete elements:

$$\Omega_{position \times size} : \{ left.small, left.medium, left.large, middle.small, middle.medium, \\ middle.large, right.small, right.medium, right.large\}.$$

If we define the position and size universes to be *[0, 100]* and *[0, 100]* respectively then the definitions of the fuzzy sets in partitions $P_{position}$ and P_{size} (in Fril notation [5])[3] could be:

left:[0:1, 50:0]	*small*:[0:1, 50:0]
middle:[0:0, 50:1, 100:0]	*medium*:[0:0, 50:1, 100:0]
right:[50:0, 100:1] and	*large*:[50:0, 100:1].

Then taking a sample data tuple (in the form *<position, size>*) *<60, 80>* yields two fuzzy sets *{middle/.8+ right/.2}* and *{medium/.4+ large/.6}*. Next we form the Cartesian product of these fuzzy data to yield a fuzzy set in Cartesian granule space:

{middle.medium/.32 + middle.large/.48 + right.medium/.08 + right.large/.12}.

Here we have interpreted the combination operator $\wedge$ as product.

---

[3] A fuzzy set definition in Fril such as *middle*:[0:0, 50:1, 100:0] can be rewritten mathematically as follows (denoting the membership value of x in the fuzzy set *middle*):

$$m_{middle}(x) = \begin{cases} 0 & \text{if } x \leq 0 \\ \dfrac{x}{50} & \text{if } 0 < x \leq 50 \\ \dfrac{100-x}{50} & \text{if } 50 < x \leq 100 \\ 1 & \text{if } x \geq 100 \end{cases}$$

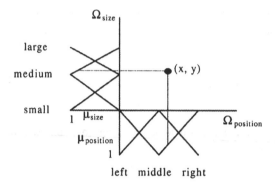

Figure 1 Fuzzy partitions of universes Ω_{size} and $\Omega_{positilon}$.

3.1.2 Cartesian Granule Fuzzy Sets Induction Algorithm

Notions fundamental to the formation of Cartesian granule features and fuzzy sets were presented in the previous sections. Here we extend these basic notions and show how they can be applied in a machine learning context. We present an induction algorithm that extracts concepts from example data in terms of Cartesian granule fuzzy sets.

Our proposed learning algorithm falls into the category of supervised learning algorithms. Within this framework databases of examples of the form:

$$< \vec{i}, output >$$

are utilised (for both training and testing) where $\vec{i}$ is a vector of values (where each value can be numeric or linguistic i.e. a single value, an interval value, or a fuzzy value) defined over the input attributes and are used to predict the output attribute value (which may be a single value, an interval value, or a fuzzy value). More formally a database D is defined over a set of attribute features $\{F_1, F_2...F_m\}$ defined in turn over the universes $\Omega_1, \Omega_2, ...,\Omega_m$. Here we have extended the notion of a conventional database attribute value to the case where uncertain or vague information can specified in terms of fuzzy subsets or interval values. Supervised learning algorithms normally address two types of problems, namely classification problems and prediction/regression problems. We present the induction algorithm from a classification problem perspective. A similar approach can be followed for prediction problems; instead of using the natural data partitioning provided by the output classification feature to build cartesian granule fuzzy sets corresponding to each class value, we generate a fuzzy partition in the output space (continuous) [42] and build Cartesian granule fuzzy sets corresponding to each concept (fuzzy set) in the output space.

3.1.2.1 Initialisation

We begin the whole induction process by selecting which features should be combined into Cartesian granule features. On this front we have proposed an automatic, near optimal, feature discovery algorithm based upon a genetic search, G_DACG, which will be presented in Section 4. However for now we can assume we will combine all the available input features into a Cartesian granule feature. Subsequently we form linguistic partitions over all attribute universes (both continuous and discrete) in the input space. The feature discovery algorithm will also determine automatically the granularity of the base feature universes and the granule characterisations. For the purposes of presenting this algorithm we assume that we have an expert who can indicate good linguistic partitions of the base feature universes. Having generated linguistic partitions over the universes of the selected features, we form the Cartesian granule universe Ω_{CG}. Next we split the database of examples into 2 parts namely the training database D_{train} and the testing database D_{test}. Subsequently we partition the database D_{Train} using the output classification values.

3.1.2.2 Extraction of Cartesian Granule Fuzzy Sets from Example Data

We extract a fuzzy set defined over the Cartesian word universe from example data, corresponding to each class in the output space. We begin by initialising a frequency distribution $DIST_{CG}$ defined over all the Cartesian granules in Ω_{CG}. We then take each training tuple for a class T_{ci} and construct the corresponding Cartesian granule fuzzy set (i.e. linguistic description of the data vector) CGF_{Ci} using the approach outlined in Section 3.1.1. Subsequently we form the least prejudiced distribution LPD_{Ci} [2, 5] corresponding to this fuzzy set CGF_{Ci} via its mass assignment. Next we update the overall frequency distribution $DIST_{CG}$ with this least prejudiced distribution LPD_{Ci}. We repeat this process for all training tuples in this class C_C. This results in frequency distribution $DIST_{CG}$ defined over the Cartesian granules corresponding to the class C_C. We take this distribution to correspond the least prejudiced distribution LPD_{CG}. We can then form a mass assignment corresponding to LPD_{CG}. Using the assumption of the least-prejudiced distribution we distribute probability masses uniformly within focal elements of the mass assignment and solve to find the associated Cartesian Granule Fuzzy Set. We repeat the above steps for each output classification C_C thereby extracting the corresponding class Cartesian granule fuzzy sets. These induced Cartesian Granule fuzzy sets can then be utilised to solve both classification and regression problems by incorporating them in to Fril product or evidential rules [4]. The induction algorithm for prediction problems is described in [8].

3.1.3 Additive Cartesian Granule Feature Models

[9, 42] highlighted the need for discovering structural decomposition of input spaces in order to generate Cartesian granule feature models that provide good generalisation and knowledge transparency. Cartesian granule features incorporated into evidential logic rule structures [4] provide a natural mechanism for capturing this type of decomposed approach to systems modelling [42] and is referred to as an additive model. The use of additive Cartesian granule feature models can lead to greatly simplified models which are comptractable (computationally tractable) and are amenable to human inspection, thus providing insight to the system being modelled, while also enhancing model generalisation.

The evidential logic rule structure [4] captures very naturally additive Cartesian granule feature models. Here classification problems are presented (see [8, 42] for prediction problems). A sample evidential logic rule structure is depicted in Figure 2. Here *CLASS* can be viewed as a fuzzy set consisting of a single crisp value (in the case of classification type problems). Each rule characterises the relationship between input and output data for a particular region of the output space i.e. a concept. An equivalence rule is normally used i.e. the support intervals associated with the rule are $((1\ 1)(0\ 0))$. In the case of classification problem domains a rule is generated for each class in the output space.

The body of each rule consists of information expressed in terms of a list of problem domain features. Here each F_i represents a feature, which is either a single attribute feature, or Cartesian granule feature or some other type of derived feature. The values F_{iCLASS} of these features will typically be fuzzy sets defined over corresponding universe Ω_i (again it can be a fuzzy set defined over a single attribute universe or Cartesian granule universe and so on) corresponding to the output variable value *CLASS*. Notice how naturally we can treat features of heterogeneous forms in a very homogeneous manner using these representations.

((classification is *CLASS*) /* if */	*Head/Consequent*

(evlog FILTER
    $(F_1$ is $f_{1CLASS})$ w_1
    :
    $(F_i$ is $f_{iCLASS})$ w_i
    :
    $(F_m$ is $f_{mCLASS})$ w_m
	*Body/Antecedents
	and associated weights*

)):$((1\ 1)(0\ 0))$	*Rule Supports*

Figure 2 Fril evidential logic rule structure.

The weight term w_i associated with each body term in the evidential logic rule indicates its contributing weight of importance to this rule's conclusion. In generating evidential logic rules we need the additional step of calculating the weights associated with each body term. Since the values of each the body terms are fuzzy sets, regardless of the feature type being flat or Cartesian granule in nature, the weights can be estimated by measuring the semantic separation of the inter class fuzzy sets using semantic discrimination analysis (as presented in Section 4.2). Each rule body is associated with a filter or linguistic quantifier (expressed as a fuzzy set) that lends a linguistic interpretation to the support value generated by the rule body. This filter can be determined automatically from example data as discussed in Section 4.4.

3.1.4 Inference and Decision Making

Here we consider the general **inference** and **decision-making** processes used within this framework of knowledge representation for the classification problem domain - discrete output variable - (see [8, 42] for the prediction problem domain). As described in detail in the previous section, each rule consists of a body of features and their corresponding fuzzy set values. These features may be flat or Cartesian granule in nature. In the case of Cartesian granule features, when performing inference we require the additional inference step that interprets the input data vector $\vec{x}$ linguistically (see Section 3.1.1) which results in the Cartesian granule fuzzy set description *CGD* of $\vec{x}$. Then we merely carry out the semantic unification (SU i.e. the fuzzy set match via mass assignment theory [5]) between the class fuzzy set *CGF* and the data fuzzy set *CGD*. In otherwords, in the case of Cartesian granule features

$$SU(CGF \mid \bar{x}) = SU(CGF \mid CGD)$$

where $\vec{x}$ corresponds to the input data and *CGD* to the Cartesian granule fuzzy set description of $\vec{x}$.

In general, when dealing with systems where the individual universes are granulated into fuzzy sets, multiple fuzzy sets and hence multiple fuzzy rules are called upon to deduce an answer from a particular case. For any particular test case, each rule is processed separately and then individual solutions are combined to give a final overall outcome. For each class rule in the rule set we calculate its respective level of support for the body and head of the rule. For evidential logic rules we calculate the body support B as

$$B_{Class} = \sum_{i=1}^{m} SU(f_{iClass} \mid \vec{x}_i) w_{iClass}$$

where w_{iCLASS} is the weight of importance associated with feature i for class *Class*. Since we are utilising equivalence rules the support for the head clause of each class rule is equivalent to the support for the body of that rule [5].

Having calculated the level of support for each hypothesis *(classification is CLASS)*, some decision-making needs to take place. In the case of classification problems when the rule base is presented with an unclassified vector of data, inference is performed as described previously, thus yielding a point support value S_i for the hypothesis of the form *(classification is CLASS$_i$)* associated with each class rule R_i. Then the classification of the input data vector is determined as the class *CLASS$_{max}$* associated with the hypothesis with the highest support.

4. System identification of Additive Cartesian Granule Feature Models using G_DACG

Having described parsimonious additive model structure in terms of Cartesian granule features as a potentially effective means of representing models that provide good generalisation and model transparency, and having identified their construction as a feature selection and discovery process, here we present the G_DACG constructive induction algorithm which automates the process of additive Cartesian granule feature model discovery and construction. Genetic programming [31, 32] forms an integral part of the G_DACG feature discovery algorithm. Before describing the G_DACG algorithm we present the chromosome structure and fitness function used.

4.1 Chromosome Structure

There are infinite ways of forming the membership value associated with a Cartesian granule in a Cartesian granule fuzzy set [8, 41]. This would correspond to an infinite function set in genetic programming terms. To date we have mainly used two operators, product and min operators. Both the product and min are intuitive conjunction operators [42]. However empirical evidence on various problem domains seems to suggest that there is very little difference between the effectiveness of both these operators [8, 41]. Consequently we have reduced our function set to the product operator *CGProduct*. At a later date it is hoped to allow a richer function set and genetically select appropriate conjunction operators. The arity of the *CGProduct* function can vary from one to the number of available base features, though parsimonious (low dimensional) Cartesian granule features are encouraged. This desire/behaviour is encoded in the fitness function.

Our terminal set consists of all the base features we wish to use in systems modelling along with their respective granularity range (abstraction). For example if we have 2 base features $f1$ and $f2$ and we allow a granularity range of [2..4] for each base feature, then, we would have a terminal set made up of the following:

$$\{f1\_G2, f1\_G3, f1\_G4, f2\_G2, f2\_G3, f2\_G4\}$$

where $f_i\_G_j$ corresponds to base feature i and with a granularity of j.

Since we are currently dealing with just one function, *CGProduct*, we can reduce the complexity of our chromosome structure from a tree structure to a list structure. This becomes feasible as a result of the discrete nature of Cartesian granule features. The granularity range for the base feature universes is very much feature and problem dependent, although a range of [2..15] is thought to be sufficient for most problem domains. The distribution of fuzzy sets across each of the feature universes is set, by default, to uniform, in order to decrease the search complexity. However, this could be automatically determined using the genetic search approach.

4.2 Fitness

The most important and difficult concept of genetic programming is the determination of the fitness function. The fitness function dictates how well a discovered program is able to solve the problem. The output of the fitness function is used as the basis for selecting which individuals get to procreate and contribute their genetic material to the next generation. The structure of the fitness function will vary greatly from problem to problem. In the case of Cartesian granule feature identification the fitness function needs to find Cartesian granule features which give good class separation (class corresponds to specific areas of the output variable universe) and are parsimonious. Consequently when used in fuzzy modelling these features should yield high classification accuracy with low computational overhead along with transparent reasoning. Cartesian granule features can be determined individually for each class in the problem domain (heterogeneous feature discovery) or alternatively in unison (homogeneous feature discovery). The fitness for an individual Cartesian granule feature (for a particular class or all classes) is a weighted combination of the discrimination (separation) of the individual and the parsimony of the individual, which is measured in terms of dimensionality of the individual and the size (cardinality) of the individual's universe of discourse. In order to calculate the semantic discrimination of a

Cartesian granule feature we need to construct the Cartesian granule fuzzy sets corresponding to each class in the output universe. Subsequently the process of semantic discrimination analysis determines the mutual dissimilarity of individuals, measured in terms of the point semantic unifications between the Cartesian granule fuzzy set corresponding to the current class CGF_i and the other class CG fuzzy sets CGF_j. This is written more succinctly as follows:

$$\text{Discrimination}_i = 1 - \underset{\substack{j=1 \\ j \neq i}}{\overset{C}{\text{Max}}} \; \Pr(CGF_i \mid CGF_j)$$

where C corresponds to the number of classes in the current system.

The dimensionality factor corresponds to the number of base features making up a Cartesian granule feature. The size (cardinality) of a Cartesian granule feature universe is simply the number of Cartesian granules in the corresponding universe. During the process of evolution it is important to promote individuals that have high discrimination, low dimensionality and small universe size. The latter of these two desires are expressed linguistically using the fuzzy sets depicted in Figure 3.

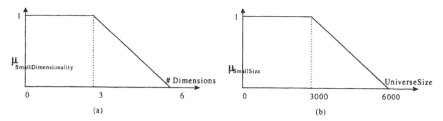

Figure 3 (a) Fuzzy set corresponding to small dimensionality in Cartesian granule features.   (b) Fuzzy set corresponding to small size of Cartesian granule feature universes.

We combine the individual factors in the following manner:

$$\text{Fitness}_i = W_{Dis} * \text{Discrimination}_i + W_{Dim} * \mu_{SmallDim}(\text{Dimensionality}_i) + W_{USize} * \mu_{SmallUinv}(\text{UniverseSize}_i)$$

where W_{Dis}, W_{Dim} and W_{USize} take values in the range [0..1] and sum to 1. Since Cartesian granule features of high discrimination are desirable regardless of other criteria W_{Dis} tends to take values in the range [0.7..0.8]. The remaining weight is split evenly amongst W_{Dim} and W_{USize}. The weights are determined heuristically from trial runs.

4.3 Genetic Discovery of Additive Cartesian Granule Feature Models (G_DACG)

The discovery of good, highly discriminating, parsimonious Cartesian granule features is an exponential search problem that forms one of the most critical and challenging tasks in the additive model identification. Obviously no parameter optimisation algorithm can overcome shortcomings in structure identification. An additive model composed of Cartesian granule features that are too simple or too inflexible to represent the data will have a large bias, while one which has too much flexibility (i.e. redundant structure) may fit idiosyncrasies found in the training set producing models that generalise poorly; in this case the model's variance is too high. This is an example of the classical bias/variance dilemma presented in [20]. Bias and variance are complementary quantities, and the best generalisation is obtained when we have the best compromise between the conflicting requirements of small bias and small variance.

In order to find the optimum balance between bias and variance we need to have a way of controlling the effective complexity of the model. This trade-off is incorporated directly into the G_DACG discovery algorithm at two levels; one in terms of a fitness function for the individual Cartesian granule features (submodel level) and the other at aggregate model level where lowly significant features based on semantic discrimination analysis are eliminated. In the case of additive Cartesian granule features models, both the bias and variance can be drawn towards their minimum, by adding, removing, or altering (granularities, granule characterisations) the constituent Cartesian granule features, thereby generating models which tend to generalise better and have a simpler model structure; i.e. Occam's razor, where all things being equal the simplest is most likely to be the best.

As was seen earlier in Section 2.1, the search algorithm plays a big part in the discovery of good features. It can influence what parts of the parameter space are or are not evaluated due to local minima, starting states and computational constraints. Each state in the parameter space corresponds to a feature subset and the granularity of the individual base features i.e. the feature selection and feature abstraction steps are combined. The size of the finite space of all possible Cartesian granule features for any problem given a finite number of base features is given by the following equation:

$$\sum_{granularity=min\,Gran}^{max\,Gran} \sum_{dim=1}^{MaxDim} NumOfFeatu\,res\, C_{dim} * (granularit\,y)^{dim}$$

Note that in this case, the granule characterisations are assumed to be fixed (for example triangular fuzzy sets), otherwise, the complexity could potentially increase by another order of magnitude. For a sample problem, like the Pima Indian diabetes problem presented later in Section 5.2, the number of possible Cartesian granule features runs into millions if the eight base features are considered with base feature granularity ranges of [2, 15]. In general the search space will be of the order of millions, increasing exponentially with the permitted Cartesian granule features dimensionality. Consequently, traditional approaches to feature discovery would prove computationally intractable even for low-dimensional problems. Here we propose an additive Cartesian granule feature model constructive induction algorithm centred around a pseudo-random, distributed search paradigm based upon natural selection and population genetics; genetic programming. The genetic search paradigm, due to its distributed nature, avoids pitfalls such as local minima by exploring large areas of the search space in parallel. Currently we use the steady state flavour of genetic programming (SSGP) [31, 47]. SSGP permits overlapping generations and when used in conjunction with k-tournament selection avoids the problem of losing good individuals. We use a flavour of

SSGP where duplicate children are discarded rather than inserted into the population [47]. This helps promote diversity and avoids premature convergence in the population. Furthermore since the individuals will solve problems collectively (rather than individually), in the case of additive Cartesian granule feature modelling, this flavour of genetic programming is deemed to be appropriate. From a feature selection point of view, the G_DACG algorithm could be classified as wrapper feature selection algorithm in that it uses the Cartesian granule feature induction algorithm to evaluate the relevance of the individual Cartesian granule features.

The key steps involved in the G_DACG algorithm are as follows (see Figure 4 for a schematic):

- Generate a random set of individual Cartesian granule features
- Assign a fitness value to each individual
- REPEAT
  - Generate n new fitnessed children
  - Insert new children into population
  - Eliminate n individuals from the population
  - Determine best Additive Model
- UNTIL a satisfactory solution or the number of generations expires.
- Determine best Additive Model

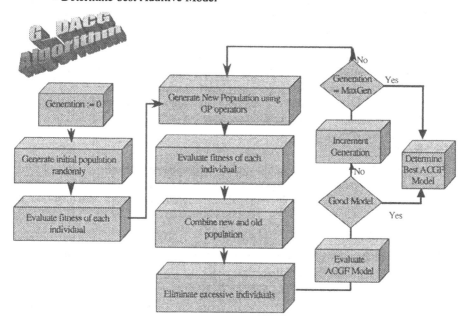

Figure 4: G_DACG constructive induction algorithm.

Determining the best additive model from the discovered Cartesian granule features can be performed at the end of each iteration of the genetic search or at the termination of the algorithm. This takes the form of selecting n of the best features (either heterogeneous or homogeneous discovered features) from the current population and constructing the corresponding additive model (i.e. determine the parameters of the model, see next section). Then superfluous Cartesian granule features are removed from the model by eliminating lowly contributing features, using a process known as backward elimination [17], thereby decreasing the additive model's bias and its variance. Alternatively, using the final population of individuals (or a subset), a genetic search can be performed of the possible additive models (of limited dimensionality). Structure identification is also concerned with the number of rules (and hence the number of classes in the output space) in our model. When dealing with classification type problems, structure identification of this type reduces to building one rule for each class. One technique that has been developed to speed up the evaluation process is to cache the fitnesses of the hypothesised Cartesian granule features. In genetic searches, while diversity tends to be relatively high, Cartesian granule features can be visited repeatedly. Exploiting the cached results can lead to significant computational gains.

4.4 Parameter Identification

Parameter identification is concerned primarily with setting up the class aggregation rules for the constituent Cartesian granule features: i.e. estimating the weights associated with the individual Cartesian granule feature (submodels) and tuning the class rule filters. We estimate the weights associated with each Cartesian granule feature using semantic discrimination analysis. Other optimisation techniques could be used. Since the submodels are being aggregated using the evidential logic rule another degree of parameter identification needs to be performed; that of learning the filter. This is addressed in [42] where a data driven optimisation algorithm centred on Powell's direction set minimisation technique is presented. An alternative parameter identification technique based upon the Mass Assignment Neuro Fuzzy (MANF) framework, where neural network learning algorithms can be applied to learn the submodel aggregation function, is also considered in [42].

5. Results

The C_DACG algorithm has been illustrated and compared with other machine learning approaches on a variety of problem domains including object recognition [42] and plant control [10]. Here illustrate the approach on some benchmark machine learning problems.

5.1 Ellipse Problem

The ellipse problem is a binary classification problem based upon artificially generated data from the universe $\Re \times \Re$. Points satisfying an ellipse inequality are classified as legal while all other points are classified as illegal. This is graphically depicted in Figure 5 for the ellipse inequality

$$x^2 + 2y^2 \leq 1.$$

Thus there are two single attribute input features, X and Y. The universe of X, Ω_X is taken to be [-1.5, 1.5] and similarly the universe of Y, Ω_Y is taken to be [-1.5, 1.5]. Different training, control (validation) and test datasets, comprising of 1000, 300 and 1000 data vectors respectively, were generated using a pseudo-random number stream.

An equal number of data samples for each class were generated. Each data sample consists of a triple <*X, Y, Class*>, where *Class* adopts the value *0* for *illegal* indicating that the point <*X, Y*> does not satisfy the ellipse inequality, and the value *1* for *legal* otherwise.

5.1.1 A G_DACG Run on the Ellipse Problem

Here we present the steps and parameter settings involved in a typical run of the G_DACG constructive induction algorithm; we construct an additive Cartesian granule feature model for the Ellipse problem. Genetic programming is integral part of the G_DACG algorithm genetically evolving Cartesian granule features. As a result a lot of the algorithm parameters are GP related. In a typical GP run the population size is limited to 20 chromosomes, due to the small nature of the problem. Initial populations are generated using the ramped-half-and-half procedure [31] i.e. half-random length chromosomes and half full-length chromosomes. The length of chromosome range, in the initial population and in subsequent generations is problem dependent but parsimony is promoted. The k-tournament selection parameter *k* was set to 3 for this problem. The G_DACG algorithm iterated for thirty generations (or if the stopping criterion was satisfied it halted earlier, arbitrarily set at 100% accuracy) and at the end of each generation three of the best Cartesian granule features were selected from the current population. The selected features were then used to form an additive Cartesian granule feature model – best of generation model. Backward elimination based on fitness was employed, eliminating extraneous lowly contributing features. Once the main part of the G_DACG algorithm finished three of the best features that were discovered during the G_DACG iterations were combined to form an ACGF model – overall best model. Again backward elimination based on fitness was employed. Subsequently the model with the highest accuracy was selected from the best of generation models and the overall best model as a suitable ACGF model for ellipse problem. In the case of this problem the best discovered ACGF model was generated by taking the three best Cartesian granule features from generation 10 of a G_DACG run. This yielded the rule-based model depicted in Figure 6. The rule corresponding the legal class consists of three Cartesian granule features, while the rule for the illegal case consists of just 2 features. Backward elimination based upon semantic discrimination eliminated the third feature from the illegal rule. The optimally determined filters correspond to the "true" filter for this model (not shown in Figure 6). The discovered additive model yields an accuracy of 98.7%. A trapezoidal fuzzy set with 60% overlap was determined to be the best granule characterisation in the case of the evaluated models.

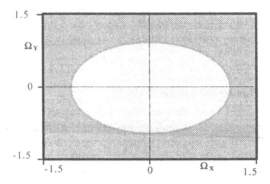

Figure 5: Ellipse inequality in Cartesian space. Points in lightly shaded region satisfy the ellipse inequality and thus are classified as legal. Points in darker region are classified as illegal.

5.1.2 Ellipse Results Comparison

Table 1 presents a summary of some of the best results achieved using various inductive learning approaches. All of the approaches examined here do very well in modelling the ellipse problem from a generalisation perspective. The discovered Cartesian granule features are very parsimonious in nature compared to the more complex two-dimensional Cartesian granule features model presented in Table 1. The granularity of the universes used in the additive models is much lower (three or four words) compared what is required in the non-additive model (11 words) in order to achieve the same level of accuracy. This reduction in granularity has been achieved by modelling the important decomposed variable interactions as opposed to focussing on the model of a single composed interaction.

```
((Predicted class for ellipse in case (CASE) is positive)
  (evlog POSITIVE_FILTER (
        (cgValue of ((X 4))) in (CASE) is positiveClass)0.2426
        (cgValue of ((Y 4))) in (CASE) is positiveClass) 0.367
        (cgValue of ((X 4)(Y 3))) in (CASE) is positiveClass) 0.39 ) ):((1 1)(0 0))

((Predicted class for ellipse in case (CASE) is negative)
  (evlog NEGATIVE_FILTER (
        (cgValue of ((Y 4))) in (CASE) is negativeClass) 0.396
        (cgValue of ((X 4)(Y 3))) in (CASE) is negativeClass) 0.604 ) ):((1 1)(0 0))
```

Figure 6: An example of an additive Cartesian feature model in Fril for the ellipse problem. This model gives over 98.7% accuracy on test cases.

Table 1: Summary of ellipse problem using various learning approaches.

Approach	Features details	% Accuracy
Additive Cartesian granule feature model	((X 4)) ((Y 4))((X 4) (Y 3)) - Legal ((Y 4))((X 4) (Y 3)) - Illegal	98.7
Two-dimensional Cartesian granule features	(X, Y), Granularity = 11, 60% Overlapping Trapezoids	98.8
Data browser(evidential logic rules)	X, Y(non-smoothed fuzzy sets)	94
Neural network	X, Y, and 3 hidden nodes	99.5
MATI	X, Y [3]	99

5.2 Modelling Pima Diabetes Detection Problem

The problem posed here is to predict whether a patient would test positive or negative for diabetes according to the World Health Organisation criteria given a number of physiological measurements and medical test results. The dataset was originally donated by Vincent Sigillito, Applied Physics Laboratory, John Hopkins University, Laurel, MD 20707 and was constructed by constrained selection from a larger database held by the National Institute of Diabetes and Digestive and Kidney Diseases [45]. It is publicly available from the machine learning repository at UCI [35]. All the patients represented in this dataset are females at least 21 years old of Pima Indian heritage living near Phoenix, Arizona, USA. There are eight input attributes the values of which are used to predict the output classification of "testing positive for diabetes" and "testing negative for diabetes". These input-output attributes and their corresponding feature numbers (used for convenience) are listed in Table 2. This is a binary classification problem with a classification value of 1 corresponding to "testing positive for diabetes" and a value of 2 corresponding to "testing negative for diabetes". There are 500 examples of class 1 (positive) and 268 examples of class 2.

Table 2: Input base Features for the Pima Diabetes Problem.

No.	Class
0	Number of times pregnant
1	Plasma glucose concentration in an oral glucose tolerance test
2	Diastolic blood pressure(mm/Hg)
3	Triceps skin fold thickness(mm)
4	2-hour serum insulin (mu/U/ml)
5	Body mass index (kg/m^2)
6	Diabetes pedigree function
7	Age(years)

5.2.1 Additive Cartesian Granule Feature Modelling of Pima Diabetes Problem

The Pima diabetes data set of 768 tuples was split class-wise, approximately as follows: 60% of data allocated to training, 15% to validation and 25% to testing. We applied the

G_DACG constructive induction algorithm to the Pima diabetes problem. All eight base features were considered and Cartesian granule features of dimensionality up to five with granularity ranges of [2, 12] were considered (while parsimony was promoted in the form of the fitness function used) thus yielding a multi-million node search space. The k-tournament selection parameter k was set to 4 for this problem. The G_DACG algorithm iterated for thirty generations (or if the stopping criterion was satisfied it halted earlier, arbitrarily set at 90% accuracy) and at the end of each generation five of the best Cartesian granule features were selected from the current population. The selected features were then used to form an additive Cartesian granule feature model – best of generation model. Backward elimination based on fitness was employed, eliminating extraneous lowly contributing features. Once the main part of the G_DACG algorithm finished five of the best features that were discovered during the G_DACG iterations were combined to form an ACGF model – overall best model. Again backward elimination based on fitness was employed. Subsequently the model with the highest accuracy on test data was selected from the best of generation models and the overall best model as a suitable ACGF model for diabetes detection in Pima Indians. In the case of this problem the best discovered ACGF model was generated by taking the five best Cartesian granule features that were visited during the genetic search phase. During the genetic search process the granule characterisations were set to trapezoidal fuzzy sets with 50% overlap. However in this phase of the process, a variety of granule characterisations were investigated. A trapezoidal fuzzy set with 70% overlap was determined to be the best granule characterisation in the case of the evaluated models. The best discovered model from both a model accuracy and simplicity perspective consists of two Cartesian granule features (arrived at by backward elimination), yielding a model accuracy on test data of 79.7%. The Fril code corresponding to this model is presented in Figure 7. The negative class rule filter in this case is more disjunctive or optimistic in nature than its positive counterpart. This optimism may arise from the fact that a single feature may be adequate to model this class.

```
?((def_itype POSITIVE_FILTER [0.0:0.0 1.0:1.0 ]))
?((def_itype NEGATIVE_FILTER [0.0:0.0 0.79:1.0 ]))


((Predicted class for diabetes in case (CASE) is positive)
(evlog POSITIVE_FILTER (
(cgValue of ((pregnancyCount 10) (glucoseConcentration 4)
            (bodyMassIndex 11) (Age 3))
         in case (CASE) correspond to positiveClass) .49
(cgValue of ((pregnancyCount 8) (glucoseConcentration 10)
            (bloodPressure 2) (tricepsSkinThickness 12))
         in case (CASE) correspond to positiveClass) .51  ) ) ):((1 1)(0 0))
```

Figure 7: An example of an additive Cartesian feature model in Fril for Pima diabetes detection. This model gives over 79.69% accuracy on test cases. Note only the positive rule is shown here. The negative rule has a similar structure.

5.2.2 Pima Diabetes Results Comparison

The Pima diabetes dataset serves as a benchmark problem in the field of machine learning and has been tested on many learning approaches. Table 3 compares some of the results of the more common machine learning techniques with the ACGF modelling approach. The Pima diabetes database illustrates a parity-problem-type/chaotic behaviour (i.e. change one input feature value and the classification also changes) especially when the data is projected onto lower dimensional feature spaces. This is reflected in the lack of semantic separation of concepts represented in lower dimensional Cartesian granule features. The discovered ACGF models support this in that they consist of submodels of high dimensionality.

Table 3: Comparison of results for the Pima diabetes detection problem.

Approach.	Accuracy(%)
Additive Cartesian granule feature Model	79.7
Mass Assignment based MATI [3]	79.7
Oblique Decision Trees [16]	78.5
Neural Net (normalised Data)	78
C4.5 [38]	73
Data browser	70

The Pima diabetes problem is a notoriously difficult machine learning problem. Part of this difficulty arises from the fact the dependent output variable is really a binarised form of another variable which itself is highly indicative of certain types of diabetes but does not have a one-to-one correspondence with the condition of being diabetic [37]. To date no machine learning approach has obtained an accuracy higher than 78% [35]. The discovered ACGF models have yielded very high accuracies (79.7%), outperforming other machine learning approaches (see Table 3).

6. Conclusions

The focus and motivation behind this work was the development of an automatic system identification process that leads to additive Cartesian granule feature models that are ultimately understandable not only by computers but also by experts in the domain of application and that perform effectively. This has resulted in the development of a new constructive induction algorithm – G_DACG. G_DACG avoids many of the pitfalls of other induction algorithms that arise from poor feature selection and abstraction. G_DACG was illustrated on variety of problems (synthetic and real world) and the discovered models in general performed as well or outperformed (in terms of accuracy) other well-known techniques in the field. From a model transparency perspective, the G_DACG algorithm, while yielding glassbox models in particular for the ellipse problem, needs further work when applied to real world problems. This is highlighted by the models discovered in the Pima diabetes problem where the Cartesian granule feature are of high dimensionality and consist of relatively high granularity. Cartesian granule features do however lay the foundations for a learning paradigm that provides the accuracy of mathematical approaches, while also achieving model transparency. Current work [43] is addressing the transparency issue as follows:

- Increase the expressiveness of the hypothesis language from attribute-value to relational.

- Hierarchical modelling (somewhat related to relational descriptions of concepts) is a promising approach that facilitates the capture of deep knowledge representation as opposed to the relatively shallow representations (considered here) and in most learning approaches.

References and Related Bibliography

1. **H. Almuallim and T. G. Dietterich** (1991), *"Learning with irrelevant features"*, in Proc. AAAI-91, Anaheim, CA, pp 547-552.

2. **J. F. Baldwin** (1991) *"A Theory of Mass Assignments for Artificial Intelligence"*, in IJCAI '91 Workshops on Fuzzy Logic and Fuzzy Control, Sydney, Australia, Lecture Notes in Artificial Intelligence, A. L. Ralescu, Editor 1991, pp. 22-34.

3. **J. F. Baldwin, J. Lawry and T.P. Martin** (1997), *"Mass assignment fuzzy ID3 with applications"*, in Proc. Fuzzy Logic: Applications and Future Directions Workshop, London, UK, pp 278-294.

4. **J. F. Baldwin, T. P. Martin and B. W. Pilsworth** (1988) *"FRIL Manual"*, FRIL Systems Ltd, Bristol, BS8 1QX, UK.

5. **J. F. Baldwin, T. P. Martin and B. W. Pilsworth** (1995) *"FRIL - Fuzzy and Evidential Reasoning in A.I."*, Research Studies Press(Wiley Inc.), ISBN 086380159 5.

6. **J. F. Baldwin, T. P. Martin and J. G. Shanahan** (1996) *"Modelling with Words using Cartesian Granule Features"*, (Report No. ITRC 246), Advanced Computing Research Centre, Dept. of Engineering Maths, University of Bristol, UK.

7. **J. F. Baldwin, T.P. Martin and J. G. Shanahan** (1997), *"Fuzzy logic methods in vision recognition"*, in Proc. Fuzzy Logic: Applications and Future Directions Workshop, London, UK, pp 300-316.

8. **J. F. Baldwin, T. P. Martin and J. G. Shanahan** (1997), *"Modelling with words using Cartesian granule features"*, in Proc. FUZZ-IEEE, Barcelona, Spain, pp 1295-1300.

9. **J. F. Baldwin, T.P. Martin and J. G. Shanahan** (1998), *"Aggregation in Cartesian granule feature models"*, in Proc. IPMU, Paris, pp 6.

10. **J. F. Baldwin, T. P. Martin and J. G. Shanahan** (1998) *"Controlling with words using automatically identified fuzzy Cartesian granule feature models"*, (To Appear) International Journal of Approximate Reasoning - Special issue on Fuzzy Logic Control: Advances in Methodology, N/A, pp. 37.

11. **J. F. Baldwin and B. W. Pilsworth** (1997), *"Genetic Programming for Knowledge Extraction of Fuzzy Rules"*, in Proc. Fuzzy Logic: Applications and Future Directions Workshop, London, UK, pp 238-251.

12. **A. Bastian** (1995) *"Modelling and Identifying Fuzzy Systems under varying User Knowledge"*, PhD Thesis, Meiji University, Tokyo,

13. **A. Ben-Davis and J. Mandel** (1995) *"Classification accuracy: machine learning vs. explicit knowledge acquisition"*, Machine Learning, **18**, pp. 109-114.

14. **A. L. Blum and P. Langley** (1997) *"Selection of relevant features and examples in machine learning"*, Artificial Intelligence, **97**, pp. 245-271.

15. **K. M. Bossley** (1997) *"Neurofuzzy Modelling Approaches in System Identification"*, PhD Thesis, Department of Electrical and Computer Science, Southampton University, UK,

16. **N. Cristianini** (1998) *"Application of oblique decision trees to Pima diabetes problem"*, Personal Communication, Department of Engineering Mathematics, University of Bristol, UK.

17. **P. A. Devijer and J. Kittler** (1982) *"Pattern Recognition: A Statistical Approach"*, Prentice-Hall, Englewood Cliffs, NJ.

18. **W. J. Frawley, G Piatetsky-Shapiro and C. J. Matheus** (1991) *"Knowledge Discovery in Databases: An Overview"*, in Knowledge Discovery in Databases, G. Piatetsky-Shapiro and W. J. Frawley, Editors 1991, AAAI Press/MIT Press. Cambridge, Mass, USA. pp. 1-27.

19. **J. H. Friedman** (1991) *"Multivariate Adaptive Regression Splines"*, The Annals of Statistics, **19**, pp. 1-141.

20. **S. Geman, E. Bienenstock and R Doursat** (1992) *"Neural networks and the bias/variance dilemma"*, Neural computation, **4**, pp. 1-58.

21. **J. Hertz, K. Anders and R. G. Palmer** (1991) *"Introduction to the Theory of Neural Computation"*, Addison-Wesley, New York.

22. **A. G. Ivanhnenko** (1971) *"Polynomial theory of complex systems"*, IEEE Transactions on Systems, Man and Cybernetics, **1**(4), pp. 363-378.

23. **I. T. Jolliffe** (1986) *"Principal Component Analysis"*, Springer, New York.

24. **T. Kalvi** (1993) *"ASMOD: an algorithm for Adaptive Spline Modelling of Observation Data"*, International Journal of Control, **58**(4), pp. 947-968.

25. **M. Kay, J. M. Gawson and P. Norvig** (1994) *"Verbmobil: A translation system for face-to-face dialog"*, CSLI Press, Stanford, California, USA.

26. **K. Kira and L Rendell** (1992), *"A practical approach to feature selection"*, in Proc. 9th Conference in Machine Learning, Aberdeen, Scotland, pp 249-256.

27. **G. J. Klir and B. Yuan** (1995) *"Fuzzy Sets and Fuzzy Logic, Theory and Applications"*, Prentice Hall, New Jersey.

28. **R Kohavi and G. H. John** (1997) *"Wrappers for feature selection"*, Artificial Intelligence, **97**, pp. 273-324.

29. **I. Kononenko** (1993) *"Inductive and Bayesian learning in medical diagnosis"*, Artificial Intelligence, **7**, pp. 317-337.

30. **I. Kononenko and S J Hong** (1997) *"Attribute selection for modelling"*, FGCS Special Issue in Data Mining, (Fall), pp. 34-55.

31. **J. R. Koza** (1992) *"Genetic Programming"*, MIT Press, Massachusetts.

32. **J. R. Koza** (1994) *"Genetic Programming II"*, MIT Press, Massachusetts.

33. **P. Langley** (1996) *"Elements of Machine Learning"*, Morgan Kaufmann, San Francisco, CA, USA.

34. **L. Ljung** (1987) *"System identification: theory for the user"*, Prentice Hall, Englewood Cliffs, New Jersey 07632.

35. **C. J. Merz and P. M. Murphy** (1996) *"UCI Repository of machine learning databases [http://www.ics.uci.edu/~mlearn/MLRepository.html]. Irvine, CA"*, University of California, Irvine, CA.

36. **R. S. Michalski, I. Bratko and M. Kubat** (Ed), (1998), *"Machine Learning and Data Mining"*, Wiley, New York.

37. **D. Michie, D. J. Spiegelhalter and C. C. Taylor** (1993) *"Dataset Descriptions and Results"*, in <u>Machine Learning, Neural and Statistical Classification</u>, D. Michie, D. J. Spiegelhalter and C. C. Taylor, Editors 1993,

38. **D. Michie, D. J. Spiegelhalter and C. C. Taylor** (Ed), (1993), *"Machine Learning, Neural and Statistical Classification"*,

39. **J. R. Quinlan** (1986) *"Induction of Decision Trees"*, Machine Learning, **1**(1), pp. 86-106.

40. **B. Schweizer and A. Sklar** (1961) *"Associative functions and statistical triangle inequalities"*, Publ. Math. Debrecen, **8**, pp. 169-186.

41. **J. G. Shanahan** (1996) *"Automatic Synthesis of Fuzzy Rule Cartesian Granule Features from Data for both Classification and Prediction"*, (Report No. ITRC 247), Advanced Computing Research Centre, Dept. of Engineering Maths, University of Bristol, UK.

42. **J. G. Shanahan** (1998) *"Cartesian Granule Features: Knowledge Discovery of Additive Models for Classification and Prediction"*, PhD Thesis, Dept. of Engineering Maths, University of Bristol, UK,

43. **J. G. Shanahan** (1998) *"Inductive logic programming with Cartesian granule features"*, Personal Communication, Dept. of Engineering Maths, University of Bristol, UK.

44. **H. A. Simon** (1983) *"Why should machine learn?"*, in <u>Machine Learning: An Artificial Intelligence Approach</u>, R. S. Michalski, J. G. Carbonell and T. M. Mitchell, Editors 1983, Springer-Verlag. Berlin. pp. 25-37.

45. **J. W. Smith, et al.** (1988), *"Using the ADAP learning algorithm to forecast the onset of diabetes mellitus"*, in <u>Proc. Symposium on Computer Applications and Medical Care</u>, , pp 261-265.

46. **M. Sugeno and T. Yasukawa** (1993) *"A Fuzzy Logic Based Approach to Qualitative Modelling"*, IEEE Trans on Fuzzy Systems, **1**(1), pp. 7-31.

47. **G. Syswerda** (1989), *"Uniform crossover in genetic algorithms"*, in <u>Proc. Third Int'l Conference on Genetic Algorithms</u>, , pp 989-995.

48. **W. A. Tackett** (1995) *"Mining the Genetic Program"*, IEEE Expert, (6), pp. 28-28.

49. **R. R. Yager** (1994) *"Generation of Fuzzy Rules by Mountain Clustering"*, J. Intelligent and Fuzzy Systems, **2**, pp. 209-219.

50. **L. A. Zadeh** (1994) *"Soft Computing and Fuzzy Logic"*, IEEE Software, **11**(6), pp. 48-56.

51. **L. A. Zadeh** (1996) *"Fuzzy Logic = Computing with Words"*, IEEE Transactions on Fuzzy Systems, **4**(2), pp. 103-111.

Deep Fusion of Symbolic and Computational Processing for Next Generation User Interface

Shun'ichi Tano

Graduate School of Information Systems, University of Electro-Communications
1-5-1 Chofugaoka, Chofu, Tokyo 182-8585, JAPAN
e-mail: tano@is.uec.ac.jp

Abstract. We proposed the new design concept of the next generation user interface and developed a system, called RVI-desk, which provides with the intelligent user interface in which a user can communicate with the computing environment through multi modalities, such as voice, handwriting, pen gesture, printed material, touch screen and keyboard. Through the development of the system, we found that it was indispensable deeply to combine the symbolic and computational processing in order to realize a software architecture for the next generation user interface. Potentially the fuzzy methodologies play an important role to combine the symbolic and computational processing due to the inherent nature of fuzzy theory. The purpose of this paper is (i) to show that the next generation user interface is the attractive field for fuzzy methodologies, (ii) to clarify that the breakthrough is the deep fusion of the symbolic and computational processing, (iii) to introduce two leading systems we have developed as examples of the fusion of the symbolic and computational processing, and (iv) to appeal that further research is needed.

1 Introduction

Recently, the multi media technology and the network technology enable us freely to access various multi media information spread in the world. It seems that we are now in the second era of an information-oriented society. However, people is tied up in front of a small CRT screen, such as 19 inches or 21 inches, and the input modalities to the computer are also limited to a keyboard and a mouse. This sever limitation on the personal computing environment prevents the novice users from the full utilization of the computing power which the personal computer brings us.

We proposed the new design concept of the next generation user interface, called RVI-concept, which is an acronym of the real virtual intelligent user interface concept[1], [2], [3]. To show that our RVI-concept is effective and feasible, we developed a system, called RVI-desk, which provides with the intelligent user interface in which a user can communicate with the computing environment through multi modalities, such as voice, handwriting, pen gesture, printed material, touch screen and keyboard.

Through the development of the system, we found that it was indispensable deeply to combine the symbolic and computational processing in order to realize a software architecture for the next generation user interface. Now we believe that fuzzy methodologies play an important role to combine the symbolic and computational processing due to the inherent nature of fuzzy theory. However, at this point, there is not appropriate fuzzy methodologies for the software architecture.

The purpose of this paper is (i) to show that the next generation user interface is the attractive field for fuzzy methodologies, (ii) to clarify that the breakthrough is the deep fusion of the symbolic and computational processing, (iii) to introduce two leading systems we have developed as examples of the fusion of the symbolic and computational processing, and (iv) to appeal that further research is needed to realize the next generation user interface such as an intelligent multi modal computer system.

In the following section, the concept of the next generation user interface is briefly explained and RVI-desk, which we have developed as the next generation user interface, is reviewed. In the section 3, the software architecture is shown and the fusion of symbolic and computational processing is addressed. In the section 4 and 5, two systems we have developed are shown as examples of the fusion of symbolic and computational processing. In the section 4, the extension of symbolic and computational nature of conventional fuzzy reasoning is described. In the section 5, the fusion of symbolic AI (Artificial Intelligence) and fuzzy methodologies is described. In the last section, the summary is given.

2 Next Generation User Interface

2.1 Trend of User Interface Design

The user interface design moves from CLI (Command Line Interface) to GUI (Graphical User Interface). CLI is composed of a keyboard and a text display. GUI has extended the input and output media to a mouse as an additional input medium and a graphical display.

There was no critical paradigm shift when MMI (Multi Modal Interface) appeared, because the movement can be understandable that the media are extended merely straight to the other available modalities such as the voice and the gesture. In other words, the evolution from CLI to MMI can be seen as a straight forward extension of available input and output media.

Recently, several new approaches were proposed toward a novel user interface which is essentially different from current user interface, that is, GUI.

2.2 RVI-concept

We have analyzed this new trend and divided it into three categories, i.e. the virtual world-centered UI, the real word-centered UI and the intelligent UI. In the following subsections, the essence of each concepts is summarized.

Virtual World-centered UI [4]

Basic idea is to realize a virtual desk or a virtual office environment in a computer by the virtual reality technology and the computer graphics technology. In other words, they try to build a real world in virtual (computer) world.

Real Word-centered UI [5]

A completely opposite way of thinking is to augment a real world by a computer power. The paradigm is refereed as terms of "back to real world", "ubiquitous computing" and "augmented reality".

Intelligent UI [6]

Intelligent processing, i.e. problem solving and learning, is usually applied in the industrial world to solve the complex problems such the diagnosis of the furnace. Someone believes that the user interface should be intelligent in order to move from the direct manipulation to the indirect management. Recently software becomes too complex to understand the full specifications. So the shift toward the Intelligent UI is inevitable.

As explained above, leading concepts are categorized into three by our analysis. Fig.1 illustrates the traditional user interfaces categorized by three axes which correspond to the three leading concepts.

The key idea of our new design concept is the combination of these three conflicting concept at the adequate level. At the first glance, the three leading concepts looks quit different. But look carefully, and you can see that they compensate each other. Moreover they can synergetically combined. Our new concept "Fusion of Three Exclusive Concepts" is indicated by a thick dotted line in the middle of virtual world-centered UI, real world-centered UI and intelligent UI. This idea is so simple that it is applicable to any field. We call it RVI-concept.

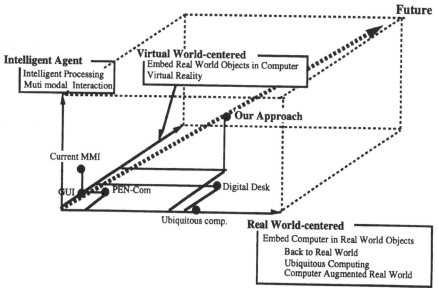

Fig. 1 Fusion of Three Exclusive Concepts

2.3 Experimental System : RVI-DESK

For the feasibility study, the RVI-concept has been applied to the design of the desk environment. We developed RVI-desk based on RVI-concept and evaluated it.

Appearance of RVI-desk is shown in fig.2. RVI-desk consists of :
- Monitor with touch sensor x 1
- Pen Pad x 3 or more
- Pen with Scanner x 1
- Microphone & Speaker x 1 set
- Keyboard x 1

Three workstations and six PCs are needed for the recognition and the synthesis of multi media data and the intelligent processing.

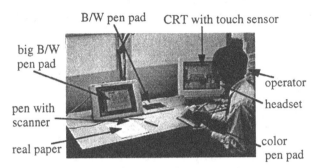

Fig. 2 Photograph of current RVI-Desk

We introduced the following three special devices.

- InformationViewer

InformationViewer is a kind of a pen computer. It substitutes both the real paper in the real world and the CRT monitor in PC-based desk environment. As it is intended as a real paper, it supports the following situation:
- Many InformationViewers can be put on the desk.
- User can put additional InformationViewers on the desk whenever user wants.
- Several InformationViewers can act as a big paper when they are set side by side.

It has a truly pen-based user interface (Other media are also available. See below.). For example, it has the search mechanism by a handwriting.

- EnvironmentViewer

EnvironmentViewer is a CRT monitor with touch sensor. Usually it displays the desk environment quit similar to fig.2. At a glance, it looks like a desk top displayed in a conventional PCs.

However, it displays three qualitatively different objects;
- real object,
- virtual object, and
- real & virtual object.

In this case, "virtual" means to exist only in a computer and "real & virtual" means to exist both in a computer and a real world. For example, on Environment Viewer, you can see a real paper (i.e. a real object), a virtual folder (i.e. a virtual object) which does not exit on the real desk but in a computer, and the InformationViewer whose hardware exists on real world and whose substance exists in a computer. In other word,

EnvironmentViewer displays the mixed situation of a real world and a virtual world.

Moreover it can display several different places such as your study in your home at the same time. EnvironmentViewer is intended to provide a user with general view of current working environment. On the other hand, it also defines the working environment where an Intelligent Agent does its job. It will be explained later.

- Pen with scanner

There still exits a real paper. So it is very important to exchange the information on a real paper and a virtual paper (InformationViewer in case of RVI-desk). For this reason, we attached a stylus pen with a very small CCD camera that the diameter is about 5 mm (a quarter inch) and the length is about 5 cm (two inches). We call this "a pen with scanner."

Two types of intelligent processing were realized in RVI-desk.

- Multi media input/output recognition

Recently the recognition algorithms have been greatly improved. Concerning the speech recognition, the accuracy and the vocabulary are almost at level of practical use [7]. But it is still difficult to use as a prime input medium, except for Japanese handwriting. Actually Japanese handwriting can be recognized at quit high accuracy. So we have decided the pen input as the primary input medium and that the recognition results of other media are corrected by the semantic consistency. Of course, it is possible to use single modality such as speech through microphone and printed material through a pen with scanner. But, practically, single modal input except handwriting should not be used due to the low accuracy of recognition.

Intelligent processing is adopted to check the semantic consistency among the information form several modalities.

- Intelligent multi modal agent

To realize the movement from the direct manipulation to the indirect management, we developed an agent whose face, as a symbol of an agent, is displayed in the EnvironmentViewer. The agent always listens and watches users' input. So the agent always checks the semantic consistency among the inputs from many modalities and corrects them. At the same time, the agent always looks for the command which the agent can perform. When the agent succeeds in finding a command, the agent smiles and waits for the allowance of execution. Facial expression and the understood command are displayed in the EnvironmentViewer. Then the agent generates either the command sequence to control several applications or multi modal output to a user.

This agent is built by the knowledge-based approach. It has a knowledge base which store information concerning applications as well as the linguistic knowledge [3].

3. Software Architecture for Next Generation User Interface
- Fusion of Symbolic and Computational Processing -

We believe that RVI-concept plays an important role to realize the future user interface. There exits two main problems.

First one is how to harmonize three exclusive concepts into one system. One possible fusion is RVI-desk. But the best fusion varies on the characteristics and the purpose of target fields.

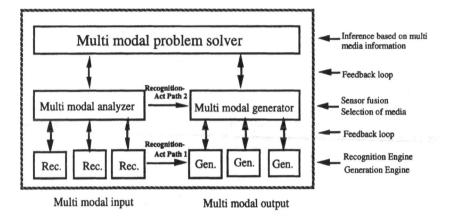

Fig. 3 Basic Software for RVI-Concept

Second problem is how to realize the system. Eventually RVI-concept leads a certain system which is intelligent and can handle the multi modal input and output. So the architecture shown in fig.3 will be a common architecture. The architecture shown in fig.3 should be regarded as basic software for the future user interface. Although the software architecture of RVI-desk shown in fig.2 is similar to that of fig.3. But there are two fundamental differences. All blocks of fig.3 are connected bidirectionally. On the other hand, in RVI-desk, the bidirectional connection was realized only between recognition units and MMA. Moreover, the architecture in fig.3 has two recognize-act short cut paths, but the current RVI-desk does not have. It keeps the system fast enough to react in the emergent cases.

How should we implement this architecture? Candidates are the computational AI, e.g. a neural system, and the symbolic AI, e.g. rule-based systems. Generally speaking, the former is suitable for recognition of raw data and the latter is suitable for high level inference. Actually, many system adopt two layers structure where low level recognition is realized by a neural system and the correction and the problem solving in the upper layer are realized by the logical inference mechanism. Our RVI-desk is not the exception. But we found that symbolic AI is needed even in recognition of raw data for more accurate recognition and computational AI is needed even in high level problem solving for more robust inference and meta-level analogical reasoning. We started the study on the fusion of computational AI and symbolic AI. Note that it is not "hybrid" but "fusion."

We considered that fuzzy methodologies play an important role to combine the symbolic and computational processing due to the inherent nature of fuzzy theory. However, at this point, there is not appropriate fuzzy methodologies.

In the following section, our two systems are shown and evaluated as the possible fusion of the symbolic and computational processing. Although we have developed these two systems for other purpose, they can be seen as early works for the fusion of the symbolic and computational processing.

4 Extension of Symbolic and Computational Nature of Fuzzy Reasoning   - Example 1 -

4.1 Overview of FINEST

We developed FINEST(Fuzzy Inference Environment Software with Tuning) [8], [9]. It is actually a software environment for fuzzy inference with a mechanism to tune the inference method as well as fuzzy predicates. Since it has an improved fuzzy reasoning, it can be seen as an example of the extension of the symbolic and computational nature of fuzzy reasoning.

FINEST has the following three special features.
(1) Improved generalized modus ponens
(2) Mechanism which can tune the inference method as well as fuzzy predicates
(3) Software environment for debugging and tuning

Concerning (1), the generalized modus ponens is improved in the following four ways: (a) aggregation operators that have synergy and cancellation nature, (b) a parametrized implication function, (c) a combination function which can reduce fuzziness, and (d) backward-chaining based on generalized modus ponens. The (a)-(c) extend the symbolic nature of the fuzzy reasoning.

4.2 Extension of Symbolic and Computational Nature of Fuzzy Reasoning

(1) Computational Nature of Fuzzy Reasoning
Consider the following fuzzy rules and facts.

$$Rule\,i: If\ x_1\ is\ A_{i1}\ and\ ...and\ x_n\ is\ A_{in}\ then\ y\,is\,B_i$$

$$Fact\,j: x_j\,is\,A_j' \qquad \left(j=1,...,n, \quad i=1,...,m\right)$$

In FINEST, they are converted into a neural-network-like structure, as shown in fig.4, where fuzzy data are processed and flown. The input values (x_i) of the network are the facts, and the output value (y) is the conclusion of the fuzzy inference.

This network shows that computational model of fuzzy inference. Namely, the calculation of each layer in this figure corresponds to the following step1, 2, 3 and 4.

Step 1: Converse truth value qualification for the condition j of the *Rule i*

$$\tau_{A_{ij}}\left(a_{ij}\right) = \sup_{\mu_{A_{ij}}\left(x_j\right)=a_{ij}} \mu_{A_j'}\left(x_j\right)$$

Step 2: Aggregation of the truth values of the conditions of the *Rule i*

$$\tau_{A_i}\left(a_i\right) = \sup_{and_i\left(a_{i1},...,a_{in}\right)=a_i} \left\{\tau_{A_{i1}}\left(a_{i1}\right)\wedge \cdots \wedge \tau_{A_{in}}\left(a_{in}\right)\right\}$$

Step 3: Deduction of the conclusion from the *Rule i*

$$\mu_{B_i'}(y) = \sup_{a_i}\left\{\tau_{A_i}(a_i) \wedge I_i\left(a_i, \mu_{B_i}(y)\right)\right\}$$

Step 4: Combination of the conclusions derived from all the rules

$$\mu_{B'}(y) = comb\left(\mu_{B_1'}(y)\wedge\cdots\wedge\mu_{B_m'}(y)\right)$$

In the above equations, τ_{Aij}, τ_{Ai} and B_i' represent the truth value of the condition "x_j is Aij" of the *Rule i*, the truth value of the condition part of the *Rule i* and the conclusion derived from the *Rule i*, respectively. Besides, the functions and$_i$, I$_i$ and *comb* represent the function characterizing the aggregation operator of the *Rule i*, the implication function of the *Rule i* and the global combination function, respectively .

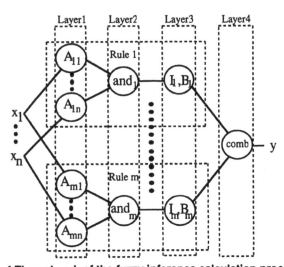

Fig.4 The network of the fuzzy inference calculation process

(2) Extension of Symbolic Nature of Fuzzy Reasoning
The flow of fig.4 shows only the computational procedure. In other words, we can observe that the data are computed in some manner in the network, but we can not symbolically understand the meaning of the calculation and the calculated result flown in the network. The only exceptions are the fuzzy predicates. We can observe fuzzy sets flown in the network and at the same time we can understand the symbolical meaning, i.e., as the name of the fuzzy set.

To extend the symbolic nature of the fuzzy reasoning, it is necessary to clarify the symbolic meaning of the aggregation functions, the implication functions and the combination functions.

We have clarified and defined the symbolic meaning of these three functions, then we developed the fuzzy inference software environment called FINEST. In the following subsections, our extensions are described as early works of the fusion of the symbolic and computational processing.

(a) Extended Aggregation Function

Even though, in many cases, a rule is simply expressed in the form " If X and Y Then Z", the "and" operator has a vague meaning. It may have a strict "and" nature, or a weak one.

We defined a new aggregation operator '*and*' by adding a synergistic effect to an ordinary t-norm operator (denoted by 'basic(x,y)' in (1)). The following formula defines the *and* operator when the basic function 'basic(x,y)' is Dombi's t-norm.

$$*And*(x,y) = w \times synergy(x,y) + (1-w) \times basic(x,y)$$
$$w = equal(x,y) \times high(x,y) \times \gamma$$
$$equal(x,y) = almost(0, x-y, \alpha)$$
$$high(x,y) = almost(1, x, \beta) \times almost(1, y, \beta)$$
$$almost(a,x,b) = \exp(\ln 0.5 \times (x-a)^2 / b^2)$$
$$synergy(x,y) = 1$$
$$basic(x,y) = \cfrac{1}{1 + \sqrt[p]{\left(\cfrac{1-x}{x}\right)^p + \left(\cfrac{1-y}{y}\right)^p}}$$

$$(1)$$

This operator has four parameters representing respectively the strength of the synergistic effect (γ), the area where this effect is required (α, β), and Dombi's t-norm parameter (p). Furthermore, the cancellation property, which is of the same nature as the synergistic effect, can be expressed as a special kind of synergistic effect.

(b) Extended Implication Function

There are various implication functions. They can be classified based on the relations that are generally considered to be satisfied between the premise "x is A' " and the conclusion "y is B' " deduced by a rule "IF x is A THEN y is B" using fuzzy inference (see Table 1).

In Table 1, "P⇒Q" means that the conclusion should be Q when P is given as the premise. RI corresponds to classical modus ponens. RII-1 expresses that the modification of the fuzziness of the conclusion is influenced by the reduction of that of the premise. We extended the basic idea shown in Table 1 to the classification shown in Table 2

The following (2) is our extended implication function which can be uniquely drawn by the constraints shown in Table 2. In (2), α represents the degree to which fuzziness reduction of the condition part affects that of the conclusion part, β represents the degree to which the fuzziness reduction of the condition part of the converse rule affects that of the conclusion part of the converse rule and γ represents the degree to which the converse rule is satisfied. Of course, β does not make sense when γ=0.

Table 1 Relations to be satisfied

	Relations
RI	x is A $\Rightarrow$ y is B
RII-1	x is very A $\Rightarrow$ y is very B
RII-2	x is very A $\Rightarrow$ y is B
RIII	x is more or less A $\Rightarrow$ y is more or less B
RIV-1	x is not A $\Rightarrow$ y is unknown
RIV-2	x is not A $\Rightarrow$ y is not B

Table 2 Extended relation

	Extended relation
I	included by the extended relations of RII and RIII
II	x is $A^{m} \Rightarrow y$ is $B^{m^{\alpha}}$ $\quad m \geq 1,\ 0 \leq \alpha \leq 1$
III	x is $A^{m} \Rightarrow y$ is $B^{m^{\delta}}$ $\quad 0 < m \leq 1,\ \delta = 1$
IV	x is $(not\,A)^{m} \Rightarrow y$ is $\left(\gamma\,not\,B + (1-\gamma)unknown\right)^{m^{\beta}}$ $\quad m \geq 1,\ 0 \leq \beta \leq 1,\ 0 \leq \gamma \leq 1$ x is $(not\,A)^{m} \Rightarrow y$ is $\left(\gamma\,not\,B + (1-\gamma)unknown\right)^{m^{\rho}}$ $\quad 0 < m \leq 1,\ \rho = 1,\ 0 \leq \gamma \leq 1$

$$I(a,b) = \begin{cases} \begin{bmatrix} 1 - \gamma b & \text{if } \beta = 0 \\ 0 & \text{else if } \beta = 1 \text{ or} \\ & a = 0 \text{ or } \gamma b = 1 \\ (1-a)^{(\log 1 - \gamma b / \log 1 - a)^{1/(1-\beta)}} & \text{else} \end{bmatrix} & 0 \le a < \gamma b \\[2pt] 1 &] \gamma b \le a \le b \\[2pt] \begin{bmatrix} b & \text{if } \alpha = 0 \\ 0 & \text{else if } \alpha = 1 \text{ or} \\ & a = 1 \text{ or } b = 0 \\ a^{(\log b / \log a)^{1/(1-\alpha)}} & \text{else} \end{bmatrix} & b < a \le 1 \end{cases} \tag{2}$$

(c) Extended Combination Function

A combination operation is defined as a method of getting one result A''' when two fuzzy sets A' and A'' are deduced by two inference processes.

Many systems use the max operator as a combination method, but this causes a constant increase of the fuzziness. To resolve the problems, we introduce two new parameters, equilibrium E, and dependence factors α and β.

An equilibrium parameter E is introduced to provide a tradeoff point which is interpreted as neither a positive belief nor a negative belief. The meaning of the grade is divided at E. Values greater then E correspond to positive belief, whereas values lower than E correspond to negative belief.

The property of reinforcement is indispensable for combination operations. It is also important to take into account of the dependence of evidence.

Since it is possible to think of dependence as the underlying derivation relation, a pair of stochastic rules can represent it. The following stochastic rules represent the dependence between the evidence in groups A and B.

$$A \to B : \alpha$$
$$B \to A : \beta$$

The first rule says that the evidence in A induces the evidence in B with the probability α.

Here is the calculation flow.

Assumption: "$\mu_S(x)=a$" was deduced from an evidence A, and the equilibrium is E_1. "$\mu_S(x)=b$" was deduced from the other evidence B, and the equilibrium is E_2. The equilibrium of the combined result is E_3. The dependency between the evidence A and B is represented above.

Step1: The degrees of belief of the premises, i.e. a and b, are transformed into normalized degrees of positive or negative belief. A grade bigger than E, i.e. in [E,1], is transformed into a PB-value in [0,1] by the function PB (PB means positive belief). The function NB transforms a grade in [0, E] into a NB-value in [0,1].

$$PB(x:E) = \frac{x-E}{1-E}$$

$$NB(x:E) = \frac{E-x}{E}$$

In this step, a and b are transformed into u and v respectively.

Step2: In case both u and v are PB-values or NB-values, the combined PB-values or NB-values becomes:

$$\max((1-\alpha)u+v-(1-\alpha)uv, u+(1-\beta)v-(1-\beta)uv)$$

In case u or v is a PB-value and the other one is a NB-value, the absolute value of the combined values is | u - v |.

Step3: PB^{-1} and NB^{-1} defined below transform PB-values and NB-values into a grade value.

$$PB^{-1}(x:E) = E + (1-E)x$$

$$NB^{-1}(x:E) = E - Ex$$

It covers the range of conventional combination functions, such as the max-based combination function, min-based combination function, voting-model-based combination function, probability-based combination.

4.3 Evaluation of the Extension

As explained in the above sections, the symbolic meaning of the aggregation functions, the implication functions and the combination functions has been clarified. So now we can understand the symbolic meaning of all of the calculation and all of the calculated result flown in the network as well as the fuzzy predicates.

This extension enables to quantify the fuzzy meaning of sentences expressed in the form of fuzzy rules. For example, aggregation operators, implication methods, combination methods as well as fuzzy predicates can be tuned with FINEST, and as a result the nature of the sentences is made clear because the symbolic nature is clarified. The interpretation is, for example, "the 'and' in this rule has a strong synergistic nature," "the 'or' has a weak cancellation property," or "this rule expresses knowledge of the form 'the more ..., the more....' ." It can be said that ordinary tools can quantify the meaning of fuzzy predicates such as "tall" and "big" because fuzzy predicates can be learned. FINEST, however, expands the range of quantification into the meaning of natural language sentences.

This work can thus be regarded as the first step of the deep fusion of symbolic and computational processing of the fuzzy inference.

5. Fusion of Symbolic AI and Fuzzy Methodologies
- Example 2 -

5.1 Overview of FLINS

We developed a natural language communication system called 'FLINS', which is short for Fuzzy Lingual System [10], [11]. FLINS has three-layered fuzzy inference to understand the meaning of natural language. It can be seen as an example of the fusion of symbolic AI and fuzzy methodologies.

5.2 Fusion of Symbolic AI and Fuzzy Theory

Fig.5 shows the structure of three-layered fuzzy inference developed for FLINS. It consists of three layers, i.e., basic inference layer, fuzzy inference layer, and fuzzy CBR layer.

Fuzzy CBR	
Fuzzy Inference	On Fuzzy Set
	On Fuzzy Symbol
Basic (Non-fuzzy) Inference	

Fig. 5 Hierarchy of Fuzzy Inference

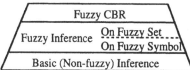

(a) First layer   (b) Second layer   (c) Third layer

Fig.6 Inference model

(1) Basic Inference Layer
The basic inference mechanism is an ordinary (non-fuzzy) inference, that is regular modus ponens shown in Fig.6(a). In this base layer, text symbols are treated simply as labels.

(2) Fuzzy Inference Layer
The second layer is a fuzzy inference on fuzzy sets or fuzzy symbols. In this layer, a symbol is treated as either a fuzzy set (i.e., a sort of distribution over a universe of discourse) or a fuzzy symbol (i.e. words that can be calculated). For example, 'a tall boy' and 'a boy of 180 cm height' in natural languages can be matched in this layer although they can not be matched in the basic inference layer.

The typical example for this layer is the deduction of 'the apple is very ripe' from the gradual rule 'the more apple is red, the more apple is ripe' and the information 'the apple is very red'. Since this can be formalized as $(A{\to}B, A'){\Rightarrow}B'$ where A and A' are the similar fuzzy sets as shown Fig. 6 (b), this inference can be regarded as a type of case-based reasoning. Current CBR methodologies gives only a vague outline of the inference method, but the generalized modus ponens in fuzzy theory provides a concrete algorithm for executing a very simple type of CBR.

The following natural language proposition (NLP) is the canonical form of a standard fuzzy sentence in FLINS. This shows what kind of fuzziness FLINS can deal with.

$(QA$ is F is τ) * $(QA$ is F is τ) *...

where   Q : fuzzy quantifier : most

A : fuzzy quantity : foreigner

F : fuzzy predicate : tall

τ : fuzzy qualifier : true

$*$: and, or, implication,...

(3)Fuzzy CBR Layer

Top layer is a fuzzy case-based reasoning. It is the case-based reasoning (CBR) extended by fuzzy theory, which tries to match cases (which are also represented as texts) on the basis of their fuzzy relations which are deduced by using the knowledge in 'Text Base'. This can be formalized as $(A \rightarrow B, C) \Rightarrow D$ where C is different from A as shown Fig.6(c)

Fig.7 illustrates the basic flow of F-CBR. Inputs to F-CBR are called events which are represented a set of sentences. Note that, in FLINS, a case is composed of sentences and a case is not characterized by the fixed attributes as the conventional CBR systems.

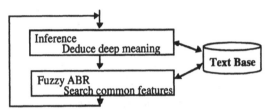

Fig. 7 Basic flow of F-CBR

Many types of knowledge are stored in 'Text Base'. F-CBR tries to find out the deep meaning by applying the knowledge in Text Base. After the deduction of the deep meaning, the common features of two events are searched by fuzzy analogy-based reasoning (FABR). FABR extend the ordinal analogy-based reasoning in the following three points.
- Matching by grade of membership
- Matching by shape of membership
- Matching by fuzzy modifier

Cooperation of Three Layers

In the problem solving phase, the three-layered fuzzy inference mechanism is used in the bottom to the top manner (i.e. the ordinary inference, the fuzzy inference and the fuzzy CBR are evoked in this order) and *recursively*. When a user asks a question, the question is inputted to the basic layer where the question is processed by the ordinary (non fuzzy) inference. When the question can not be solved by the basic layer, the question is passed into the fuzzy inference layer. Finally, it may be passed in the fuzzy CBR layer. In real problems, since it is often the case that some part of the question can be dealt by the basic layer, some part by the fuzzy inference layer and some part by the fuzzy-CBR, so the structure is not simple as explained above but very complicated. The calling sequence are illustrated in Fig.8. Note that the calling sequence is structured *recursively*.

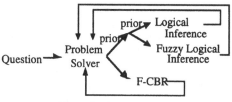

Fig.8 Calling Sequence

Inference Control by Self-wondering

In the conventional Knowledge Engineering (KE) tool, meta-knowledge is represented in a special form and is processed by a supervisor inference unit.

This separation of ordinal knowledge and meta-knowledge enables the system to control the system's behavior by using the meta-knowledge prior to the ordinal knowledge. However, the mechanism cannot be adopted because all knowledge in a text base is uniformly represented.

We designed a new inference mechanism which wonders 'What should I do?'(WSID) every time an inference proceeds one step. All knowledge is used as meta-knowledge in the wondering phase. For example, the knowledge 'if a user asks a question, the system must answer the question' is used as meta-knowledge during the wondering 'what should I do?' that follows the user's first inquiry.

By this control schema, ordinal knowledge may serve as meta-knowledge at the same time. Even if an item of knowledge looks like ordinal knowledge (e.g., a domain-dependent know-how), the knowledge may be used as meta-knowledge by the fuzzy CBR. Since the fuzzy CBR tends to interpret the meaning of the sentence widely, the applicable range of the sentence is greatly extended. Robust and flexible meta inference is realized by the fusion of symbolic AI and fuzzy methodologies.

Thus FLINS can use the past experience as meta knowledge in the much more flexible way than the well-known CBR system, MEDIATOR, applies the experience of a quarrel between brothers to the resolution of the international conflict.

5.3 Evaluation of the Fusion

The development of FLINS is a new challenge to apply the fuzzy theory in the natural language understanding system. Especially it is important of FLINS to combine the classical non fuzzy logic, the fuzzy logic and the analogical reasoning.

The weak point of classical inference is compensated by the fuzzy inference and the weak point of fuzzy inference is compensated by the CBR. Moreover the loop of the compensation is structured recursively. As a result, the three-layered fuzzy inference realized the robust and high level logical inference.

6. Discussion

First, I pointed out that the current user interface should be drastically changed because of its unfriendliness and non-intelligence. Then I proposed the new design concept called RVI-concept and demonstrated an experimental system, called RVI-desk.

Through the development of the system, we found that it was indispensable deeply to combine the symbolic and computational processing in order to realize a software architecture for the next generation user interface.

Although the fuzzy methodologies potentially play an important role to combine the symbolic and computational processing due to the inherent nature of fuzzy theory, there is not appropriate fuzzy methodologies for the purpose.

In this paper, I introduced our two early works toward the deep fusion of symbolic and computational processing. These two systems are originally developed for the other purpose. But they can be seen the first step toward the fusion of symbolic and computational processing.

The first example can be regarded as an example of fusion of symbolic and computational processing at the shallow semantic level since FINEST can not handle such a deep meaning as a metaphor. On the other hand, the second example realized the fusion of symbolic and computational processing at the deep semantic level.

Actually, these two systems are the leading examples, however, the level of the fusion is not high and widely-applicable enough to use the common algorithm for the all of blocks in fig.3. Further research is needed. Please refer [12] for the recent progress.

References

1. Tano, S., et. al. Design Concept Based on Real-Virtual-Intelligent User Interface and Its Software Architecture, HCI-97, pp.901-904,1997.
2. Tano, S. Research Trend of Next Generation User Interface, Journal of Japan Society for Fuzzy Theory and Systems, Vol. 8, No. 2, pp. 216-228, 1996 (Japanese)
3. Namba, Y. Tano, S., et. al. Complex Chained Function Structure for Human-Computer Interface, HCI International '95 Poster Session, pp. 32-32, 1995
4. Kruger, W., et. al. The Responsible Workbench: A Virtual Work Environment, IEEE COMPUTER, Vol. 28, No. 7, pp.42-48, 1995
5. Wellner, P. Interactive With Papers on the DigitalDesk, Communications of the ACM, Vol. 36, No. 7, pp.87-97, 1993
6. Maes, P. Agent that Reduce Work and Information Overload, CACM, Vol. 37, No. 7, 30-40,1994
7. Rudnicky, A.I., Hauptmann, A. and Lee, K.F. Survey of Current Speech Technology, CACM Vol.37, No.3, pp. 52-57, 1994
8. Tano, Miyoshi, Kato, Oyama, Arnould and Bastian: Fuzzy Inference Software - FINEST: Overview and Application Examples, IEEE International Conference on Fuzzy Systems - FUZZ-IEEE'95 , pp. 1051-1056, 1995
9. Tano, Oyama and Arnould : Deep Combination of Fuzzy Inference and Neural Network in Fuzzy Inference Software - FINEST, International Journal of Fuzzy Set and Systems,1996
10. Tano, Okamoto and Iwatani : New Design Concepts for the FLINS-Fuzzy Lingual System: Text-based and Fuzzy-centered Architectures, International Symposium on Methodologies for Intelligent Systems-ISMIS '93, pp.285-294 , 1993
11. Tano, S., et. al. Three-layered Fuzzy Inference and Self-wondering Mechanism as Natural Language Processing Engine of FLINS, IEEE International Conference on Tools with Artificial Intelligence - TAI'94, pp. 212-218, 1994
12. papers in the invited session "Deep Fusion of Symbolic and Computational Processing", IEEE World Congress on Computational Intelligence, FUZZ-IEEE'98, 1998.

Reasoning with Words about Geographic Information

Hans W. Guesgen

Computer Science Department, University of Auckland
Private Bag 92019, Auckland, New Zealand

Abstract. Geographic information systems have gained an increasing interest over the recent years. However, their abilities are restricted in that they usually reason about precise quantitative information only, which means that they fail whenever exact matches cannot be found. They do not allow for any form of reasoning with imprecision.

In this article, we describe a way of incorporating imprecise qualitative spatial reasoning with quantitative reasoning in geographic information systems. In particular, we show how tessellation data models can be extended to allow for qualitative spatial reasoning. The idea is to associate qualitative information with fuzzy sets whose membership grades are computed by applying the concept of proximity.

In addition, we will show how images like geographic maps or satellite images can be analyzed by computing the distances between given reference colors and the colors that occur in the image, and how the results of this analysis can be used in the fuzzy spatial reasoner.

1 Introduction

Geographic information systems have been in use for nearly thirty years, but there has been little change in the functionality of the systems. The way in which they perform spatial reasoning, i.e., the extraction of new information from stored spatial data, has been quantitative in nature. On the other hand, human beings often prefer a qualitative analysis over a quantitative one, as this is more adequate in many cases from the cognitive point of view.

In the following, we will look at qualitative spatial reasoning in geographic information systems. We will develop a data model to support qualitative spatial reasoning based on constraints, and we will provide an example to illustrate our model.

A geographic information system is viewed here as a special case of a spatio-temporal information system, i.e., a set of procedures to store and manipulate spatially and temporally referenced data. The data used in a spatio-temporal information system may be of any scale. However, the most common systems use data at a geographic scale, i.e., they describe features of our world like roads, lakes, rivers, land, trees, etc.

Geographic information systems require data models (see, for example, [12] for an elaborate introduction to these models). These models vary from GIS to

GIS. If the locations in the GIS need to be classified by the value of one of their attributes (e.g., temperature, type of vegetation, rainfall, etc.), then tessellation models are generally used. A tessellated data model is a model in which data is stored in tiles which cover a given area.

Classification is done by assigning values to each tessellation based on ranges defined by an operator. For example, a digitized map from a satellite may show areas of desert, bush, and water at a particular wavelength. By assigning water as 0–20%, vegetation as 21–65%, and desert as 66-100%, a false-color map can be produced which clearly outlines each area on the map.

The most common tessellated model is the raster model, in which an area is split into a matrix of squares. There are three main problems with the raster data model:

1. The size of each tessellation must be determined prior to the entry of data. Therefore it is not possible to change the resolution of the data once it is in the system.
2. The value assigned to a tessellation is assumed to apply evenly over the entire area of the tessellation. If a scale is selected that does not uniquely define the attribute represented in the tessellation, i.e., more than one attribute value may reside within a tessellation, then the value assigned to that tessellation will not accurately describe the contents of the tessellation.
3. The model requires a huge amount of storage space. For example, covering an area of one square kilometer to a resolution of five meters requires 40,000 squares of data. When a data set contains large areas of a single attribute value, many data squares are stored which contain the same data. This is obviously very redundant.

A way of solving most of these problems is to use a many-level tessellation (see Fig. 1) and to implement it by a quadtree. This approach has the advantage that the size of each square is determined solely by whether it has been reduced to cover a single attribute value, i.e., large areas containing the same data are stored as one large data square, thus reducing storage space and removing redundancy.

2   Quantitative Reasoning

There are various types of spatial reasoning used in standard geographic information systems, one of which is the creation of new maps from existing ones. We will illustrate this type of reasoning by using the city dump scenario as an example. In this example, the task is to find a suitable location for a new city dump given certain constraining factors that depend on the road network, waterways like rivers, lakes, and sea, classification of property into residential, commercial, industrial, rural, and parks, and various types of vegetation. In particular, there are the following constraints:

1. To limit the cost of transporting garbage and to maximize the useful life of the new dump, the city council has decided the following:

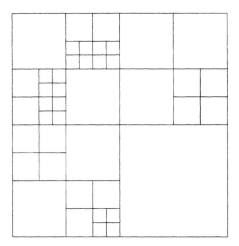

Fig. 1. A many-level tessellation. Each area is divided into four smaller areas until each contains only one data value.

(a) The dump must be within 500 meters of an existing road.
(b) The dump must have an area of more than 1000 square meters.
2. Environmental legislation has further limited the possible locations for the new dump:
   (a) The dump must be at least 1000 meters from residential or commercial property.
   (b) The dump must be at least 500 meters from any water.
   (c) The dump must not be situated on land covered in native vegetation.

In existing geographic information systems, this type of reasoning uses the concept of map overlay. This is a method for merging different datasets to produce a final output. Various functions are available, including a buffer operator, which increases the size of an object by extending its boundary, and logical operators, such as ¬, ∧, and ∨.

A possible solution to the city dump problem might be as follows:

1. Select all property which is residential or commercial.
2. Buffer the property selections by 1000 meters.
3. Use ¬ to select everything outside this area.
4. Perform similar actions for water.
5. Buffer the road data by 500 meters.
6. Select all vegetation that is not native.

At this point, we have a map showing all locations that are more than 1000 meters from residential or commercial property, a second one showing all locations that are more than 500 meters from water, a third map with all locations that are within 500 meters of a road, and a fourth one with all non-native vegetation.

These maps are now overlaid to produce composite maps using the logical operators ¬, ∧, and ∨. The property and vegetation maps are merged using ∧ to produce a map showing all areas that are more than 1000 meters from residential or commercial property and that do not contain native vegetation. The water and road maps are merged to produce a map showing all areas within 500 meters of a road that are also more than 500 meters from water. Finally, the resulting two maps are merged to produce a map showing all possible locations for the city dump. A selection can then be made from all locations that are more than 1000 square meters in area.

3 Qualitative Reasoning

Quantitative spatial reasoning, as described in the previous section, delivers precise results, but is often too rigid and therefore not applicable to scenarios like the city dump scenario. The reason is that quantitative statements like *All locations that are more than 500 meters from water* and *All locations that are within 500 meters of a road* may eventually result in an empty map, as they restrict the search space too dramatically by excluding any areas, for example, which are 490 meters from water or 510 meters of a road. Such an area, however, might be the best choice available and therefore perfectly acceptable.

This problem can be solved by using qualitative spatial statements rather than quantitative ones. Instead of *All locations that are more than 500 meters from water*, we would put in the restriction *All locations that are far from water*. The system would then analyze the qualitative relation *far from* that is used in this restriction and would find the areas that best match this restriction and that are compatible with the other restrictions.

To achieve this goal, we interpret spatial relations among objects as restrictions on linguistic variables which represent spatial information about the objects.[1] Consider, for example, the position x of some object O in the city. A qualitative approach would specify x in terms of qualitative values like *near church*, *at harbor*, *downtown*, etc. This approach can be translated directly into an approach using linguistic variables.

Informally, a linguistic variable is a variable whose values are words or phrases in a natural or artificial language. The values of a linguistic variable are called linguistic values. For example, the position of O can be represented by a linguistic variable x whose linguistic values are from the following domain:

$$\{downtown, near\ church, at\ harbor, \ldots\}$$

Using the notation from [16], we denote the domain of a linguistic variable as follows:

$$L(x) = downtown + near\ church + at\ harbor + \cdots$$

---

[1] This step is just a shift in terminology rather than an introduction to a new reasoning method. The motivation for this step is the attempt to stay within the terminology used in fuzzy set theory.

To express spatial information, we introduce restrictions on the values of the linguistic variables that represent these relations. For example, if O is either downtown or at the harbor, we restrict the value of x to $\{downtown, at\ harbor\}$ and denote this restriction as follows:

$$R(x) = downtown + at\ harbor$$

Spatial relations between objects can be represented by restrictions on composite linguistic variables. For example, the spatial relation between two objects O_1 and O_2 can be represented by introducing a binary composite variable (x_1, x_2), the values of which are from the domain $L(x_1, x_2) = L(x_1) \times L(x_2)$, and a restriction $R(x_1, x_2) \subseteq L(x_1) \times L(x_2)$ on the values of (x_1, x_2). In other terms, a spatial relation is a relation on linguistic variables representing spatial information.

In general, one can distinguish between noninteractive and interactive variables. Two variables x_1 and x_2 are noninteractive if the restriction on (x_1, x_2) is identical with the Cartesian product of the marginal restrictions on x_1 and x_2 [16]. For example, let x_1 and x_2 denote the positions of Ernie and Bert, respectively. Then a restriction like *Ernie and Bert are sitting at the table* would make x_1 and x_2 noninteractive, since Ernie's position at the table does not depend on Bert's position at the table (if we disregard the fact that usually Ernie can't sit where Bert is sitting). On the other hand, a restriction like *Ernie and Bert are sitting side by side at the table* would make x_1 and x_2 interactive, since Ernie's position at the table depends on Bert's position at the table (and vice versa).

Usually, spatial relations between objects are represented by restrictions on the values of interactive rather than noninteractive variables. For example, if we want to express the distance between two objects O_1 and O_2, then the relation on the composite variable (x_1, x_2), where x_1 and x_2 are the positions of O_1 and O_2, respectively, causes the variables x_1 and x_2 to interact with each other.

Linguistic variables provide us with a convenient means to express qualitative spatial relations. However, they alone aren't sufficient to integrate qualitative and quantitative spatial reasoning. Only when combined with fuzzy sets, they allow us to add quantitative aspects to the qualitative ones. The next section will discuss this issue.

4 Fuzzy Sets

A fuzzy subset $\tilde{R}$ of a domain D is a set of ordered pairs, $\langle d, \mu_{\tilde{R}}(d) \rangle$, where $d \in D$ and $\mu_{\tilde{R}} : D \to [0, 1]$ is the membership function of $\tilde{R}$. The membership function replaces the characteristic function of a classical subset $R \subseteq D$, which maps the set D to $\{0, 1\}$ and thereby indicating whether an element belongs to R (indicated by 1) or not (indicated by 0). If the range of $\mu_{\tilde{R}}$ is $\{0, 1\}$, $\tilde{R}$ is nonfuzzy and $\mu_{\tilde{R}}(d)$ is identical with the characteristic function of a nonfuzzy set.

Fuzzy sets can be used to associate quantitative information with qualitative one. Consider, for example, a linguistic value like *downtown*. We can associate this qualitative value with a fuzzy set that characterizes for each coordinate on some given street map to which extend this coordinate represents some location downtown. Assuming that D represents the possible coordinate (usually a set of character–digit combinations), *downtown* may be represented by a fuzzy set such as the following:

$$\tilde{R} = \langle M5, 1 \rangle + \langle M4, 0.8 \rangle + \langle M6, 0.8 \rangle + \langle L5, 0.8 \rangle + \\ \langle N5, 0.8 \rangle + \langle L4, 0.7 \rangle + \langle L6, 0.7 \rangle + \cdots$$

In other words, each location on the city map is considered to be more or less downtown. If its membership grade equals 1, the location is definitely downtown. If it equals 0, then it isn't downtown at all.

If it doesn't cause any confusion, we denote a fuzzy set as follows:

$$\tilde{R} = \sum_{d \in D} \mu_{\tilde{R}}(d)\, d$$

In general, the fuzzy set corresponding to a spatial linguistic value may be a continuous rather than a countable or even finite set. For example, the spatial linguistic value *illuminated*, which specifies that an object is near some light source, may be associated with a fuzzy set $\tilde{R}$ in the domain of real numbers, $\mathbb{R}$. An element $d \in \mathbb{R}$ then indicates the distance of the object to the light source. If the distance is 0, then the object is definitely considered to be illuminated. The greater (the square of) the distance to the light source, the less we consider the object to be illuminated. Since $\tilde{R}$ is a continuous set, we denote it as follows, assuming that $\mu_{\tilde{R}}(d) = 1/(1 + d^2)$:

$$\tilde{R} = \int_0^\infty \left\langle d, \frac{1}{1 + d^2} \right\rangle$$

In the following, we will discuss in more detail how to compute the membership grades for a qualitative spatial description. Since many qualitative descriptions use the concept of proximity, like in *close to a main road*, we will start with discussing the factors that influence the human perception of proximity.

5 Proximity Factors

There are numerous studies over a wide range of different data domains, including geographical space, of how humans make subjective judgements regarding distances. According to [6], the human perception of closeness or proximity is influenced by the following:

1. In the absence of other objects, humans reason about proximity in a geometric fashion. Furthermore, the relationship between distance and proximity can be approximated by a simple linear relationship.
2. When other objects of the same type are introduced, proximity is judged in part by relative distance, i.e., the distance between a primary object and a reference object.

3. Distance is affected by the size of the area being considered, i.e., the frame of reference.

Proximity measures in spatial reasoning must behave in a way that follows the human perception of proximity. Otherwise, the result of the GIS is counterintuitive and therefore unreliable. In the following, we will address the factors that influence proximity in more detail.

Absolute Distance The simplest form of reasoning about proximity is based on the absolute (or physical) distance between objects. Absolute distance is the major factor that affects proximity. It can be defined by a symmetric Euclidean distance matrix, in which an entry $\delta(O_1, O_2)$ specifies the distance between an object O_1 with coordinates (x_1, y_1) and O_2 with coordinates (x_2, y_2):

$$\delta(O_1, O_2) = \sqrt{(x_1 - x_2)^2 + (y_1 - y_2)^2}$$

Figure 2 shows the Euclidean distance matrix for a simple map.

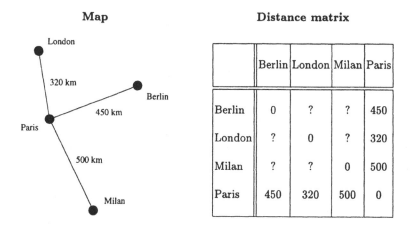

Fig. 2. Simple map and the corresponding Euclidean distance matrix showing the (absolute) distances between Berlin, London, Milan, and Paris.

Relative Distance In the presence of other objects, the pattern of how the other objects are distributed should be considered in addition to the absolute distance. Taking the distribution from Figure 2, London and Milan are considered to be far apart, because Paris is closer to London than Milan. On the other hand, Milan might be considered to be close to London if Paris were absent from the map. Thus the perceived distance between Milan and London will depend on the presence of the other objects, in particular on the presence of Paris.

Frame of Reference The reference frame plays a significant role in comparing distances between objects. It defines the maximal distance, and therefore an upper bound on all distances under consideration. The maximal distance is given by the length of the diagonal of the boundary of the reference frame.

In Figure 2, Milan may be far from London in a European reference frame, but they are close to each other in a world reference frame. The scale of the reference frame influences the perceived distance. What might be considered as being close in one scale may be regarded as being far away in another scale.

Object Size Sometimes the object size will have an effect on proximity. The larger the size of an object, the closer the objects appear to be. For example, 100 kilometers is regarded as being far apart if we consider two houses, but as being close if we are looking at two cities.

Traveling Costs and Reachability Traveling costs can be expenses, effort, time, etc. Generally speaking, the lesser the traveling costs, the smaller the perceived distance between two objects. For example, it may take less time or money to travel from Paris to Milan, and therefore a traveler may regard Milan as being closer to Paris as London.

Reachability is related to traveling costs. If a city isn't reachable from another city, the costs for getting to that city are infinitely high, and therefore the perceived distance is huge. Or if the other city can't be reached easily because of a missing direct flight connection, then the perceived distance to that city is greater than to a similar city with a direct flight connection.

Traveling Distance In some sense traveling distance is related to reachability. If two objects are connected, then we can establish a traveling distance between the objects by the length of the path that we have to travel on to get from the one object to the other. The path can be a straight line, in which case the traveling distance is equal to the absolute distance. It is more likely, however, that the path is some curved line, which makes the traveling distance greater than the absolute distance.

Attractiveness of Objects Different types of objects involve different types of proximity. The perceived attractiveness of an object is a major factor that affects proximity. For example, *close to the park* may be 500 meters or less, whereas *close to the sewage ponds* may be 10 kilometers or less.

6   A Case Study

To find the most adequate measure of proximity for a GIS, we conducted a survey consisting of 10 questions like the one in Figure 3. Each of the questions referred to two maps, each map consisting of a primary object (O) and a reference object (A or B). The subjects were asked to determine which reference object is closer to the primary object.

O is closer to A than to B .... □
O is closer to B than to A .... □

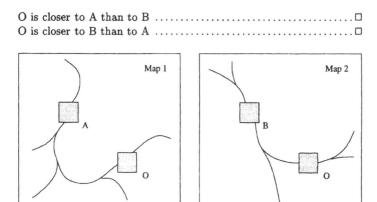

Fig. 3. Sample question from a survey for the exploration of the human perception of proximity.

Each question catered for a different proximity factor. The distance between O and A is identical with the distance between O and B in every question. If the proximity factor doesn't have any effect on the perception of proximity, then half the subjects should have chosen A as the answer, whereas the other half should have chosen B.

The survey was distributed locally through the internet and attracted 55 participants. Assuming that the subjects did the survey independently and that the probability of the outcome is constant across different subjects, then we can model the distribution of the number of subjects selecting answer A as a binomial distribution with parameters $n = 55$ and $p = 0.5$. Since n and p are large enough, we can use a normal approximation for this binomial distribution.

Although the calculations of critical standard derivations, critical values, etc. on the basis of a sample size of 55 may be inconclusive, they can at least be used as a first indication of the significance of certain proximity factors. In summary, these indications include the following:

- All factors have an effect on the human perception of proximity.
- The absolute distance is the most important proximity factor.
- As the problem reaches a certain degree of complexity, humans cannot reason about absolute distance any more.

7 Grades of Proximity

Since absolute distance seems to be the most important factor that affects the perception of proximity, we can apply the Euclidean distance between the primary object and a given reference object with coordinates (x_r, y_r) to calculate a grade of proximity. This grade can then be used to define a fuzzy set $\tilde{R}$ of reference objects that are in the proximity of the given primary object:

$$\tilde{R} = \int_{x,y \in [0,\infty)} \langle (x,y), \frac{1}{1 + (x - x_r)^2 + (y - y_r)^2} \rangle$$

Although this approach works well for queries related to one particular reference object, like *a place close to the town hall*, it becomes more complex if the spatial query refers to a class of objects, like *a place close to a waste dump*. In the latter case, the query doesn't specify a particular waste dump, but can refer to any waste dump available through the GIS, i.e, it uses a non-deterministic reference object. This type of query is commonly found in applications like resource planning and allocation.

The fuzzy set $\tilde{R}$ for a non-deterministic reference object is defined as the union of the fuzzy sets $\tilde{R}_i$ for the reference objects that belong to the class represented by the non-deterministic reference object:

$$\tilde{R} = \bigcup_{i=1}^{n} \tilde{R}_i$$

In general, computing this fuzzy set is a computationally expensive task. If we assume, however, that computing the union of fuzzy sets means maximizing the proximity grades, then it is sufficient to compute the proximity grade with respect to the closest reference object:

$$\tilde{R} = \int_{x,y \in [0,\infty)} \langle (x,y), \max_{i=1,\ldots,n} \frac{1}{1 + (x - x_{r_i})^2 + (y - y_{r_i})^2} \rangle$$

This means that finding the distance to a non-deterministic reference object is equivalent to searching for the closest reference object.

To find the closest reference object, we developed an algorithm which is related to the nearest neighbor searching algorithm introduced in [15]. Unlike Samet's algorithm, we don't dynamically update our search criteria but use a static criteria computed at the beginning of the search. The idea of the algorithm is to find a good candidate for the closest reference object and restrict the search to the circle that has the primary object at its center and the candidate reference object on its radius. If there are no other reference objects within the circle, then the candidate object is the closest reference object and its distance to the primary object determines the proximity grade of the primary object. Otherwise, we have to search for the closest reference object within the circle.

Assuming that we have stored the information about the reference objects in a quadtree as suggested above, the algorithm recursively proceeds down the tree until it finds the leaf node that corresponds to the location of the primary object. The reference object found in the leaf node becomes the candidate object (see Figure 4). If the leaf node that corresponds to the primary object is empty, we have to enlarge the search area. Every quadtree has the property that at least two of the siblings of an empty node are not empty. This means that the quadrant represented by the parent of an empty node must contain at least

Map of reference objects   **Corresponding quadtree**

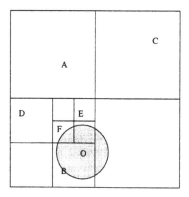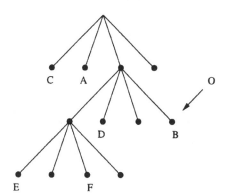

Fig. 4. Finding a candidate reference object in a quadtree. In the case shown here, the primary objects corresponds to a quadrant that contains a reference object. The circle given by the primary object and the reference object limits the search space.

Map of reference objects

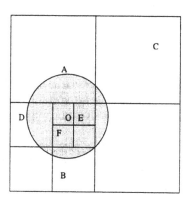

Fig. 5. Extended search space for finding a candidate reference object. The primary object corresponds to an empty quadrant, so the search space is extended to include the parent quadrant.

two reference objects (see Figure 5). Extending the search circle such that the parent quadrant is contained in the circle therefore guarantees finding a suitable candidate object.

In summary, the whole algorithm can be divided into the following steps:

1. Compute a search circle that is as small as possible but guarantees containing the closest reference object.
2. Compile a list of the locations of all reference objects in the search circle.
3. Calculate the distance between the primary object and each of the reference objects in the search circle.
4. Select the reference object with the smallest distance.

It can be shown that the algorithm has a linear worst time complexity, due to the fact that the depth of the quadtree is $O(\log \sqrt{m})$, where m is the maximal number of reference objects.

8 Fuzzifying the Distances between Colors

The algorithm introduced in the previous section uses geographic maps as input. So far, we have always assumed that the information to produce these maps is already available in electronic form. This assumption is certainly valid for a large amount of geographic information. On the other hand, there is also a significant proportion of information that isn't yet available online, like old maps. Producing an online version of such maps is often not straightforward, as colors may have faded, lines may have become invisible, etc. In the following, we will develop a framework for converting such 'fuzzy' maps into a representation that can be incorporated with the fuzzy spatial reasoner. The main idea of our approach is to determine a set of reference colors, each color corresponding to an object of a particular type.

Usually, there is some standard as to how certain areas of a map are colored. For example, blue areas on a map most often represent areas of water, whereas green areas stand for rural land. A brute-force approach to analyzing color maps would be to scan in the map and look for certain colors in the resulting file. However, this approach fails in most situations, as colors differ slightly from map to map.

So instead of searching for a particular color, we look for colors in a particular range, like all areas from light to deep blue. In other words, we are looking for a color that is close to a given reference color, which means that we need to define distances between colors. The smaller the distance of some color to the reference color, the more we consider this color to be the same as the reference color. By mapping distances to fuzzy values such that a distance of 0 is mapped to a fuzzy value of 1, we are able to define a fuzzy set for the reference color.

The distance between colors depends on the color space that is used to specify the colors. A popular color space is the RGB color space in which each color is split into its red, green, and blue component, similar to how the color is generated on a CRT tube. Most visible colors can be generated that way. Our first attempt was to use the RGB color space to compute distances between colors. Let $c_1 = (r_1, g_1, b_1)$ and $c_2 = (r_2, g_2, b_2)$ be two colors, then the distance between c_1 and c_2 would be defined as follows:

$$\Delta(c_1, c_2) = \sqrt{(r_2 - r_1)^2 + (g_2 - g_1)^2 + (b_2 - b_1)^2}$$

Each color in the RGB color space can be associated with a fuzzy set for that color. Since the largest distance in the RGB cube is $\sqrt{3}$, we define this fuzzy set as follows:

$$\tilde{R}_c = \{\langle c', \mu(c')\rangle \mid \mu(c') = (\sqrt{3} - \Delta(c', c))/\sqrt{3}\}$$

Although this looks reasonable at first sight, it has a major drawback: it is not consistent with how humans perceive color differences. Given two colors, c_1 and c_1', and two other colors, c_2 and c_2', then c_1 and c_1' might look more different than c_2 and c_2', even if $\Delta(c_1, c_1')$ is equal to $\Delta(c_2, c_2')$. A way to solve this problem is to switch to a color space that—although not as well known as the RGB color space—reflects human color perception more accurately. This color space is the CIE Luv color space [3].

Coordinates in the RGB color space can be transformed into coordinates in the CIE Luv color space by first mapping them to coordinates (x, y, z) in the CIE space and then mapping the result to coordinates (L, u, v) in the CIE Luv space. In particular, the transformations are as follows. Given a color (r, g, b) in the RGB color space, a transformation matrix M can be used to calculate the corresponding color (x, y, z) in the CIE space:

$$\begin{pmatrix} x \\ y \\ z \end{pmatrix} = M \begin{pmatrix} r \\ g \\ b \end{pmatrix} \qquad \text{with} \qquad M = \begin{pmatrix} x_r & x_g & x_b \\ y_r & y_g & y_b \\ z_r & z_g & z_b \end{pmatrix}$$

where x_r, x_g, and x_b are the weights applied to the monitor's RGB colors to find x, and so on.

After obtaining the coordinates of the color in the CIE space, we are able to calculate the coordinates (L, u, v) of the color in the CIE Luv space by applying the following formulas:

$$L = 116 \sqrt[3]{y/y_n} - 16$$

$$u = 13 L (u' - u_n')$$

$$v = 13 L (v' - v_n')$$

$$u' = \frac{4x}{x + 15y + 3z} \qquad v' = \frac{9y}{x + 15y + 3z}$$

$$u_n' = \frac{4x_n}{x_n + 15y_n + 3z_n} \qquad v_n' = \frac{9y_n}{x_n + 15y_n + 3z_n}$$

where (x_n, y_n, z_n) are the coordinates of the color that is defined as white.

The new coordinates are in a color space that is perceptually uniform, which means that the distance between, for example, two reds is comparable with the distance between two greens, etc. In other words, given a reference color for a certain area like water, we can now associate with each point on the map a fuzzy value that indicates the degree to which the area is considered to be water. Analogously, we can determine the degree to which the point is considered to be part of rural land, a road, etc.

The fuzzy spatial reasoner can use both information about colors and information about spatial relations to deduce new information from the given geographic information. This is achieved in two steps:

1. Analyze the color of each point on the map and compute fuzzy values by comparing that color to reference colors for water areas, roads, rural land, etc.
2. Combine the resulting fuzzy values with the fuzzy values obtained from the qualitative spatial relations, yielding fuzzy values that indicate the degree to which a certain area satisfies the set of initially given restrictions.

9 Conclusion

Qualitative reasoning is reasoning in terms of linguistic values, whereas quantitative reasoning is reasoning based on numerical values such as measurements. Both qualitative and quantitative reasoning are used by humans to deduce new information from given one. However, it is believed that there is a preference towards qualitative reasoning, and that often some sort of translation takes place from quantitative to qualitative information:

Humans often convert precise quantitative information into qualitative values (or categories) to gain insight into the truth meaning of the data.
[2]

In this article, we introduced a scheme of representing qualitative spatial information by associating qualitative relations with fuzzy sets. We argued that there are several factors that influence the perception of closeness (or proximity), but that the absolute distance is the main factor. Based on the concept of absolute distance, we introduced an algorithm for computing proximity grades. In particular, we focussed on the problem of computing proximity grades for non-deterministic reference objects. The algorithm has been implemented in Java and is part of a workbench for exploring new concepts and algorithms in the field of spatial reasoning.

Beyond that, we outlined a system for fuzzy spatial reasoning. The system takes an image (geographic map, satellite image, etc.) and analyzes the colors in that image by first transforming the colors into a perceptually uniform color space and then associating fuzzy values with the colors. These fuzzy values are combined with the fuzzy values that are obtained from analyzing spatial relation like *close to* or *far from*. As a result, we get a fuzzy classifications of all points in the image.

The work described in this article is more or less closely related to other work on data models for geographic information systems [4, 7, 8, 10, 11, 14].

From the viewpoint of AI, the work described here is related to work on qualitative spatial reasoning in the form of reasoning about spatial relations. This has been addressed in a number of papers.

Both Freksa [5] and Hernández [9] introduced an extension of Allen's temporal logic [1] to spatial reasoning. The basic idea of these papers is to describe the relationship between two objects by one or several relations from a set of thirteen basic relations.

A similar approach is described in [13], where objects of a two-dimensional world are characterized by the directions in which the objects are moving and by associating with the objects trajectories along which they are moving.

10 Acknowledgement

This article is based on research work previously published by Jonathan Histed, Ute Lörch, David Poon, and the author. We are grateful for the support that we received from the University of Auckland Research Committee under the grant numbers A18/XXXXX/62090/F3414025, A18/XXXXX/62090/F3414052, and A18/XXXXX/62090/F3414065.

References

1. J.F. Allen. Maintaining knowledge about temporal intervals. *Communications of the ACM*, 26:832–843, 1983.
2. L.C. Booth. *Qualitative Reasoning.* Morgan Kaufmann, San Mateo, California, 1989.
3. J.D. Foley, A. van Dam, S.K. Feiner, and J.F. Hughes. *Computer Graphics: Principles and Practice.* Addison Wesley, Readings, Massachusetts, second edition, 1990.
4. A.U. Frank. Spatial concepts, geometric data models, and geometric data structures. *Computers and Geosciences*, 18:409–417, 1992.
5. C. Freksa. Qualitative spatial reasoning. In *Proc. Workshop RAUM*, pages 21–36, Koblenz, Germany, 1990.
6. M. Gahegan. Proximity operators for qualitative spatial reasoning. In A.U. Frank and W. Kuhn, editors, *Spatial Information Theory: A Theoretical Basis for GIS*, Lecture Notes in Computer Science 988. Springer, Berlin, Germany, 1995.
7. M.F. Goodchild. Geographic data modeling. *Computers and Geosciences*, 18:401–408, 1992.
8. A. Gupta, T.E. Weymouth, and R. Jain. An extended object-oriented data model for large image bases. In O. Günther and H.-J. Schek, editors, *Advances in Spatial Databases*, Lecture Notes in Computer Science 525, pages 45–61. Springer, Berlin, Germany, 1991.
9. D. Hernández. Relative representation of spatial knowledge: The 2-D case. In D.M. Mark and A.U. Frank, editors, *Cognitive and Linguistic Aspects of Geographic Space*, pages 373–385. Kluwer, Dordrecht, The Netherlands, 1991.
10. J.R. Herring. The mathematical modeling of spatial and non-spatial information in geographic information systems. In D.M. Mark and A.U. Frank, editors, *Cognitive and Linguistic Aspects of Geographic Space*, pages 313–350. Kluwer, Dordrecht, The Netherlands, 1991.

11. J.R. Herring. TIGRIS: A data model for an object-oriented geographic information system. *Computers and Geosciences*, 18:443–452, 1992.

12. R. Laurini and D. Thompson. *Fundamentals of Spatial Information Systems*. Academic Press, London, England, 1992.

13. A. Mukerjee and G. Joe. A qualitative model for space. In *Proc. AAAI-90*, pages 721–727, Boston, Massachusetts, 1990.

14. J.F. Raper and D.J. Maguire. Design models and functionality in GIS. *Computers and Geosciences*, 18:387–394, 1992.

15. H. Samet. *The Design and Analysis of Spatial Data Structures*. Addison-Wesley, Reading, Massachusetts, 1990.

16. L.A. Zadeh. The concept of a linguistic variable and its application to approximate reasoning—I. *Information Sciences*, 8:199–249, 1975.

Fuzzy Morphology and Fuzzy Distances: New Definitions and Links in both Euclidean and Geodesic Cases

Isabelle Bloch

École Nationale Supérieure des Télécommunications, département Images
CNRS URA820
46 rue Barrault, 75013 Paris, France
Tel: 33 1 45 81 75 85, Fax: 33 1 45 81 37 94, E-mail : bloch@ima.enst.fr

Abstract. The aim of this paper is to establish links between fuzzy morphology and fuzzy distances. We show how distances can be derived from fuzzy mathematical morphology, in particular fuzzy dilation, leading to interesting definitions involving membership information and spatial information. Conversely, we propose a way to define fuzzy morphological operations from fuzzy distances. We deal with both the Euclidean and the geodesic cases. In particular in the geodesic case, we propose a definition of fuzzy balls, from which fuzzy geodesic dilation and erosion are derived, based on fuzzy geodesic distances. These new operations enhance the set of fuzzy morphological operators, leading to transformations of a fuzzy set conditionally to another fuzzy set. The proposed definitions are valid in any dimension, in both Euclidean and geodesic cases.

1 Introduction

Although the literature witnesses a growing interest for fuzzy distances and fuzzy mathematical morphology, with several applications (e.g. in image processing both are needed), both topics are generally unrelated to each other. Several works have been dedicated to fuzzy morphology [1, 9, 11, 15, 21] without direct reference to metrics or distances, a fortiori to fuzzy distances. On the other hand, several works have been done in order to propose definitions of fuzzy distances (see e.g. [5] for a comparative review).

The aim of this paper is to establish links between fuzzy morphology and fuzzy distances, and constitutes an extended version of [6, 7]. This follows our work in [2] where we defined distances from a point to a fuzzy set and distances between fuzzy objects based on fuzzy dilation. These definitions were most interesting since they involve at the same time membership information and spatial information, both being very important for applications like image processing or spatial reasoning.

In this paper, we extend these relationships between fuzzy morphology (and in particular fuzzy dilation) and fuzzy distances, and we propose a way to define fuzzy morphological operations from fuzzy distances, in both Euclidean and geodesic cases. Thus the contribution of this paper is twofold, and concerns both the proposition of original definitions along with the study of their properties, and the establishment of links between fuzzy morphology and fuzzy distances.

In Section 2 we recall the main ways to derive fuzzy distances from fuzzy dilation in the Euclidean case. In Section 3, we address the opposite question, i.e. defining fuzzy dilation from a fuzzy distance. In Section 4 we recall and discuss our definition of fuzzy geodesic distances, as defined in [3]. From this definition, we propose definitions of fuzzy distances in the geodesic case in Section 5.

2 Fuzzy distances from fuzzy dilation: Euclidean case

The main ways for defining a fuzzy operator from its binary equivalent are based either on computations on the α-cuts (using e.g. the extension principle [23]), or on a direct translation of binary equations into fuzzy ones, according to the following table:

crisp concept	equivalent fuzzy concept
set X	fuzzy set / membership function μ
complement of a set	fuzzy complementation c
intersection $\cap$	t-norm t
union $\cup$	t-conorm T
existence $\exists$ / universal symbol $\forall$	supremum / infimum

This second way to proceed has proven to lead to fuzzy definitions having good formal properties, good intuitive behavior, and efficient computation, for several types of operations (mathematical morphology [9], adjacency [10], distances [2, 5], etc.). In particular for distances, we have shown that this construction principle can be applied easily as soon as the distance can be expressed in set theoretical and logical terms. It is the case for distances having a direct expression in terms of mathematical morphology (e.g. nearest point distance, Hausdorff distance, or distance from a point to a set). Therefore we defined in [2] the fuzzy equivalent of these distances in terms of fuzzy mathematical morphology.

We summarize below the main steps of the construction, the obtained definitions and their properties.

Let us denote by μ a fuzzy set defined on the space $\mathcal{S}$. Equivalently μ is a function from $\mathcal{S}$ into $[0, 1]$ and, for each point x of $\mathcal{S}$, $\mu(x)$ is a value representing the membership degree of x to the fuzzy set μ, also called fuzzy object.

2.1 Distance from a point to a fuzzy set

In this section, we describe the approach proposed in [2] for defining the distance $d(x, \mu)$ from a point x of $\mathcal{S}$ to a fuzzy set μ defined on $\mathcal{S}$ as a fuzzy number, by translating crisp equations into their fuzzy equivalent. The easiest way to perform this translation is to express the distance in set theoretical terms, through mathematical morphology.

In the crisp case, and in a finite discrete space, the distance from a point x to a crisp set X is defined by:

$$d_B(x, X) = 0 \Leftrightarrow x \in X \tag{1}$$

$$d_B(x, X) = n \Leftrightarrow x \in D^n(X) \text{ and } x \notin D^{n-1}(X) \tag{2}$$

where D^n denotes the dilation by a ball of radius n centered at the origin of $\mathcal{S}$ (and $D^0(X) = X$). In this case, the extensivity property of the dilation holds [19], and $x \notin D^{n-1}(X)$ is equivalent to $\forall n' < n, x \notin D^{n'}(X)$. Equation 2 is equivalent to:

$$x \in D^n(X) \cap [D^{n-1}(X)]^C, \tag{3}$$

where A^C denotes the complement set of A in $\mathcal{S}$. This is a pure set theoretical expression, that we can now translate into fuzzy terms. This leads to the following definition of the degree to which $d(x, \mu)$ is equal to n:

$$\delta_{(x,\mu)}(0) = \mu(x), \tag{4}$$

$$\delta_{(x,\mu)}(n) = t[D_\nu^n(\mu)(x), c[D_\nu^{n-1}(\mu)(x)]], \tag{5}$$

where t is a t-norm (fuzzy intersection), c a fuzzy complementation (typically $c(a) = 1 - a$), and ν a fuzzy structuring element used for performing the dilation. Several choices of ν are possible. It can be simply the unit ball, or a fuzzy set representing for instance the smallest sensitive unit in the image, along with the imprecision attached to it. In this case, ν has to be equal to 1 at the origin of $\mathcal{S}$, such that the extensivity of the dilation still holds [9]. Note that for the definition of fuzzy dilation relying on t-norms and t-conorms, the iterativity property holds (see [9] for details), and therefore we have:

$$D_\nu^n(\mu) = D_\nu[D_\nu^{n-1}(\mu)] = D_\nu[D_\nu[D_\nu^{n-2}(\mu)]] = \ldots \tag{6}$$

The properties of this definition are the following [2]: If $\mu(x) = 1$, $\delta_{(x,\mu)}(0) = 1$ and $\forall n > 0, \delta_{(x,\mu)}(n) = 0$, i.e. the distance is a crisp number in this case. If μ and ν are binary, the proposed definition coincides with the binary one. $\delta_{(x,\mu)}$ can be interpreted as a density distance, from which a distance distribution can be deduced by integration. $\delta_{(x,\mu)}$ is a non normalized fuzzy number (in the discrete finite case).

From this definition, distances between two fuzzy sets can be derived using supremum or infimum computation of fuzzy numbers using the extension principle [12]. The details are given in [2].

2.2 Distances between two fuzzy sets

We consider here the examples of nearest point distance (denoted by d_N) and Hausdorff distance (denoted by d_H) since they have a direct morphological expression that will be used in the following:

$$d_N(X, Y) = \inf\{n, X \cap D^n(Y) \neq \emptyset\}$$
$$= \inf\{n, Y \cap D^n(X) \neq \emptyset\}. \tag{7}$$

$$d_H(X, Y) = \inf\{n, X \subset D^n(Y) \text{ and } Y \subset D^n(X)\}. \tag{8}$$

In these equations, X and Y denote two crisp sets of the considered space $\mathcal{S}$, and $D^n(X)$ the dilation of size n of X. Although these notions are usually called distances, this terminology is improper for the first one, because of its properties. Indeed, the properties of a (true) distance are: positivity, separability, symmetry and triangular inequality. For the nearest point distance, positivity and symmetry hold, but separability and triangular inequality are not satisfied. In particular, we have $d_N(X, X) = 0$ for any set X, but $d_N(X, Y) = 0$ does not necessarily imply $X = Y$ (it only implies $X \cap Y \neq \emptyset$). For the Hausdorff distance, all properties hold, and therefore it is a true distance (note that the morphological expression given by equation 8 allows for a straightforward proof of triangular inequality).

A direct morphological expression of the fuzzy extension of nearest point distance is obtained by translating equation 7. We define a distance distribution $\Delta_N(\mu, \mu')(n)$ that expresses the degree to which the distance between two fuzzy sets μ and μ' is less than n by:

$$\Delta_N(\mu, \mu')(n) = f[\sup_{x \in \mathcal{S}} t[\mu(x), D^n_\nu(\mu')(x)],$$
$$\sup_{x \in \mathcal{S}} t[\mu'(x), D^n_\nu(\mu)(x)]], \tag{9}$$

where t is a t-norm and f is a symmetrical function. A distance density, i.e. a fuzzy number $\delta_N(\mu, \mu')(n)$ representing the degree to which the distance between μ and μ' is equal to n can be obtained implicitly by [17]:

$$\Delta_N(\mu, \mu')(n) = \int_0^n \delta_N(\mu, \mu')(n') dn'. \tag{10}$$

Clearly, this expression is not very tractable and does not lead to a simple explicit expression of $\delta_N(\mu, \mu')(n)$. Therefore, we suggest to use an explicit method, exploiting the fact that, for $n > 0$, we have:

$$d_N(X, Y) = n \Leftrightarrow D^n(X) \cap Y \neq \emptyset \text{ and } D^{n-1}(X) \cap Y = \emptyset \tag{11}$$

and the symmetrical expression. For $n = 0$ we have:

$$d_N(X, Y) = 0 \Leftrightarrow X \cap Y \neq \emptyset. \tag{12}$$

The translation of these equivalences provides, for $n > 0$:

$$\delta_N(\mu, \mu')(n) = t[\sup_{x \in \mathcal{S}} t[\mu'(x), D^n_\nu(\mu)(x)],$$
$$c[\sup_{x \in \mathcal{S}} t[\mu'(x), D^{n-1}_\nu(\mu)(x)]]] \tag{13}$$

or a symmetrical expression derived from this one, and:

$$\delta_N(\mu, \mu')(0) = \sup_{x \in \mathcal{S}} t[\mu(x), \mu'(x)]. \tag{14}$$

From equation 8, a distance distribution for Hausdorff distance can be defined, by introducing fuzzy dilation:

$$\Delta_H(\mu, \mu')(n) = t[\inf_{x \in S} T[D^n_\nu(\mu)(x), c(\mu'(x))],$$

$$\inf_{x \in S} T[D^n_\nu(\mu')(x), c(\mu(x))]], \tag{15}$$

where c is a complementation, t a t-norm and T the dual t-conorm. Like for the nearest point distance, a distance density can be derived implicitly from this distance distribution. A direct definition of a distance density can be obtained from:

$$d_H(X, Y) = 0 \Leftrightarrow X = Y, \tag{16}$$

and for $n > 0$:

$$d_H(X, Y) = n \Leftrightarrow X \subset D^n(Y) \text{ and } Y \subset D^n(X)$$
$$\text{and } (X \not\subset D^{n-1}(Y) \text{ or } Y \not\subset D^{n-1}(X)). \tag{17}$$

Translating these equations leads to a definition of the Hausdorff distance between two fuzzy sets μ and μ' as a fuzzy number:

$$\delta_H(\mu, \mu')(0) = t[\inf_{x \in S} T[\mu(x), c(\mu'(x))],$$

$$\inf_{x \in S} T[\mu'(x), c(\mu(x))]], \tag{18}$$

$$\delta_H(\mu, \mu')(n) = t[\inf_{x \in S} T[D^n_\nu(\mu)(x), c(\mu'(x))],$$
$$\inf_{x \in S} T[D^n_\nu(\mu')(x), c(\mu(x))],$$
$$T(\sup_{x \in S} t[\mu(x), D^{n-1}_\nu(\mu')(x)],$$
$$\sup_{x \in S} t[\mu'(x), D^{n-1}_\nu(\mu)(x)])]. \tag{19}$$

The previous definitions of fuzzy nearest point and Hausdorff distances (defined as fuzzy numbers) between two fuzzy sets do not necessarily share the same properties as their crisp equivalent. This is due in particular to the fact that, depending on the choice of the involved t-norms and t-conorms, excluded middle and non contradiction laws may not be satisfied. All distances are positive, in the sense that the defined fuzzy numbers have always a support included in $\mathbb{R}^+$. By construction, all defined distances are symmetrical with respect to μ and μ'. The separability property is not always satisfied. However, if μ is normalized, we have for the nearest point distance $\delta_N(\mu, \mu)(0) = 1$ and $\delta_N(\mu, \mu)(n) = 0$ for $n > 1$. For the Hausdorff distance, $\delta_H(\mu, \mu')(0) = 1$ implies $\mu = \mu'$ for T being the bounded sum $(T(a, b) = \min(1, a + b))$, while it implies μ and μ' crisp and equal for $T = \max$. Also the triangular inequality is not satisfied in general.

3   Fuzzy dilation from fuzzy distance: Euclidean case

In this Section, we address the opposite question: how to define a fuzzy dilation from a fuzzy distance? The binary dilation by an Euclidean ball of size n is expressed in terms of distance as:

$$D^r(Y) = \{x \in \mathcal{S}, d(x, Y) \leq n\} \tag{20}$$

where $d(x, Y)$ denotes the Euclidean distance from x to Y. The form of this equation suggests to define fuzzy dilation as a fuzzy distance distribution, since a natural fuzzy extension of this equation consists in defining the fuzzy dilation at a point x as the degree to which its distance to a fuzzy set μ (replacing the crisp set Y) is less than n.

3.1   Two simple examples

Let us first consider two simple examples. In the first one, we consider that the fuzzy distance distribution Δ is defined by the extension principle from the Euclidean distance between points, typically as:

$$\forall x \in \mathcal{S}, \forall n \geq 0, \ \Delta(x, \mu)(n) = \sup_{d(x,y) \leq n} \mu(y). \tag{21}$$

Defining directly the fuzzy dilation at x as the value given by the distance distribution leads to the following result:

$$D^n(\mu)(x) = D_{B_n}(\mu)(x) \tag{22}$$

where B_n is the Euclidean ball of size n. This shows that, in this first example, we just end up with the dilation of the function μ by the binary structuring element B_n. No fuzziness appears at the level of the structuring element.

In the second example, we consider fuzzy distance density and distribution defined from fuzzy dilation, as in Section 2. In the case where we use the Lukasiewicz t-norm ($t(a, b) = \max(0, a + b - 1)$), the distance density and distribution take the following forms (for $n > 0$):

$$\delta(x, \mu)(n) = D_\nu^n(\mu)(x) - D_\nu^{n-1}(\mu)(x), \tag{23}$$

$$\Delta(x, \mu)(n) = D_\nu^n(\mu)(x). \tag{24}$$

In this case, if we define a fuzzy dilation from the distance distribution, we recover exactly the fuzzy dilation used for the construction of the distribution, with the same fuzzy structuring element. This loop is in accordance with the interpretation of dilation in terms of distance distribution, and guarantees the consistency of the approach described below when the distance distribution is itself issued from a dilation.

3.2 General case

Based on the previous observations and examples, we address now the more general case, where we define a fuzzy dilation from any fuzzy distance distribution, as:

$$\forall x \in \mathcal{S}, \forall n \in \mathbb{N}, \ D^n(\mu)(x) = \Delta(x, \mu)(n). \tag{25}$$

The fuzzy structuring element is defined implicitly, and depends on the shape of the distance distribution Δ.

Now the question is: what are the properties that the distance distribution should satisfy in order to actually define a fuzzy dilation, with nice properties?

Let us consider a fuzzy distance distribution Δ having the following properties:

1. $\forall x \in \mathcal{S}, \forall n \in \mathbb{N}, \Delta(x, \mu)(n) \in [0, 1]$,
2. $\forall x \in \mathcal{S}, \Delta(x, \mu)(0) = \mu(x)$,
3. if μ is a crisp set, then $\Delta(x, \mu)$ is a binary distribution, i.e. takes the value 0 everywhere except at $n = d(x, \mu)$,
4. Δ is increasing in n, i.e. $n \leq n' \Rightarrow \Delta(x, \mu)(n) \leq \Delta(x, \mu)(n')$,
5. Δ is increasing in μ, i.e. $\forall y, \mu(y) \leq \mu'(y) \Rightarrow \Delta(x, \mu)(n) \leq \Delta(x, \mu')(n)$,
6. Δ is invariant with respect to geometrical transformations, i.e. $\Delta(x, \mu)$ does not change if x and μ are translated or rotated.

These properties are rather intuitive and are likely to be satisfied by most distance distributions. Typically, the distance distributions obtained in Section 2 satisfy them.

From these properties, we can prove the following properties on the derived fuzzy dilation:

1. $\forall x \in \mathcal{S}, \forall n \in \mathbb{N}, D^n(\mu)(x) \in [0, 1]$,
2. $\forall x \in \mathcal{S}, D^n(\mu)(x) \geq \mu(x)$, which means that the fuzzy dilation is extensive (it follows that the second property of Δ induces that the implicit fuzzy structuring element ν satisfies $\nu(0) = 1$, which is the usual condition to have an extensive dilation [9]),
3. the fuzzy dilation is increasing in n,
4. the fuzzy dilation is increasing in μ,
5. the fuzzy dilation is invariant with respect to geometrical transformations,
6. fuzzy erosion can be defined by duality:

$$E^n(\mu)(x) = c[D^n(c(\mu))(x)] = c[\Delta(x, c(\mu))(n)], \tag{26}$$

which corresponds to the degree to which x satisfies $\Delta(x, c(\mu)) \geq n$, in accordance to the binary case.

This shows that the fuzzy dilation derived from a distance distribution has most of the basic properties expected for a dilation. One property that does not appear in the previous list and that is very important in the binary case is the compatibility with union. In order to get a fuzzy dilation satisfying this property, the distance distribution has to be itself compatible with union, i.e. for any two fuzzy sets μ and μ', Δ has to satisfy:

$$\forall x \in \mathcal{S}, \forall n \in \mathbb{N}, \Delta(x, T(\mu, \mu'))(n) =$$

$$T[\Delta(x, \mu)(n), \Delta(x, \mu')(n)] \tag{27}$$

where T is a t-conorm (fuzzy union). This property is clearly not always satisfied by a distance distribution. On the other hand, there exist distance distributions that satisfy this property. If Δ is not compatible with union, then the derived fuzzy dilation has weaker properties than in the crisp case (this is also the case for several fuzzy dilations that have been defined in the literature, see [9]).

This construction shows that we can derive fuzzy dilations having good formal properties from fuzzy distance distributions. The next step will be to examine the particular forms of the obtained dilations for several examples of distance distributions, e.g. derived from nearest point or Hausdorff distance. This is left for future work.

Another possible direction is to define fuzzy dilations from fuzzy distance densities (instead of distributions), by looking at the degree to which $\delta(x, \mu)$ is less than n, for instance using comparison of fuzzy numbers. This leads to an approach similar to the one described in Section 5 for the geodesic case and will not be detailed here.

4   Fuzzy geodesic distance

We proposed in [3] an original definition for the distance between two points in a fuzzy set, extending the notion of geodesic distance. We recall here the main results we obtained.

The geodesic distance in μ between two points x and y represents the length of the shortest path between x and y that "goes out of μ as least as possible". We have proposed several formalisms for this notion. Here we recall only the one having the best properties. This definition relies on the degree of connectivity, as defined by Rosenfeld [16]. In the case where $\mathcal{S}$ is a discrete bounded space (as is usually the case in image processing), the degree of connectivity in μ between any two points x and y of $\mathcal{S}$ is defined as:

$$c_\mu(x, y) = \max_{L(x,y)} [\min_{t \in L(x,y)} \mu(t)], \tag{28}$$

where $L(x, y)$ denotes a path from x to y, constituted by a sequence of points of $\mathcal{S}$ according to the discrete connectivity defined on $\mathcal{S}$.

We denote by $L^*(x, y)$ a shortest path (in the Euclidean sense) between x and y on which c_μ is reached (this path, not necessarily unique, can be interpreted as a geodesic path descending as least as possible in the membership degrees), and we denote by $l(L^*(x, y))$ its length. Then we define the geodesic distance in μ between x and y as:

$$d_\mu(x, y) = \frac{l(L^*(x, y))}{c_\mu(x, y)}. \tag{29}$$

It corresponds to the weighted geodesic distance (in the classical sense) computed in the α-cut of μ at level $\alpha = c_\mu(x, y)$. In this α-cut, x and y belong to the same connected component (for the considered discrete crisp connectivity).

This definition satisfies the following set of properties (see [3] for the proof):

1. positivity: $\forall (x, y) \in \mathcal{S}^2, d_\mu(x, y) \geq 0$;
2. symmetry: $\forall (x, y) \in \mathcal{S}^2, d_\mu(x, y) = d_\mu(y, x)$;
3. separability: $\forall (x, y) \in \mathcal{S}^2, d_\mu(x, y) = 0 \Leftrightarrow x = y$;
4. d_μ depends on the shortest path between x and y that "goes out" of μ "as least as possible", and d_μ tends towards infinity if it is not possible to find a path between x and y without going through a point t such that $\mu(t) = 0$;
5. d_μ is decreasing with respect to $\mu(x)$ and $\mu(y)$;
6. d_μ is decreasing with respect to $c_\mu(x, y)$;
7. d_μ is equal to the classical geodesic distance if μ is crisp.

The triangular inequality is not satisfied, but from this definition, it is possible to build a true distance, satisfying triangular inequality, while keeping all other properties. This can be achieved in the following way:

$$d'_\mu(x, y) = \min_{t \in \mathcal{S}} \left[\frac{l(L^*(x, t))}{c_\mu(x, t)} + \frac{l(L^*(t, y))}{c_\mu(t, y)} \right].$$

These properties are in agreement with what can be required from a fuzzy geodesic distance, both mathematically and intuitively.

In this approach, the geodesic distance between two points is defined as a crisp number. It could be also defined as a fuzzy number, taking into account the fact that if the set is imprecisely defined, geodesic distances in this set can be imprecise too. All what follows can be applied for any definition of a fuzzy geodesic distance.

5 Fuzzy dilation from fuzzy distance: geodesic case

In mathematical morphology, an important set of operations is constituted by geodesic transformations [19, 13, 18, 14]. They are particularly useful in image processing, where transformations may have to be performed conditionally to a restriction of the spatial domain. Applications can be found for defining operators under reconstruction (e.g. filtering operators), in image segmentation, in pattern recognition, where operations have to be constrained by results of other transformations.

In this paper, we propose to define geodesic transformations on fuzzy sets. To our knowledge, this is the first attempt towards extending geodesic morphology to fuzzy sets, in contrary to Euclidean morphology, that has already motivated several works, e.g [8, 9, 20, 1, 11, 15, 22] and several others since these original works. The aim of this extension is to provide geodesic operators for image processing under imprecision, where image objects are represented as spatial fuzzy sets. We will consider mainly dilation and erosion, which are the two main operators, from which a large set of operators can be built, by iterating and combining these two basic ones.

In the binary case, geodesic dilation and erosion of a set Y conditionally to a set X of size r are defined as:

$$D_X^r(Y) = \{x \in S, B_X(x, r) \cap Y \neq \emptyset\}, \tag{30}$$

$$E_X^r(Y) = \{x \in S, B_X(x, r) \subset Y\}. \tag{31}$$

In these equations, $B_X(x, r)$ denotes a geodesic ball of size r and center x, defined as:

$$B_X(x, r) = \{y \in X, d_X(x, y) \leq r\}, \tag{32}$$

where d_X denotes the geodesic distance in X.

Since these definitions involve geodesic distance through the geodesic balls, we propose to generalize first equation 32, and then equations 30 and 31 to fuzzy sets.

5.1 Fuzzy geodesic balls

Definitions In this Section, we define fuzzy geodesic balls. Let us denote by $\beta_\mu(x, \rho)$ the fuzzy geodesic ball of center x and radius ρ, conditionally to μ. We define $\beta_\mu(x, \rho)$ as a fuzzy set on S. Intuitively, given that x is in μ, for each point y the value $\beta_\mu(x, \rho)(y)$ should represent the fact that y belongs to μ and that it is at a geodesic distance in μ from x less than ρ. Therefore, $\beta_\mu(x, \rho)(y)$ has to be defined as a conjunction of three terms: the degree to which x belongs to μ, the degree to which y belongs to μ, and the degree $\delta(d_\mu(x, y) \leq \rho)$ to which $d_\mu(x, y) \leq \rho$, i.e.:

$$\forall y \in S, \ \beta_\mu(x, \rho)(y) = t[\mu(x), \mu(y), \delta(d_\mu(x, y) \leq \rho)], \tag{33}$$

where t is a t-norm.

Obviously, $\delta(d_\mu(x, y) \leq \rho)$ should be a decreasing function of $d_\mu(x, y)$. If we consider that ρ is a crisp number, we can choose a simple Heaviside function, such that:

$$\delta(d_\mu(x, y) \leq \rho) = \begin{cases} 1 & if \ d_\mu(x, y) \leq \rho \\ 0 \ else \end{cases} \tag{34}$$

Then we derive, $\forall y \in S$:

$$\beta_\mu(x, \rho)(y) = \begin{cases} t[\mu(x), \mu(y)] & if \ d_\mu(x, y) \leq \rho \\ 0 & else \end{cases} \tag{35}$$

A fuzzy ball is therefore a subset of μ constituted of points y which are at a geodesic distance from x less than ρ, and whose membership degrees are bounded by $\mu(x)$.

This assumes that the value of interest ρ is precisely defined, which may appear as restrictive in a fuzzy context.

If we consider that some imprecision is attached to ρ, rather than considering it as crisp, then we can choose a smoother function, depending on the amount of imprecision attached to ρ. The problem with this approach is that the chosen decreasing function is somewhat arbitrary, and probably difficult to tune for specific applications.

Therefore, we propose another approach, where the link between this function and the imprecision of ρ is made more explicit. For this aim, we consider ρ as a fuzzy number. Defining $\delta(d_\mu(x,y) \leq \rho)$ calls then for the comparison of fuzzy numbers: $d_\mu(x,y)$ is less than ρ iff $d_\mu(x,y)$ is equal to the minimum of $d_\mu(x,y)$ and ρ. The minimum between two fuzzy numbers has been defined in [12] as follows. Let ν and ν' be two fuzzy numbers. From the definition of fuzzy numbers, the α-cuts of ν and ν' are bounded intervals, denoted as $[\nu_\alpha{}^-, \nu_\alpha{}^+]$ and $[\nu'_\alpha{}^-, \nu'_\alpha{}^+]$ respectively. The minimum of ν and ν' is then the fuzzy number the α-cuts of which are:

$$\min(\nu, \nu')_\alpha = [\min(\nu_\alpha{}^-, \nu'_\alpha{}^-), \min(\nu_\alpha{}^+, \nu'_\alpha{}^+)]. \tag{36}$$

Here, we have to compute the minimum between $d_\mu(x,y)$ and ρ. Let us denote by $[\rho_0, \rho_2]$ the support of ρ and by ρ_1 its modal value. Applying equation 36 in the case where $d_\mu(x,y)$ is a crisp number, we come up with the following result, for all real number z:

- if $d_\mu(x,y) \leq \rho_0$:

$$\min(d_\mu(x,y), \rho)(z) = \begin{cases} 1 \; if \; z = d_\mu(x,y) \\ 0 \; if \; z \neq d_\mu(x,y) \end{cases} \tag{37}$$

- if $\rho_0 \leq d_\mu(x,y) \leq \rho_1$:

$$\min(d_\mu(x,y), \rho)(z) = \begin{cases} \rho(z) \; if \; z < d_\mu(x,y) \\ 1 \quad\; if \; z = d_\mu(x,y) \\ 0 \quad\; if \; z > d_\mu(x,y) \end{cases} \tag{38}$$

- if $\rho_1 \leq d_\mu(x,y) \leq \rho_2$:

$$\min(d_\mu(x,y), \rho)(z) = \begin{cases} \rho(z) \; if \; z \leq d_\mu(x,y) \\ 0 \quad\; if \; z > d_\mu(x,y) \end{cases} \tag{39}$$

- if $d_\mu(x,y) \geq \rho_2$:

$$\min(d_\mu(x,y), \rho)(z) = \rho(z). \tag{40}$$

To have $d_\mu(x,y) \leq \rho$ is equivalent to $d_\mu(x,y) = \min(d_\mu(x,y), \rho)$, or to $d_\mu(x,y) \subset \min(d_\mu(x,y), \rho)$ and $\min(d_\mu(x,y), \rho) \subset d_\mu(x,y)$. This last form can be easily translated into fuzzy terms, in a way similar to the one used in [9], as:

$$\delta(d_\mu(x,y) \leq \rho) = t[\inf_z T[c(d_\mu(x,y))(z), \min(d_\mu(x,y), \rho)(z)],$$

$$\inf_z T[d_\mu(x,y)(z), c(\min(d_\mu(x,y), \rho))]],$$

where t is a t-norm, c a fuzzy complementation (typically $c(z) = 1 - z$) and T a t-conorm, dual of t with respect to c. This leads to the following result (taking into account that ρ is increasing on $[\rho_0, \rho_1]$):

$$\delta(d_\mu(x,y) \leq \rho) = \begin{cases} 1 & if\ d_\mu(x,y) \leq \rho_0 \\ c(\rho)(d_\mu(x,y)) & if\ \rho_0 \leq d_\mu(x,y) \leq \rho_1 \\ 0 & if\ d_\mu(x,y) \geq \rho_1 \end{cases} \tag{41}$$

Finally, we obtain, $\forall y \in \mathcal{S}$:

$$\beta_\mu(x,\rho)(y) = \begin{cases} 0\ if\ d_\mu(x,y) \geq \rho_1 \\ t[\mu(x), \mu(y), c(\rho)(\delta(d_\mu(x,y)))]\ else \end{cases} \tag{42}$$

If t is chosen for instance as the product, $\mu(x)$ and $\mu(y)$ appear as weighting factors.

This definition may appear as severe. A more "optimistic" definition can be derived from the relationship "to the left of", as introduced in [4], but applied here in a simpler 1D case, as:

$$\delta(d_\mu(x,y) \leq \rho) = \begin{cases} 1 & if\ d_\mu(x,y) \leq \rho_1 \\ c(\rho)(d_\mu(x,y)) & if\ d_\mu(x,y) \geq \rho_2 \end{cases} \tag{43}$$

These definitions are illustrated in **Figure 1**.

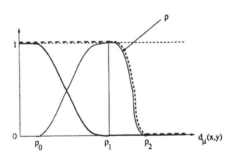

Fig. 1. Illustration of the definition of $\delta(d_\mu(x,y) \leq \rho)$ using the minimum of two fuzzy numbers (continuous dark line) and using the relation "left to" (dashed line).

The two proposed definitions, one being severe and the other more optimistic, can be interpreted as necessity and possibility degrees in the context of possibility theory, or as lower-bound and upper-bound of $\delta(d_\mu(x,y) \leq \rho)$ considered as a rough set. A compromise solution would consist in taking a mean of both values.

Properties The proposed definitions of fuzzy geodesic balls share the following properties (whatever the fuzzy geodesic distance used):

1. $\beta_\mu(x, \rho)(x) = \mu(x)$;
2. $\beta_\mu(x, \rho)(y) \leq \mu(x)$;
3. $\beta_\mu(x, \rho)(y) \leq \mu(y)$;
4. if ρ is a crisp number, $\delta(d_\mu(x, y) \leq \rho)$ is binary, and equal to 1 iff $d_\mu(x, y) \leq \rho$;
5. if μ and ρ are crisp, then $\beta_\mu(x, \rho)$ is the crisp geodesic ball, therefore compatibility with the binary case is achieved;
6. spatial invariance: $\beta_\mu(x, \rho)$ is invariant by translation and rotation;
7. monotony with respect to ρ: if ρ and ρ' are such that $\rho_1 \leq \rho'_1$ and $\rho \leq \rho'$ on $[\rho_0, \rho_1]$ (which is typically the case if ρ' is just a translation of ρ), then $\beta_\mu(x, \rho) \leq \beta_\mu(x, \rho')$, expressing that a fuzzy geodesic ball is included in a fuzzy geodesic ball of same center and "larger" radius;
8. a fuzzy geodesic ball is always included in the Euclidean ball of same radius.

These properties are the fuzzy equivalents of the properties of crisp geodesic balls. This shows the consistency of the proposed extension.

5.2 Fuzzy geodesic mathematical morphology

Translating binary expressions into fuzzy ones In order to extend geodesic morphological operations to fuzzy sets, we translate equations 30 and 31 into fuzzy terms. The idea is to replace formally every binary concept by its fuzzy equivalent, as in Section 2. From these equivalences, more complex relationships can be translated. For instance, the expression $A \subset B$, which is equivalent to $A^C \cup B = S$ is translated as:

$$\inf_{x \in S} T[c(\mu_A)(x), \mu_B(x)],$$

which is a number in $[0, 1]$ representing the degree to which the fuzzy set μ_A is included in the fuzzy set μ_B.

Such translations have already been used for defining Euclidean morphological operators [9], leading to the following generic expressions for the dilation (expressed as a degree of intersection) and erosion (expressed as a degree of inclusion) of a fuzzy set μ by a fuzzy structuring element ν:

$$\forall x \in S, \ D(\mu, \nu)(x) = \sup_{y \in S} t[\mu(y), \nu(y - x)], \tag{44}$$

$$\forall x \in S, \ E(\mu, \nu)(x) = \inf_{y \in S} T[\mu(y), c(\nu(y - x))]. \tag{45}$$

These definitions have good properties in terms of both mathematical morphology and fuzzy sets, as shown in [9]. Therefore we based our work on these definitions. However, the proposed construction of geodesic operators could be applied to any other definition.

Definitions of basic fuzzy geodesic operators The translation of the equations 30 and 31 defining crisp geodesic dilation and erosion into fuzzy terms leads to the following definitions of fuzzy geodesic dilation and erosion of μ' conditionally to μ:

$$\forall x \in S, \ D_\mu^\rho(\mu')(x) = \sup_{y \in S} t[\beta_\mu(x, \rho)(y), \mu'(y)], \tag{46}$$

$$\forall x \in S, \ E_\mu^\rho(\mu')(x) = \inf_{y \in S} T[c(\beta_\mu(x, \rho)(y)), \mu'(y)]. \tag{47}$$

From these two basic operators, other can be defined, as is done in classical morphology. For instance fuzzy geodesic opening and closing are simply defined as:

$$O_\mu^\rho(\mu') = D_\mu^\rho[E_\mu^\rho(\mu')], \tag{48}$$

$$C_\mu^\rho(\mu') = E_\mu^\rho[D_\mu^\rho(\mu')]. \tag{49}$$

Properties The proposed definitions of fuzzy geodesic dilation and erosion have the following properties, which are similar to the properties of classical geodesic operators:

1. compatibility with the crisp case: if μ, μ' and ρ are crisp, the definitions are equivalent to the binary geodesic operators;
2. duality with respect to complementation:

$$\forall x \in S, \ D_\mu^\rho[c(\mu')](x) = c[E_\mu^\rho(\mu')](x),$$

   assuming that the t-norm and the t-conorm used in dilation and erosion respectively are dual with respect to the complementation c;
3. the result of the geodesic dilation of μ' conditionally to μ is included in μ:

$$\forall x \in S, \ D_\mu^\rho(\mu')(x) \leq \mu(x),$$

   expressing that the transformed set stays inside the conditioning set;
4. invariance with respect to geometrical transformations, and local knowledge property;
5. increasingness:

$$\mu' \leq \mu'' \Rightarrow \forall x \in S, D_\mu^\rho(\mu')(x) \leq D_\mu^\rho(\mu'')(x);$$

6. restricted extensivity:

$$\forall x \in S, \ D_\mu^\rho(\mu')(x) \geq t[\mu(x), \mu'(x)];$$

7. interpretation: rewriting the expression of fuzzy geodesic dilation leads to:

$$D_\mu^\rho(\mu')(x) =$$

$$\sup_{y \in S} t[t[\mu(x), \mu(y), \delta(d_\mu(x, y) \le \rho)], \mu'(y)]$$

and, since a t-norm is commutative, associative and increasing:

$$D_\mu^\rho(\mu')(x) =$$

$$t[\mu(x), \sup_{y \in S} t[\mu(y), \mu'(y), \delta(d_\mu(x, y) \le \rho)]].$$

This represents the intersection of μ with the dilation of μ' performed on a neighborhood containing the points y of μ (the conditioning aspect) such that $d_\mu(x, y) \le \rho$ (the geodesic distance aspect). This interpretation is in complete agreement with what is expected from a geodesic dilation.

6 Conclusion

We investigate in this paper links between fuzzy mathematical morphology and fuzzy distances. On the one hand, we propose to define several distances (from a point to a fuzzy set, between two fuzzy sets) from fuzzy dilation. Indeed, expressing distances in a morphological form leads to a consistent extension to fuzzy sets, having nice formal properties. On the other hand, we propose original ways to define fuzzy dilation from fuzzy distances, from which other morphological operations are derived. We deal with both the Euclidean case and the geodesic case. In the Euclidean case, several works have already been done on fuzzy distances and on fuzzy morphology, but without any link between them. Our approach establishes links and allows to propose new definitions. In particular, distances derived from mathematical morphology include spatial information in a convenient way. To our knowledge, much less attention has been paid to the geodesic case. We propose here an original approach to define fuzzy geodesic morphology, based on geodesic distances in a fuzzy set and on the notion of fuzzy ball. The proposed definitions of morphological operators and of fuzzy geodesic balls have nice features: they deal with a direct representation of spatial imprecision in the fuzzy sets, they are consistent with existing binary definitions, they have good formal properties, in agreement with the formal properties of crisp definitions and with intuitive requirements.

Future work include further developments on specific types of distances and derived dilations, and applications in image processing and spatial reasoning. Applications are foreseen for fuzzy image registration, fuzzy pattern recognition in images under imprecision, in particular in a structural framework where the spatial arrangement of objects is important (and therefore distances), and more generally management of spatial imprecision in images.

References

1. B. De Baets. Idempotent Closing and Opening Operations in Fuzzy Mathematical Morphology. In *ISUMA-NAFIPS'95*, pages 228–233, College Park, MD, September 1995.

2. I. Bloch. Distances in Fuzzy Sets for Image Processing derived from Fuzzy Mathematical Morphology. In *Information Processing and Management of Uncertainty in Knowledge-Based Systems*, pages 1307–1312, Granada, Spain, July 1996.

3. I. Bloch. Fuzzy Geodesic Distance in Images. In A. Ralescu and T. Martin, editors, *Lecture Notes in Artificial Intelligence: Fuzzy Logic in Artificial Intelligence, towards Intelligent Systems*, pages 153–166. Springer Verlag, 1996.

4. I. Bloch. Fuzzy relative position between objects in images: a morphological approach. In *IEEE Int. Conf. on Image Processing ICIP'96*, volume II, pages 987–990, Lausanne, September 1996.

5. I. Bloch. On Fuzzy Distances and their Use in Image Processing under Imprecision. Technical report, ENST Paris 97D012, 1997.

6. I. Bloch. Fuzzy Geodesic Mathematical Morphology from Fuzzy Geodesic Distance. In *ISMM'98*, Amsterdam, 1998.

7. I. Bloch. On Links between Fuzzy Morphology and Fuzzy Distances: Euclidean and Geodesic Cases. In *IPMU'98*, Paris, 1998.

8. I. Bloch and H. Maître. Constructing a fuzzy mathematical morphology: alternative ways. In *Second IEEE International Conference on Fuzzy Systems, FUZZ IEEE 93*, pages 1303–1308, San Fransisco, California, March 1993.

9. I. Bloch and H. Maître. Fuzzy Mathematical Morphologies: A Comparative Study. *Pattern Recognition*, 28(9):1341–1387, 1995.

10. I. Bloch, H. Maître, and M. Anvari. Fuzzy Adjacency between Image Objects. *International Journal of Uncertainty, Fuzziness and Knowledge-Based Systems*, 5(6), 1997.

11. V. di Gesu, M. C. Maccarone, and M. Tripiciano. Mathematical Morphology based on Fuzzy Operators. In R. Lowen and M. Roubens, editors, *Fuzzy Logic*, pages 477–486. Kluwer Academic, 1993.

12. D. Dubois and H. Prade. *Fuzzy Sets and Systems: Theory and Applications*. Academic Press, New-York, 1980.

13. J. Serra (Ed.). *Image Analysis and Mathematical Morphology, Part II: Theoretical Advances*. Academic Press, London, 1988.

14. C. Lantuejoul and F. Maisonneuve. Geodesic Methods in Image Analysis. *Pattern Recognition*, 17(2):177–187, 1984.

15. A. T. Popov. Morphological Operations on Fuzzy Sets. In *IEE Image Processing and its Applications*, pages 837–840, Edinburgh, UK, July 1995.

16. A. Rosenfeld. The Fuzzy Geometry of Image Subsets. *Pattern Recognition Letters*, 2:311–317, 1984.

17. A. Rosenfeld. Distances between Fuzzy Sets. *Pattern Recognition Letters*, 3:229–233, 1985.

18. M. Schmitt and J. Mattioli. *Morphologie mathématique*. Masson, Paris, 1994.

19. J. Serra. *Image Analysis and Mathematical Morphology*. Academic Press, London, 1982.

20. D. Sinha and E. Dougherty. Fuzzy Mathematical Morphology. *Journal of Visual Communication and Image Representation*, 3(3):286–302, 1992.

21. D. Sinha and E. R. Dougherty. Fuzzification of Set Inclusion: Theory and Applications. *Fuzzy Sets and Systems*, 55:15–42, 1993.

22. D. Sinha, P. Sinha, E. R. Dougherty, and S. Batman. Design and Analysis of Fuzzy Morphological Algorithms for Image Processing. *IEEE Trans. on Fuzzy Systems*, 5(4):570–584, 1997.

23. L. A. Zadeh. The Concept of a Linguistic Variable and its Application to Approximate Reasoning. *Information Sciences*, 8:199–249, 1975.

An Application of Possibility Theory Information Fusion to Satellite Image Classification

Ludovic ROUX

NASDA–EORC
1—9—9 Roppongi, Minato-ku
TOKYO 106—0032
JAPAN

Abstract. This paper presents the application of an adaptive information fusion operator developed in the framework of possibility theory for the supervised classification of multisource remote sensing images. This operator is low CPU time consuming and carries out classification rates comparable to maximum likelihood.

The adaptive operator has been designed to merge several agreeing information sources which might be in conflict from time to time. It has been used for the classification of two data sets: a Landsat MSS image and GIS data on the one hand, and multitemporal SPOT XS visible images on the other hand. Satellite images of the same scene are redundant and complementary, and this operator is efficient at handling this kind of data.

1 Introduction

Satellite images are used to monitor land cover use, vegetation distribution, sea surface temperature... For any of these applications, a classification of pixels of an image is carried out. To classify a pixel consists in determining to which class it may belong to. The main problem to deal with is usually a poor discrimination between several classes which leads to confusion and wrong decisions. In addition, there is a partial knowledge of classes spectral response, pixels are made up of mixed classes, and the sensor used may be not able to discriminate efficiently some classes. All these problems lead to misclassifications.

The use of several information sources of different types, such as different spectral bands of multispectral images (Landsat, SPOT), and GIS data (Geographic Information System) such as roads location, elevations, slopes, rivers location, cities location — or of multidate images (to make a better distinction of different vegetation species thanks to their different growing periods), allows to improve the discrimination of the classes and to reach a better classification. In fact, these different information sources share the knowledge concerning the classes, they are complementary each other, so their use in an information combination process is very valuable for the classification.

This paper presents the use of an adaptive information fusion operator designed to merge numerous agreeing information sources. It has been proposed by Dubois and Prade [5] in the framework of possibility theory [9] [3] [4].

2 Related Work

Data fusion in remote sensing applications usually makes use of statistical methods in which information is representing using a multivariate normal probability distribution [7] [8]. Such methods are proved to be especially efficient at classifying spectral data which have a Gaussian distribution.

Evidence theory and Dempster-Shafer combination rule have been used successfully to merge data of different types such as spectral and GIS data [7] or multispectral optical image and SAR data [6].

This paper presents the use of an adaptive information fusion method developed in the possibility theory framework for the fusion of spectral and GIS data on the one hand, and the fusion of multitemporal data on the other hand.

3 Information Fusion Operators

A large variety of information fusion operators have been designed in the possibility theory framework. They can be set into three groups, according to their main behaviour.

- Conjunctive type operators: They are useful for merging agreeing sources. They look for the values for which all the sources are agreeing.
- Disjunctive type operators: They should be used for merging conflicting sources. When it is impossible to find a common value on which most of the sources agree, then a disjunctive operator is used to keep all the available information.
- Trade-off type operators: They are used for sources partially in conflict. Means are an example of such operators.

Bloch [1] presents a classification of these operators to provide a guide to help for choosing the most appropriate one for a given problem.

3.1 Conjunctive Operators

This type of fusion operators are efficient to deal with highly agreeing sources. Their main behaviour consists in selecting the information on which all the sources are agreeing. So it is looking for unanimity. If only one source is disagreeing with the others, no common information will be found, and the result of fusion would be void. In this way, conjunctive fusion is unable to deal with conflict.

A conjunctive operator performs an intersection of several fuzzy sets. If no intersection can be found, it means that sources are disagreeing, therefore the result is empty. The most common conjunctive operator is the minimum operator.

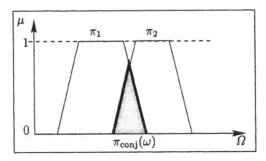

Fig. 1. Conjunctive fusion

For example, assume two sources have to be merged. Let Ω be the referential, and π_1 and π_2 be the two possibility distributions defined respectively for source 1 and source 2. Figure 1 is a simple example of the behaviour of the minimum operator. The possibility distribution π_{conj} resulting from the use of the minimum operator is defined by:

$$\forall \omega \in \Omega, \ \pi_{conj}(\omega) = \min(\pi_1(\omega), \pi_2(\omega)) \tag{1}$$

The effect of a conjunctive operator is to select the most promising information, the one for which all sources agree to say it should be the good value one is looking for.

3.2 Disjunctive Operators

To the opposite of conjunctive operators, there are disjunctive operators. They consider that sources are competing, but they are unable to say which source tells the truth. So disjunctive operators have been designed such that they keep as much information as possible because the good value one is looking for is certainly provided by at least one of the sources, but it is not known which one.

The most popular disjunctive operator is the maximum. It consists simply in selecting the union of fuzzy sets, so that all the information contained in all the sets is kept. Figure 2 shows the result of disjunctive fusion of two possibility distributions π_1 and π_2. The operator π_{disj} is defined as:

$$\forall \omega \in \Omega, \ \pi_{disj}(\omega) = \max(\pi_1(\omega), \pi_2(\omega)) \tag{2}$$

This operator is not sensitive to conflict, but of course its results are very poorly informative. Disjunctive fusion should not be used often, only to help solving cases for which there is a high conflict rate preventing from using a conjunctive operator.

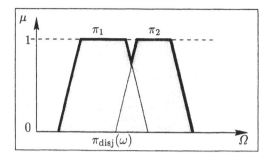

Fig. 2. Disjunctive fusion

4 Adaptive Information Fusion

4.1 Operator Description

Dubois and Prade [5] have proposed an adaptive operator able to switch smoothly from a conjunctive to a disjunctive behaviour according to the amount of conflict between all the information sources.

This operator has a conjunctive behaviour most of the time. Even though a small conflict arises between few sources, the operator will still keep its conjunctive behaviour because most of the sources are agreeing. In other words, this operator selects the agreeing sources and merges them. Sources which create the conflict are considered to be poorly informed and therefore are rejected. So the strong coherence between sources is taken into account. It is only when the conflict is too strong that the operator switches to a more disjunctive behaviour for which sources creating the conflict are not rejected from the fusion process.

It is supposed that most of the time a majority of sources are agreeing, and the true value one is looking for is certainly given by this majority of agreeing sources. One has then to determine which ones are the agreeing sources.

Let Ω be the referential, p be the number of information sources, and π_i the possibility distribution given by a source i. Information coming from the p sources has to be merged. To deal with some possible conflicts, assume that j sources out of p are reliable. The agreggation method consists in selecting a subset J of sources such that $|J| = j$, assuming sources in subset J are reliable, and combining the information they provide in a conjunctive way. But as it is not known which one of the subsets J contains the reliable sources, all the intermediary results are combined in a disjunctive way.

The number j of agreeing sources is unknown. A pessimistic estimation m and an optimistic estimation n ($m \leqslant n$) give an interval of possible values for j:

- $m = \max\{|J|, h(J) = 1\}$ (pessimistic estimation)
- $n = \max\{|J|, h(J) > 0\}$ (optimistic estimation)

$h(J) = \sup_{\omega \in \Omega} \min_{i \in J} \pi_i(\omega)$ is the agreeing degree of the subset of J sources. It corresponds to the highest intersection level reached among the sources composing subset J.

It is supposed that, among the p available sources, it exists a subset of at least m agreeing sources (pessimistic estimation), but there is no more than n agreeing sources (optimistic estimation). It is not possible to determine which sources are the m (resp. n) agreeing sources, but it is assumed it exists a subset J containing these m (resp. n) agreeing sources ($|J| = m$, resp. $|J| = n$) which will be combined in a conjunctive way. It is not known which subset J contains the m (resp. n) sources, so the intermediary results will be combined in a disjunctive way. The pooling for a group of m (resp. n) sources is achieved in the following way:

$$\forall \omega \in \Omega, \; \pi_{(m)}(\omega) = \max_{|J|=m} \min_{i \in J} \pi_i(\omega) \tag{3}$$

Finally, the adaptive information fusion operator is:

$$\forall \omega \in \Omega, \; \pi_{\mathrm{ad}}(\omega) = \max \left(\overbrace{\frac{\pi_{(n)}(\omega)}{h(n)}}^{\mathbf{A}}, \underbrace{\min(1 - h(n), \pi_{(m)}(\omega))}_{\mathbf{B}} \right)$$

where $h(n) = \max\{h(J), |J| = n\}$ is the agreeing degree for the n sources.

This operator is made up of two parts:

- Part A: Renormalized conjunctive fusion used for the most numerous agreeing sources, even though they agree a little (n sources);
- Part B: Outside the intervals defined by part A, some sources might be still agreeing, but a fewer number of sources (m sources) than for part A. Part B has a behaviour which comes closer to disjunction as the number m of agreeing sources comes small. If $m = 1$, then $\pi_{(m)}(\omega)$ of part B is truely a disjunctive fusion.

4.2 Adaptive Operator Behaviour

For example, let us have a look at this operator behaviour on an example with four sources. Each source i provides a possibility distribution π_i about the value of a parameter ω. Two exemples are presented to show the behaviour of the operator in a favourable case when most sources are agreeing, and in a less favourable case when conflict is strong.

Most sources are agreeing (small conflict) (Figure 3)

Two sources (1 and 2) are completely agreeing, so $m = 2$. Three sources (1, 2 and 3) are partially agreeing up to the level $h(\pi_1, \pi_2, \pi_3) = 0.2$, so $n = 3$.

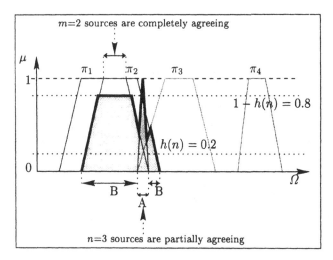

Fig. 3. Small conflict

One can observe that the area defined by the most numerous agreeing sources (part A) is stressed (it is the peak). This is because this area is the one for which most of the sources are agreeing to say it contains the true value (optimistic estimation n). Outside this area, fewer sources can be found agreeing. These sources are still considered to give possibly the good value, but their contribution is restricted up to the level $1 - h(n) = 0.8$. Source 4, which is in conflict with the others, is rejected from the fusion.

Few sources are agreeing (strong conflict) (Figure 4)

No source can be found completely agreeing, so $m = 0$. Only two sources are partially agreeing: Sources 2 and 3 up to the level $h(\pi_2, \pi_3) = 0.7$, and sources 1 and 2 up to the level $h(\pi_1, \pi_2) = 0.5$. So $n = 2$ and the agreeing degree is 0.7, the highest of the two candidates.

The areas defined by the most numerous agreeing sources (parts A) are stressed (the peaks). Outside these areas, no source could be found agreeing, so a disjunctive fusion is applied, but limited to the conflict level $1 - h(n) = 0.3$ of the n partially agreeing sources. The disjunctive behaviour is clearly showed by the part of π_4 included into the result.

5 Implementation of the Operator

The problem consists in using the adaptive fusion for a multisource image classification application. The referential Ω is the grey levels of each image, that is the set $[0, 255]$. Let p be the number of input sources. A source can be either a spectral band of a multispectral image, or a GIS image. Each pixel has to be classified into one out of k classes. Classes are represented by the distribution of

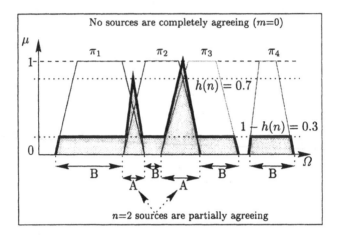

Fig. 4. Strong conflict

their characteristic grey levels. To classify a pixel consists in selecting the class which has a grey level distribution closest to the pixel grey level.

The key element of the adaptive operator is the agreeing degree h which is used to determine the estimations of agreeing sources, and therefore which controls the behaviour of the operator: Either conjunctive if many sources are agreeing or disjunctive if few sources are agreeing.

To keep a behaviour as much adaptive as possible, the determination of the agreeing sources should be made at the pixel level, allowing to have a behaviour designed specially for each pixel. Furthermore, in order to avoid creating much confusion between classes, only one global agreeing degree will be computed for all the classes. For each pixel, all the classes will be processed with the same agreeing degree. Therefore, if a class is highly supported by several sources, it will keep its strong support. But if a class is supported by few sources, it will be rejected because other classes have a better support.

The agreeing degree, *local* to each pixel, but *global* for the classes, is computed as follows:

$$h(\pi_1, \pi_2, \dots, \pi_p) = \max_{\text{class } c=1,k} (\min(\pi_1^c(\omega_1), \pi_2^c(\omega_2), \dots, \pi_p^c(\omega_p))) \qquad (4)$$

ω_i is the grey level of the pixel for image i.

Figure 5 describes the different steps of the processing. First, grey level histograms are computed for each class c and each image from training areas characteristic of classes to be recognized. These histograms are then converted into possibility distributions by using a conversion proposed by Dubois and Prade [2] [4]:

$$\pi^c(\omega) = \sum_{f^c(\gamma) \leqslant f^c(\omega)} f^c(\gamma) \qquad (5)$$

where $f(\omega)$ is the frequency of apparition of grey level ω for class c.

Then possibility measures are evaluated for each pixel of the images according to possibility distributions of each class. Finally all the possibility measures are merged together and each pixel is classified to the class which has the biggest measure.

Such processus is very different from the maximum likelihood. Adaptive fusion deals with each image *separately*, giving for each pixel a different possibility measure $\pi_i^c(\omega_i)$ to each class c.

Maximum likelihood, on the other hand, process information for a pixel as a vector of measures $< \omega_1, \omega_2, \cdots, \omega_p >$. ω_1 is the grey level of the pixel in image 1. Information about class c is represented as being a multivariate normal probability distribution. Two elements compose class c information: the vector μ^c of means of grey levels for class c and the covariance matrix Σ^c of values of measurement vectors of class c. Therefore information is processed in a *global* point of view. Distance between a pixel vector of measures and classes is computed, and the pixel is finally classified in the class which has the smallest distance.

6 Classification Results

The adaptive operator has been tested on a set of Landsat MSS multispectral image and GIS data of Palni hills area (Southern India), and on a multitemporal set of two multispectral SPOT HRV images of Kushiro wetland area (Hokkaidō island, Northern Japan).

A supervised classification is performed for both data sets. Supervised classification is performed through the training of each classifier using characteristic samples of each class. These samples are used to compute the probability and the possibility distributions. Then classifications are performed. The rating of each classification is computed by using testing samples for each class. Testing samples are different from training samples.

6.1 Palni Hills

This set is made up of a multispectral Landsat MSS satellite image (four spectral bands) and of five GIS data sources. The area of study is rather mountainous. The nine classes to be recognized are different kinds of trees and cultivated areas. The tree classes have a very close spectral definition, but the addition of GIS data (Digital Elevation Model, distance to roads, to rivers, to urban areas, and to rivers) allows to improve significantly distinction of each class.

It can be seen on table 1 and on figure 6 that the addition of GIS data helps to make each class more distinguishable from each other. The maximum likelihood classifier performs a better classification than the adaptive fusion both on the spectral bands (67.08% for maximum likelihood versus 54.24% for adaptive fusion) and on the spectral bands plus the GIS data (94.25% versus 86.76%). Data representation as global information with multivariate normal distributions is an appropriate solution. It explains why maximum likelihood performs better classication rates. But when GIS data are added to spectral images, even if maximum likelihood exhibits better classification rates, the classification produced is not much realistic. Spectral information seems to have almost disappeared, replaced by GIS data. The quality of classification provided by adaptive fusion is better. The pooling of sources made by adaptive fusion gives indirectly more importance to the spectral bands than to the GIS data. Spectral bands are highly coherent, therefore they agree most of the time. GIS data, on the other hand, are poorly coherent, and they provide often contradictory information. Therefore, by selecting the most numerous group of agreeing sources, which is often made up by a core of spectral bands, adaptive fusion gives more importance to spectral bands.

6.2 Kushiro

The Kushiro data set consists of two multispectral SPOT XS images (three spectral bands for each image) which cover two different seasons: May 22nd 1991 and July 13th 1994. The area of study is a wetland. The ten classes to be recognized are different kinds of vegetation found in this area, plus two kinds of forests, water and city. The use of multidate images allows to improve distinction of vegetation which have a different reflectance on May and on July.

SPOT spectral bands are highly coherent, there is nearly no conflict to handle. Maximum likelihood and adaptive fusion perform rather similar classifications. So even if adaptive fusion handles information of each class in a local way, separately for each image, it is able to perform classification almost as good as maximum likelihood.

7 Conclusion

The adaptive operator presented is able to handle a large number of mainly agreeing sources and to solve the conflict problems which may arise. It deals with conflict by selecting the agreeing sources and removing the conflicting sources from the fusion process.

Its application to a supervised satellite images classification example shows that it is able to perform classification almost similar as maximum likelihood. It has the advantage to require few *a priori* information, and to perform fast computations because it uses low cost operations (mainly comparisons). Furthermore, if data of different types have to be merged, such as spectral information and GIS data, the results of adaptive fusion are more realistic than those of maximum likelihood.

Acknowledgements

The Kushiro images set has been kindly provided by NASDA.

	Landsat MSS 4 bands	Landsat MSS 4 bands	Landsat 4 bands + 5 GIS data	Landsat 4 bands + 5 GIS data
	ML	**AF**	**ML**	**AF**
Class 1	74.95%	46.08%	99.13%	97.79%
Class 2	78.00%	48.53%	95.21%	96.08%
Class 3	2.29%	40.07%	98.37%	59.93%
Class 4	68.54%	46.18%	66.50%	84.41%
Class 5	63.62%	56.37%	89.54%	82.60%
Class 6	82.14%	67.40%	97.60%	85.78%
Class 7	65.58%	56.62%	99.13%	75.25%
Class 8	90.20%	72.06%	100.00%	92.89%
Class 9	57.08%	48.77%	100.00%	96,81%
Avg.	**67.08%**	**54.24%**	**94.25%**	**86.76%**

ML = maximum likelihood, AF = Adaptative Fusion
Table 1. Palni hills classification rates.

	May22,91	May22,91	July13,94	July13,94	May22,91 +July13,94	May22,91 +July13,94
	ML	**AF**	**ML**	**AF**	**ML**	**AF**
Class 1	53.57%	82.14%	51.79%	71.43%	100.00%	92.86%
Class 2	99.62%	100.00%	99.81%	98.86%	99.81%	100.00%
Class 3	76.92%	95.80%	80.42%	44.06%	75.52%	82.52%
Class 4	8.36%	20.43%	98.76%	63.78%	93.50%	88.24%
Class 5	38.89%	59.26%	3.70%	51.85%	74.07%	61.11%
Class 6	22.38%	5.59%	13.99%	14.69%	44.06%	21.68%
Class 7	97.90%	80.42%	99.30%	84.62%	100.00%	100.00%
Class 8	80.95%	76.01%	100.00%	99.12%	99.65%	98.06%
Class 9	75.81%	90.55%	83.64%	61.29%	92.86%	97.70%
Class 10	96.47%	100.00%	37.06%	93.53%	100.00%	100.00%
Avg.	**71.74%**	**75.18%**	**83.82%**	**77.60%**	**92.81%**	**91.36%**

ML = maximum likelihood, AF = Adaptative Fusion
Table 2. Kushiro classification rates.

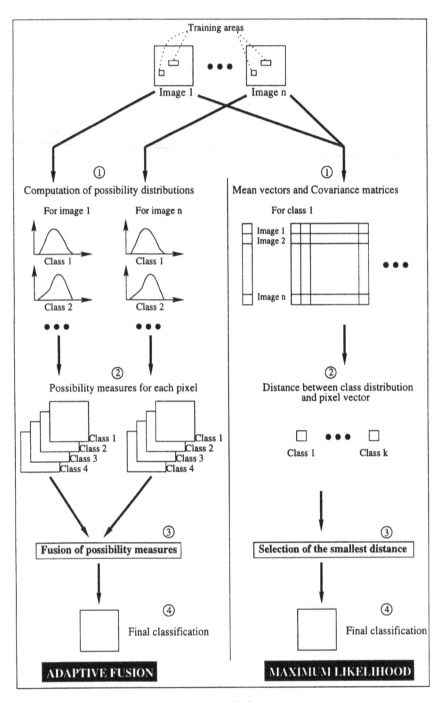

Fig. 5. Description of the processus.

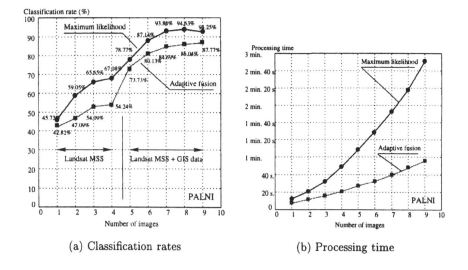

(a) Classification rates (b) Processing time

Fig. 6. Palni (images size: 512 × 512)

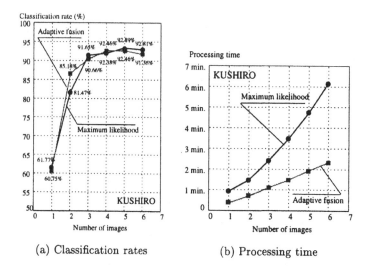

(a) Classification rates (b) Processing time

Fig. 7. Kushiro (images size: 1024 × 1024)

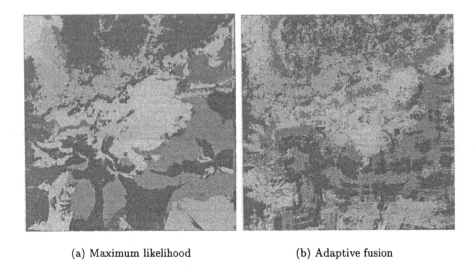

(a) Maximum likelihood   (b) Adaptive fusion

Fig. 8. Palni hills: Result images after fusion of the four spectral bands of Landsat MSS plus the five GIS data.

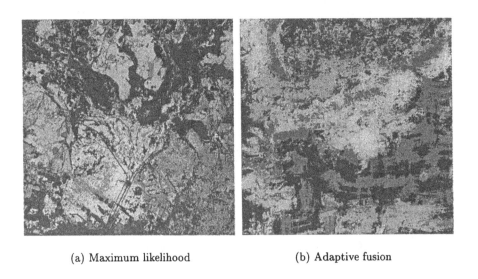

(a) Maximum likelihood   (b) Adaptive fusion

Fig. 9. Kushiro: Result images after fusion of the two SPOT HRV images.

References

1. Isabelle Bloch. Information combination operators for data fusion: A comparative review with classification. *IEEE Transactions on Systems, Man and Cybernetics, part A: systems and humans*, 26(1):52–67, 1996.
2. Didier Dubois and Henri Prade. Unfair coins and necessity measures: Towards a possibilistic interpretation of histograms. *Fuzzy Sets and Systems*, 10:15–20, 1983.
3. Didier Dubois and Henri Prade. *Théorie des possibilités, applications à la représentation des connaissances en informatique*. Masson, $2^{\text{ème}}$ edition, novembre 1987.
4. Didier Dubois and Henri Prade. *Possibility Theory, an Approach to the Computerized Processing of Uncertainty*. Plenum Press, New York, 1988.
5. Didier Dubois and Henri Prade. Possibility theory and data fusion in poorly informed environments. *Control Engineering Practice*, 2(5):811–823, 1994.
6. Sylvie Le Hégarat-Mascle, Isabelle Bloch, and D. Vidal-Madjar. Application of dempster-shafer evidence theory to unsupervised classification in multisource remote sensing. *IEEE Transactions on Geoscience and Remote Sensing*, 35(4):1018–1031, July 1997.
7. Tong Lee, John A. Richards, and Philip H. Swain. Probabilistic and evidential approaches for multisource data analysis. *IEEE Transactions on Geoscience and Remote Sensing*, GE-25(3):283–293, May 1987.
8. Anne H. Schistad Solberg, Anil K. Jain, and Torfinn Taxt. Multisource classification of remotely sensed data: Fusion of landsat tm and sar images. *IEEE Transactions on Geoscience and Remote Sensing*, 32(4):768–778, July 1994.
9. Lotfi Zadeh. Fuzzy sets as a basis for a theory of possibility. *Fuzzy Sets and Systems*, 1:3–28, 1978.

Pattern Recognition of Strong Graphs Based on Possibilistic c-means and k-formulae Matching

L. Wendling, J. Desachy

Université Paul Sabatier - IRIT
118, route de Narbonne
31062 Toulouse Cedex, FRANCE (33)
email: wendling@irit.fr

Abstract. A new graph matching approach based on 1D information is presented. Each node of the matched graphs represents a fuzzy region (fuzzy segmentation step). Each couple of nodes is linked by a relational histogram which can be assumed to the attraction of two regions following a set of directions. This attraction is computed by a continuous function, depending on the distance of the matched objects. Each case of the histogram corresponds to a particular direction. Then, relational graph computed from strong scenes are matched.

1 Introduction

In this paper a new pattern recognition system, based on sample images, is presented. An object to be recognized is described by one scene or by a set of little images. Then, a fuzzy segmentation step is performed in order to split an image into a fuzzy partition which consists in a set of fuzzy regions. For each fuzzy region both topological and relational features can be computed (methods based on atomic regions and hierarchical trees have also been proposed in previous papers [6] [20]). In the proposed approach each couple of regions of the image is linked by a histogram of forces. So, an image is defined as a relational graph. The same process is applied to another images to match. Then, a new approach of matching based on strong relational graph is defined.

2 Pattern Recognition System

Our pattern recognition system (figure 1) consists in five parts.

1. Input data (grey levels or RGB color images).
2. Fuzzy segmentation: To split the image into a set of fuzzy regions.
3. Relations, features of regions.
4. A data base composed of typical relational graphs to match.
5. Decision part to give a distance measure between two matched scenes.

Each part performs a particular process to split the image into a relational graph and to take a decision: Scenes are similar or not.

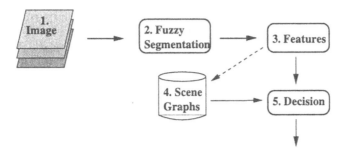

Fig. 1. System Description.

3 Fuzzy Region Definition

First part of the proposed system performs a fuzzy segmentation from the input image. The goal of fuzzy segmentation method is to manage with imprecise boundaries [18] [9] and to allow to a pixel to belong more ore less to a given region. Crisp segmentation [13] is a particular case of fuzzy segmentation and can be achieved with a max criteria applied to a fuzzy partition [3].

Most of the fuzzy segmentation methods are based on the definition of fuzzy partitions using fuzzy c-means algorithms [3]. Nevertheless these approaches give noisy and non-totally coherent results [8] [4].

A recent method proposed by Krishnapuram [10] seems to overcome these problems. His method is independent of the interclass distance and is based on a "good" membership profile [21]. The initialisation of the defined algorithm is fundamental to achieve partitions. Barny & al. [1] have shown that the use of c-means algorithm to define the input partition can fail by defining indentical clusters. This problem can be solve if possibilistic c-means algorithm [12] is used with a number of classes equal to 1.

First any point of the result cluster is set at 1. Then the most favourable cluster (defined from both validity criteria and partitions variations between two steps) is carried out. If such a class is found, points of cluster data which most verify this achieved cluster are removed from the image partition (clusters RGB in a color image, for example). Processing is runned again until the achievement of unconsistent clusters (too small for example) is performed. Currently clusters validity algorithms have generally high processing time with sometimes unconsistent results [8]. Moreover, it exists no mathematic models to define what is a "good" partition.

In the present system, this algorithm has been applied with a level cut criteria to decrease processing time (0.8s on a 100 MHz SUN SPARC 4). Then a partition composed of fuzzy clusters is achieved.

A fuzzy region is defined as being a set of connected pixels with a non-zero membership value. At this step, the system has defined the set of fuzzy regions (nodes of the graph). Then, these regions can linked with relational features to define a relational graph.

4 Fuzzy Relational Graph

First, each region is assumed to its centroid. Then, we can compute the 1D relation which links each couple of nodes.

In previous works, features, computed on pixels [16] or level-cuts [5] [7], are often used to distinguish objects. The main problem of these methods is to define the most significant features which depend on the application.

In this paper, a new relational matching based on histogram of angles and forces notion is proposed. Histogram of forces is a generalisation of Miyajima and Ralescu histogram of angles [15] with isotrop segments.

Let A and B two objects and θ a direction. The histogram value assumed to θ consists in a Riemann sum of combination of segments of A and B. An object is composed by a set of parallel segments (one pixel height) following a direction. The function apply between a segment of a region A and a segment of a region B, bear by the same straight line, takes into account the distance notion: The farer the objects, the lesser the value of the linking continuous function is. This process can be assumed to be the projection of the information onto an one dimension space in regard to both matched regions.

This approach allows to have a low processing time and to manage with non-disjoint and fuzzy objects. Such a function is entirely detailed in [14].

5 Matching between Strong Graphs

5.1 Graph Structure

It is well known that graph isomorphism problem is not deterministic (except for special kinds of graphs). The present approach manages with a particular class of graphs: Graphs with strong structure. The structure is achieved after computing histogram of forces between regions using their centroid.

In a graph G, an edge between two nodes s and t is single. A set of values is beared by each edge. Edges can be double, but as information, given by histogram of forces, is symmetric a preorder is set.

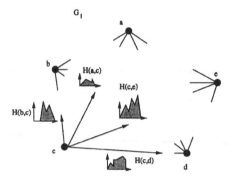

Fig. 2. Relational Graph.

5.2 Similarity Ratio

Let A be a histogram of forces linking vertex s to t in a graph G_1 and B be the histogram of forces linking vertex u to v in a graph G_2. A and B are superimposed in order to compute a distance between them from their common parts (figure 3).

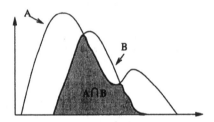

Fig. 3. Histogram Superimposition.

In the present application, a similarity ratio has been chosen to match A and B. It is obvious that other distance measures can be used. Nevertheless, the calculus of a similarity ratio is low processing time and takes into account all the histogram information. Let ν be the number of steps of each histogram, i.e. the number of digitized directions. The cardinal of intersection of histogram A and B is given by:

$$|A \cap B| = \sum_{i=1,\nu} min(A[i], B[i])$$

$|A|$ represents the cardinal of the histogram A. By definition, A and B can be null if nodes (fuzzy regions) s, t, u and v exist (that's due to the positive function applied). Then, the similarity ratio is computed as follows:

$$S(A, B) = \frac{|A \cap B|}{max(|A|, |B|)}$$

5.3 k-formula Computation

Strong graphs, i.e. rigid structures, are taken into account.

Let θ be an orientation and let s and t be two nodes of a graph G_1. Let P_t and P_s be the respective projections of s and t following a directional straight line D_θ defined with a θ angle rotation from the frame image. If P_t is lower than P_s on D_θ (figure 4.b), an edge from t to s, denoted $t \rightarrow_{G_1} s$, is carried out. Vertice are sorted (quick sort method) following an orientation θ to construct the associated k-formula.

This step is carried out for all the nodes of the Graph G_1. The set of k-formulas which defined the graph G_1, following the direction θ, is so performed.

The same processing is carried out for all the nodes of graph G_2 and following a given direction. Then, a set of k-formulas [2] has been computed from each graph (figure 4.a). At last, the k-formulas of graph G_1 are matched with the K-formulas of graph G_2.

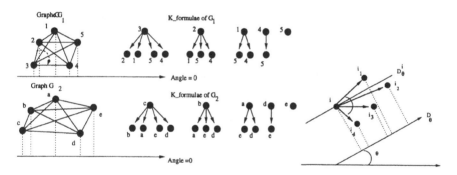

Fig. 4. k-formulae definition (projection).

The final recognition rate is given either by the mean similarity ratio following the optimal direction (which corresponds to a histogram shift) or by the minimum similarity ratio following the optimal direction.

The choice of the decision criteria (minimal or mean) can be brought by the number of nodes and depends to the kind of the current application. For example, to take a minimum criteria with graph belonging a large number of nodes can induce a drowning phenomena.

An application, of such an approach, to the case of real scenes matching is presented in section 6.

5.4 Matching Algorithm

The processing performed by our pattern recognition system can be summarized as follows:

Match(G_1, G_2)
Input: Two Graphs.
Output: Recognition Rate.
{

    Fuzzy Segmentation
    Regions Localization and Graph definition
    G_1 and G_2 Histogram of forces
    k-formulas definition of G_1 (quicksort)
    Similarity $= 0$
    For any direction θ (histogram digitization) **Do**
    {

        k-formulas definition of G_2 (quicksort)
        $\lambda \Leftarrow$ Matching between k-formulas of G_1 and G_2
        Similarity $\Leftarrow$ max(Similarity,λ)

    }

}

Fig. 5. Matching.

5.5 Complexity

The case of any k-formulae for a given graph is processed. Given an angle θ, comparisons between k-formulae of graphs G_1 and G_2 are carried out. This processing is performed for any θ and the recognition rate is set to the maximal similarity ratio.

The maximal complexity associated to the matching is in $\mathcal{O}(n^2)$ time (with $n = |G_1| = |G_2|$).

Nevertheless complexity of the method depends on the k-formulae definition. If a quicksort is used, a K-formulas with n_1 sons is build in $\mathcal{O}(n_1 \ln n_1)$ time. So, the building of all the k-formulas of a graph G, with $|G| = n+1$ needs $f = \sum_{i=1}^{n} i \ln i$ operations. Then, let us put down the following proposition:

Proposition 1. $\forall n \in \mathbf{N}^*$, we have:

$$\frac{1}{2}\left(n^2 \ln n - \frac{n^2}{2} - \frac{1}{2}\right) \leq \sum_{i=1}^{n} i \ln i \leq \frac{1}{2}\left((n+1)^2 \ln(n+1) - \frac{(n+1)^2}{2} - \frac{1}{2}\right)$$

A simple demonstration by recurrence can be used to check these two inegalities. The function f is strictly increasing (and continuous). The boundaries functions have been defined by the integration of f following the rectangle method (area of f minored and majored by both minimal and maximal rectangle integration functions).

Finally, it is easy to deduce that the maximal complexity of the proposed approach is in $\mathcal{O}(n^2 \ln n)$ time.

6 Application with Color Scenes

An application of the previous described method is given now. It consists in matching two RGB scenes supposed strong.

Scene 1, fuzzy partition (A_1, A_2, A_3) Scene 2, fuzzy partition (B_1, B_2, B_3)

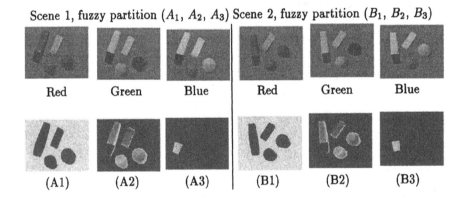

Red Green Blue Red Green Blue

(A1) (A2) (A3) (B1) (B2) (B3)

Fig. 6. Matched scenes.

Both acquisition height and orientation of images are different.

Two methods have been applied. First, an isomorphism search between graph G_1 (defined by the five regions included in clusters A_2 and A_3) and graph G_2 (clusters B_2 and B_3) is performed. For each couple of regions a histogram of forces is computed. The digitization step is equal to $1/256$. Using a lower step, value variation of the final rate is under 10^{-4} order.

Figures (i) and (ii) (next page) show similarity ratio variation from angle rotation in $[-\pi, \pi]$ interval.

A mean similarity rate of 89.84%, between the two scenes, is reached with a 28.13 degrees shift (case (i)).

Of course, if the number of regions is important then similarity ratio should be high even if a region is bad. So, it can be interesting to compute the minimal similarity ratio (following optimal angle) (case (ii)). In the present example, it reached 78.47%.

These curves (i) and (ii) show that an A^* heuristic can be useful to decrease processing time. In the present approach an A^* heuristic has been defined to find the most characteristic directed acyclic graph. This algorithm is based on distance minimal from an edge of graph G_1 and any of graph G_2 (up to a translation in the matched histograms of forces to find the best probable direction) and by building G_2 with an optimal cost.

The application of such a heuristic gives the same similarity ratio achieved result, but fastly. Moreover, this heuristic can be also applied to the case of strong subgraphs.

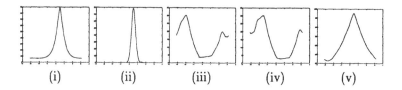

Fig. 7. (i), (ii), (v): Similarity ratio variation; (iii), (iv): Histogram of forces between clusters.

In a second approach, each cluster is assumed to be a single region. The histogram of forces linking the second and the third cluster on figures (iii) - A_2 with A_3 - and (iv) - B_2 with B_3 -. In this case, a maximal similarity ratio of 95.44% is reached for a 25.31 degrees shift.

The acquizition image height is fairly different and histogram normalized (to avoid the zoom factor) has given a weak improvement of 0.3%. Similarity ratio variations are given in figure (v).

This other approach is useful because it is not necessary to define each region (set of connected pixels with no zero membership value) contained in the clusters of a fuzzy partition. As a consequence, the number of matches is lower than in the previous method (ten time lower).

Such an approach can be assumed to be a distance measure between two models.

Hence this method is less discriminant than the previous one which takes into account any region of a partition. Then, relational information are lost. A better ratio is reached but it does not give a better idea of the reality. This result is relative to the partition quality. In the present approach the main information is located in the second cluster (B_2 and A_2).

If a cluster validity criteria is taken, which limits the number of regions per cluster and selects only the most dense part of the cluster, it is obvious to think that the number of clusters per partition should be increased and the number of regions per partition should be decreased. In this case, the second approach becomes more interesting because relational information is rather located in an inter-partition scheme.

It is possible to apply this kind of approach even with noised areas (the function used to defined histogram of forces take into account disjoint information). Moreover, in the previous approach, noise must be removed to keep "dense" areas, which induces lost of information.

The proposed approach has been applied with success on more complex scenes (up to twenty five nodes and seven clusters). When we take into account two small regions the present approach fail down. That is not the case when we work only with clusters.

Currently, our aim is to consider the search of maximal subgraph to improve the matching.

7 Conclusion

In this paper, a method of pattern recognition based on relational graphs and k-formulae definition has been proposed. This approach, which has a low processing time, has given interesting results using objects with strong structure.

Currently, the present algorithm is applied to more complex scenes (about a hundrend of nodes) and we try to extend the present approach to the case of subgraph matching in order to take into account the problem of small regions.

Nevertheless, the present approach is limited on a particular class of graphs. We try to generalize our approach to manage with non-totally ordonned graph. Our aim is to define a progressive algorithm managing with the case of strong structure to general structure.

References

1. M. Barni, V. Cappellini and A. Mecocci, *Comments on "A Possibilistic Approach to Clustering"*, IEEE Transactions on Fuzzy Systems, vol 4:3, 1996, pp 393-396

2. A.T. Berztiss, *A Backtrack Procedure for Isomorphism of Directed Graphs*, Journal of the Association for Computing Machinery, vol 20:3, 1973, pp 365-377

3. J.C. Bezdek, *Pattern Recognition with Fuzzy Objective Function Algorithms*, Plenum Press, New York, 1981

4. R.N. Dave, *Characterization and Detection of Noise in Clustering*, Pattern Recognition Letters, vol 12, 1991, pp 657-664

5. D. Dubois and M.C. Jaulent, *A General Approach to Parameter Evaluation in Fuzzy Digital Pictures*, Pattern Recognition Letters, vol 6, 1987, pp 251-261

6. P. Dhérété, L. Wendling and J. Desachy, *Fuzzy Segmentation and Astronomical Images Interpretation*, ICIAP'95-IAPR, Springer-Verlag, Lecture Notes in Computer Science 974, 1995, pp 21-27

7. R. Krishnapuram, J.M. Keller and Y. Ma, *Quantitative Analysis of Properties and Spatial Relations of Fuzzy Image Regions*, IEEE Transactions on Fuzzy Systems, vol 1:3, 1993, pp 222-233

8. R. Krishnapuram, *Generation of Membership Functions via Possibilistic Clustering*, 3rd IEEE Conference on Fuzzy System, vol 3, 1994, pp 902-908

9. J.M. Keller and C.L. Carpenter, *Image Segmentation in the Presence of Uncertainty*, International Journal of Intelligent System, vol 5:2, 1990, pp 193-208

10. R. Krishnapuram, *Fuzzy Clustering Methods in Computer Vision*, EUFIT'93, 1993, pp 720-730

11. R. Krishnapuram and J.M. Keller, *A Possibilistic Approach to Clustering*, IEEE Transactions on Fuzzy Systems, vol 1:2, 1993, pp 98-110

12. R. Krishnapuram and J.M. Keller, *The Possibilistic C-Means Algorithm: Insights and Recommendations*, IEEE Transactions on Fuzzy Systems, vol 4:3, 1996, pp 385-393

13. S. L. Horowitz and T. Pavlidis, *Picture Segmentation by a Directed Split and Merge Procedure*, 2nd International Conference on Pattern Recognition, 1974, pp 424-433

14. P. Matsakis, L. Wendling and J. Desachy, *Représentation de la position relative d'objets 2D au moyen d'un histogramme de forces*, revue Traitement du Signal, accepté, 1997.

15. K. Miyajima and A. Ralescu, *Spatial Organization in 2D Segmented Images: Representation and Recognition of Primitive Spatial Relations*, Fuzzy Sets and Systems, vol. 65, 1994, pp 225-236

16. A. Rosenfeld, *Fuzzy Geometry: An Overview*, First IEEE Conference on Fuzzy Systems, 1992, pp 113-118

17. A. Rosenfeld, R. Hummel and S. Zucker, *Scene labelling by relaxation operations*, IEEE Transactions on Systems, Man and Cybernetics, SMC-6, 1976, pp 420-433

18. E.H. Ruspini, *A New Approach to Clustering*, Inform. and Control, vol 15, 1969, pp 22-32

19. L. Wendling, *Segmentation floue appliquée à la reconnaissance d'objets dans les images numériques*, Ph.D. thesis, Université Paul Sabatier, Toulouse, 1997

20. L. Wendling, A. Pariès and J. Desachy, *Pattern Recognition by Splitting Images into Trees of Fuzzy Regions*, International Journal of Intelligent Data Analysis, 1997

21. H. J. Zimmerman and P. Zysno, *Quantifying Vagueness in Decision Models*, European J. Operational Res., vol 22, 1985, pp 148-158

A Fuzzy-Neural Model for Co-ordination in Air Traffic Flow Management

Leïla ZERROUKI [(1,2)] Bernadette BOUCHON-MEUNIER[(2)] Rémy FONDACCI [(1)]

(1) INRETS, 2 Avenue du Général Malleret-Joinville 94 114 Arcueil
(2) LIP6, tour 46-0, 4 place Jussieu 75252 Paris Cedex 05
Tel: (331) 47 40 71 05
Fax : (331) 45 47 56 06
E-Mail: zerouki@inrets.fr.

Abstract:
The paper presents a methodological approach in the area of complex system studies. It provides a description of a model aimed at protecting air traffic sectors against overload in a large-scale air traffic system. In such a problem, different aspects must be taken into account : data uncertainty, complexity due to the large dimension of the air traffic system, structural and functional interactions, etc. The model proposed is a decentralised and co-ordinated system composed of a co-ordination level and a control level. The study points on the co-ordination level which decomposes the large sector network into several smaller overlapping subnetworks that can be controlled independently. A modified interaction prediction method is developed using a fuzzy model. This model provides the co-ordination parameters on the basis of imprecise data and an approximate reasoning. A specific inference mechanism based on a neural network is adopted in order to reduce time inference costs and provide a satisfying output.

Keywords :
Large-scale System, Decomposition, Fuzzy Model, Approximate Reasoning, Neural Network, Air Traffic Flow Management.

1 Introduction

Airspace under control is composed of a set of control sectors with limited capacities. However capacity of an air traffic sector and traffic demand vary randomly over space and time, depending on several uncontrollable factors. These random aspects cause saturation of the control sectors. So as to overcome this problem Air Traffic Flow Management (A.T.F.M) activity has to distribute traffic flows and fit the air traffic demand to the system capacity by minimising costs and inconveniences [Odoni, 1987]. This activity concerns generally a large-scale air traffic system, and operates some months to few minutes before the predicted overload.

Most of existing A.T.F.M models are based on operational research techniques, Odoni [1987] ; Vranas et al [1994]; Bertsimas and Stock [1994]. These

optimisation models need a long computation time and are suitable for pre-tactical and tactical A.T.F.M filters corresponding to some days to few hours before the predicted overloads. Nevertheless, it seems interesting to develop a tool that acts 20 to 60 minutes before the overloads corresponding to a new A.T.F.M filter called the short-term filter [NOAA, 1996]. In order to cope with the computation time complexity a multi-level model was proposed in Zerrouki et al. [1997]. It is composed of a co-ordination level and a control level. In this paper we discuss the choice of an adequate fuzzy model that provides the co-ordination parameters to the control level. The fuzzy prediction model that has to be developed must respect two antagonistic properties : the accuracy of the inferred interaction prediction, and time complexity constraint.

2 Decomposition of A.T.F.M System

The model proposed attempts to overcome the computation time inconvenience by using the multilevel theory approach developed by Mesarovic et al. [1970]. Based on the system decomposition principles: the temporal, the structural and the functional decomposition, it transforms a large and complex system into several but simplified subsystems.

2.1 Structure and Time Decomposition

As it is difficult to determine a continuous model of dynamic behaviour of a large and complex air traffic network, a discrete time model is then proposed. A preventive approach is used based on a sliding prediction horizon. The large air traffic network is divided into several smaller sub-networks, the decomposition into interconnected subsystems is based on:

- data analysis of the A.T.F.M system, aggregations and global behaviours of the system are then deduced.
- spatio-temporal reasoning on the A.T.FM network.
- computation time analysis of the control units.

These tasks are achieved with the help of several modules called system analysis modules and presented below :

Prediction Module
It provides the prediction of the air traffic demand, sector capacity and weather conditions.

Simulation Module
It computes for each decision step the future sector load prediction and detects the congested sectors.

Decomposition Module
It decomposes the overall A.T. F..M network into basic subnetworks, and provides a dynamic data base associated to each subnetwork. The data base is built on the basis of the alert concept. One alert corresponds to an overload detected by the simulation module in a given sector occurring during the prediction horizon. Each

basic subnetwork is formed by the overloaded sector and its neighbourhood which is a set of sectors surrounding the saturated sector .

Interaction Evaluation Module

It has to analyse the possible effects caused by a basic subnetwork regulation action on another basic subnetwork and deduces some dependence indicators. The identification of the interaction is based on the system science [Auger, 1993], two kinds of interactions have been identified in this study: the inter-dependence which occurs when two subnetworks have common regulation sectors, and the intra-dependence occurring when there are common flows crossing both subnetworks Fig. 1 shows that sectors s and s' are common regulation sectors for a rerouting action, so there is an inter-dependence relation between the subnetworks i and j.

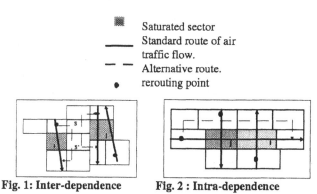

Fig. 1: Inter-dependence   **Fig. 2 : Intra-dependence**

Fig. 2 shows that the rerouting action of the subnetwork j reduces the traffic of subnetwork i and induces a decrease of the saturation of this subnetwork. There is an intra-dependence relation between the two subnetworks.

In addition to the interaction relation identification, the module evaluates the interaction indicators that give a dependence level between two subnetworks at each decision step. According to the nature of the interaction two indicators are then defined :

- Inter-dependence indicator ($INTER_{i,j}(s,kl,k)$) is evaluated at each decision step k, for each sectors s common to two inter-dependent subnetworks i and j. It is equal to the proportion of the regulated flows of subnetwork i that could arrive in the sector s at the same decision step (kl) as the flows regulated by subnetwork j.

- Intra-dependence indicator ($INTRA_{i,j}(k)$) is evaluated for each pairs of intra-dependent subnetworks i and j. It is equal to the proportion of flows of subnetwork i that could be regulated through subnetwork j.

Network Merging Module

It merges several basic subnetworks into one subnetwork according to the interaction levels and the computation capacity constraints imposed by the control units.

2.2 Functional Decomposition

The air trafic management system provides the regulation actions using two functional levels, the control level composed of several control units that are assigned to each subnetwork provided by the system analysis procedure. The actions of the control units are co-ordinated by the co-ordination level.

2.2.1 Co-ordination Level

The co-ordination task is realised by the interaction prediction module detailed in the next section. Its aim is to provide to the local control units the co-ordination parameters so as to achieve the overall optimum of the system. The strategy used for the co-ordination is the interaction prediction approach.

Interaction prediction principle :

Interaction prediction principle is to predict a set of interaction inputs α_i , i= 1..n for the n interconnected control units. Each control unit introduces the predicted values in the local optimisation computation, the control actions $M_i(\alpha_i)$ are then inferred, and induce the actual interactions denoted $U_i(\alpha_i)$. The overall optimum is achieved if the predicted interactions are equal to the actual interactions occurring when the actions $M_i(\alpha_i)$ are implemented ($\alpha_i = U_i(\alpha_i)$).

For the existing co-ordination strategies, the co-ordination is reached and effectively implemented by the control units at the end of multiple iterative data transfer between the control and co-ordination levels and it is consequently not suitable for the short-term or real-time applications. So the model proposes an improvement of the previous strategy by introducing a fuzzy interaction prediction model. This model presents some specific advantages :

* Learning :
Fuzzy model can be identified by learning techniques from analytical data obtained through the existing operational research models. Even if this existing models are not suitable in real-time for a large-scale system, they can be applied during an off-line phase, on the overall network in order to generate the necessary identification data.

* Approximation :
The basic motivation of using fuzzy models is to deduce simple and fast approximations of too complex operational research models (time computation complexity). It could use some aggregated and imprecise knowledge about the A.T.F.M network behaviour and deduce a first and accurate approximation of the interaction parameters. This accurate prediction should lead to a reduction of the data transfer between the co-ordination level and the control level.

2.2.2 Control Level

A specific control unit is assigned to each subnetwork. Because of its reduced dimension, each control unit computes independent control actions in an acceptable computation time, by using the existing classical operational research techniques. This local optimisation of the control units are co-ordinated by the interaction prediction parameters inferred by the co-ordination level. For the A.T.F.M case the co-ordination parameter is equivalent to a sector capacity variation. So each control unit takes into account the effects of another control unit, on its associated subnetwork and compensates these control action effects by using an artificial sector capacity in the local operational research model.

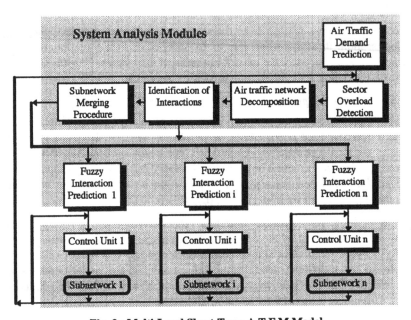

Fig. 3 : Multi-Level Short-Term A.T.F.M Model

3 Fuzzy Interaction Prediction Model (F.I.P)

Having the merged subnetworks provided by the merging model, the interaction prediction module has to define an artificial sector loads and capacities allocation for the interacted subnetworks. In fact, even if the merging model has taken into account the highest intra-dependence level, it remains some subnetworks strongly intra-dependent still not merged because of the computation capacity constraints. Hence, in order to perform a parallel and co-ordinated optimisation by the control units, according to the interaction prediction methods, this module has to predict the action effects of a subnetwork on the other subnetwork and compensate this effects by modifying artificially the sector capacities and loads.

In order to provide the interaction prediction for the control units, it is necessary to take into account all kind of available knowledge about the subnetwork behaviour. However, the knowledge gathered on the interaction relations is based on aggregated and imprecise values such as the intra-dependence, the inter-dependence indicators, the load predictions etc. For this reason, fuzzy logic seems to be the appropriate tool to deal with imprecision performing an approximate reasoning that deduces the interaction prediction. In the limit of this paper, only the inter-dependence interactions are presented, a similar model can be build for intra-dependence interaction.

3.1 Structure Identification of the Fuzzy Model

In the fuzzy prediction module, the facts in the knowledge base are represented by means of two linguistic input variables, the inter-dependence indicator provided by the Interaction Evaluation Model and the load of saturated sector provided by the simulation model. The output inferred variable represents the prediction effect of the regulation action of a subnetwork i on an inter-dependent subnetwork j. In the case of inter-dependence relation, interaction prediction is a variation of the capacity of a common sector s (Cf. Fig. 1). Actually, the output variable is equivalent to the proportion of flights that are regulated in the subnetwork i through the sector s. This value has to be subtracted from the real capacity of the common sector s in the subnetwork j in order to take into account the regulation effect of the subnetwork i. The resulting value represents the artificial capacity of the sector s, in the subnetwork j.

The input and output variables are defined respectively on the universes $X1$, $X2$ and Y and partitioned by means of fuzzy characteristics. For simplicity, we present the linguistic model for a partition composed of 3 fuzzy characteristics {Small, Medium, Large}.

Two-input variables:
$INTER_{i,j}(s,kl,k)$: inter-dependence indicator.
$SC_i(S, T)$: load of the saturated sector S of the subnetwork i, predicted for the decision step T.

Single output variable:
$\Delta CAP_{ij}(s,kl)$: the capacity variation of the common regulation sector s at the decision step kl, in the subnetwork j.
The rules of the fuzzy interaction prediction model (F.I.P) are formulated as follows:

For all non merged inter-dependent subnetworks pairs (i,j)
For all common regulation sector s of the subnetworks i and j

IF $INTER_{i,j}(s,kl,k)$ is Large AND $SC_i(S, T)$ is Large THEN $\Delta CAP_{ij}(s,kl)$ is Large.

IF $INTER_{i,j}(s,kl,k)$ is Small AND $SC_i(S, T)$ is Small THEN $\Delta CAP_{ij}(s,kl)$ is Small.

IF $INTER_{i,j}(s,kl,k)$ is Large AND $SC_i(S, T)$ is Small THEN $\Delta CAP_{ij}(s,kl)$ is Medium.

IF $INTER_{i,j}(s,kl,k)$ is Medium AND $SC_i(S, T)$ is Medium THEN $\Delta CAP_{ij}(s,kl)$ is Medium.

IF $INTER_{i,j}(s,kl,k)$ is Small AND $SC_i(S, T)$ is Large THEN $\Delta CAP_{ij}(s,kl)$ is Medium.

The structure of this fuzzy rules is constructed subjectively from the prior knowledge about the behaviour of the system we describe, which induces a uniform and gradual variation of the input and output variables. Actually, it is reasonable to think that the higher the inter-dependence of subnetwork i relatively to the common sector s and the saturation of S, the higher the necessity of using the sector s for the regulation actions of subnetwork i.

3.2 Reasoning Mechanism

The choice of the reasoning mechanism is a fundamental task in the context of this study for two essential reasons. The first one concerns the accuracy of the output, the second concerns time complexity constraint. As the model is aimed at reducing the number of data transfers between the co-ordination and control levels, it should deduce a fast and good approximation of the interaction prediction parameters. In order to choose the most appropriate mechanism to infer the conclusion of the fuzzy model with regard to the computation time complexity and the prediction accuracy we study and discuss the properties of the principal fuzzy reasoning mechanisms. The classical compositional rule of inference (C.R.I) and some fuzzy interpolation methods are then compared.

3.2.1 C.R.I Approach

A classical fuzzy control model (with fuzzification, inference and defuzzification steps) could provide an accurate crisp value of the interaction prediction. However, obtaining an accurate approximation of the interactions means the use of a dense fuzzy rule-base. The more rules there are the more exactly the interactions are predicted and a shorter time is needed to achieve the co-ordination between the interconnected control units. On the other hand, more rules mean a higher computational complexity. If L is the number of labels for the partition of the universes X1, X2 and Y used in the fuzzy prediction model, the number of rules covering $X=X1 \times X2$ is equivalent to the function $o(L^2)$ and the fuzzy inference has the following time complexity $o(3.L^3)$. For example, with 20 labels C.R.I approach needs 24 000 steps to infer an interaction prediction.

3.2.2 Fuzzy Interpolation Approaches

In order to reduce time complexity of the conclusion inference, one has to analyse the property of the fuzzy rule-base and see if it is possible to use another inference method. As it is already noticed the fuzzy rules of the model present some gradual property in the sense that the rule " If X is U then Y is V " could be written " The more X is U the more Y is V ". The gradual reasoning and the analogical reasoning [Bouchon-Meunier and Desprès, 1990], [Dubois and Prade, 1992] would be suitable techniques of inference but they are limited to the single input variable fuzzy models. Nevertheless, the gradual properties presented by the input and output variables imply the existence of full orderings and metrics in their respective universes of discourse. This property induces the possibility of using interpolation methods which are characterised by a reduced time complexity cost and the possibility of deducing an output from a sparse fuzzy rule-base. We have studied two interpolation approaches, the first one was developed by Koczy and Hirota [1993] ; [Koczy and Zorat, 1997], and consists in an extension of classical linear interpolation techniques. The second one was presented in Ishibushi et al. [1993] ; [Chin-Teng and Ya-Ching, 1995] which is based on a neural network interpolator.

- *Fuzzy Linear Interpolation (F.L.I)*

This method is applied on convex and normal fuzzy sets, with triangular or trapezoidal shape. The extension of the classical linear interpolation to linear fuzzy rule interpolation is based on the α-cut concept. If we use a small number m of sparse fuzzy rules, and a number h of α-cut levels, the fuzzy interpolation time complexity corresponds to a polynomial function $o(m+2.h)$. With the linear interpolation approach time complexity can be strongly reduced. However, the characteristics of the fuzzy output inferred are not always satisfying : the approach preserves the convexity property but it often infers abnormal output.

- *Fuzzy Neural Interpolation (F.N.I)*

This approach can interpolate sparse fuzzy rules by a neural network which has leant its weights and biases from a fuzzy input-output data during a preliminary off-line procedure. Fuzzy triangular and normalised learning input-output data are transformed into crisp learning values using α-cuts. An extension of the classical back-propagation algorithm to interval computation was developed in order to deduce the upper and lower limits of the output α-cuts. After learning the parameters from the fuzzy rule base, the neural network becomes able to deduce from any fuzzy convex and normal input a corresponding fuzzy output satisfying the convexity and normality properties. The approach was simulated with triangular fuzzy number data and infers a pseudo-triangular fuzzy output number.

Concerning time complexity of the fuzzy-neural interpolation, it depends on the number n of hidden units, the number h of α-cut levels used to determine the fuzzy output, and the number of the input variables k (k=2, for the prediction model). We have estimated time complexity of this approach with a polynomial function $o(n+2.h)$. We notice that time complexity of the fuzzy-neural interpolation does not depend on the number of rules. This time cost function implies that using a dense rule base for the learning procedure allows the interpolator to improve the accuracy of the input value without increasing time complexity cost.

3.2.3 Comparison

The summary of the previous comparative study between fuzzy reasoning methods is presented in the following table :

	Normality	Convexity	Complexity	Accuracy
C.R.I	-	-	$O(3.L^3)$	good
F.L.I	not always	satisfied	$O(m+2.h)$	not always
F.N.I	satisfied	satisfied	$O(n+2.h)$	good

Tab. 1 : Some Inference Mechanism Methods.

The discussion shows that the most appropriate tool in the context of the study is the fuzzy-neural interpolation approach because it needs a short computation time for the deduction of the output value and can provide an accurate output. In addition, the normalised fuzzy number inferred is adequate for symbolic-numeric interface between the co-ordination level and the control level. Actually, the co-ordination parameter used in the local optimisation modules must be a crisp and integer number. The core of the fuzzy number output if it is integer or its nearest integer neighbour can be an adequate interface value as it corresponds to the highest level of certainty of the fuzzy output.

3.3 Fuzzy Partitioning

The choice of the fuzzy rule base density determines the universe partitioning and the rule base dimension. There is no general answer to the question of determining how fine the fuzzy model should be in order to achieve the highest speed of conclusion computation. However, graduality property of the input and output variables, and the fuzzy-neural interpolation approach chosen for deducing the conclusion value allow us to use a sparse partitioning. We then choose three fuzzy triangular and normalised values {Small, Medium, Large} for the partitioning of X1, X2 and Y considering that they are sufficient to describe extreme and medium scenario of the system behaviour and we can deduce the other intermediate cases by fuzzy-neural interpolation method. In this case, the fuzzy model obtained corresponds to the five rule-based model presented in section 3.1.

3.4 Parameter Identification

Parameter identification corresponds to the evaluation of the membership function parameters of the linguistic labels. Having the set of fuzzy attributes corresponding to the universe partition, we have to determine the support and the core of the triangular labels. The identification approach we choose is inspired from the template method suggested by Tong [1979]. This method uses both expert knowledge and input-output data for the identification process.

In order to get the learning data we take into account the available regulation tools of A.T.F.M problem. In fact, it is interesting to exploit the existing operational research model in the sense that it could provide useful input-output data for the identification of the fuzzy model. Actually, even if this numerical model is not suitable for real-time application, we use it in an off-line step, on the overall A.T.F.M network, for extreme and medium scenario of air traffic demand in order to deduce a variation interval of the input variables and the corresponding interval of the output variable. The intervals found are associated to the support of the fuzzy numbers : Large, Small, and Medium describing both input and output variables. The core of the fuzzy numbers is deduced with the help of an expert.

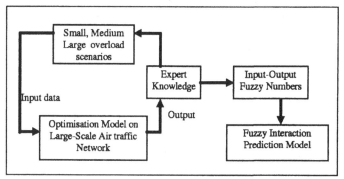

Fig. 4 : Identification of Fuzzy Interaction Prediction Model

3.5 Learning a Neural Network from Fuzzy Rules

After the fuzzy prediction model has been constructed, it can constitute a learning data base for a neural network. The learning data base is formed by five pairs of fuzzy input-output describing the fuzzy prediction model : {((Small, Small) ; Small), ((Small, Large) ; Medium), ((Medium, Medium) ; Medium), ((Medium, Small) ; Medium), ((Large, Large) ; Large)}.

The learning algorithm proceeds as follows :

For a number h of α-cut levels.

For all pairs of fuzzy input-outputs.
• Determine the upper and lower limits of the α-cuts.

The learning data base is formed by 5 vectors of 6 components, 4 for the input data, and 2 for the target data.

• Apply the back-propagation algorithm adapted to interval computation (I.B.P) of Ishibushi et al. to update the weights of the neural network. For more details concerning the architecture of the neural network and the learning algorithm see Ishibushi et al. [1994].

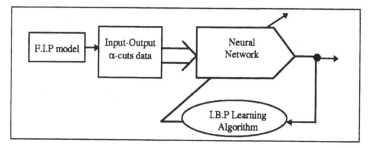

Fig. 5 : Fuzzy Neural Interpolator : Off-line Learning Phase

3.6 Inference Mechanism

Having the neural network parameters after the learning phase the neural network can be used to infer a fuzzy number output for any fuzzy number inputs. The inference mechanism proceeds as follows :

For each fuzzy input number

For a number h of α-cut levels.
- Determine the upper and lower limits of inputs α-cuts.

- Use the input-output relations of the neural network to compute the output α-cuts and build the output fuzzy number.

- Infer the integer value with the highest membership function as the co-ordination parameter for control level.

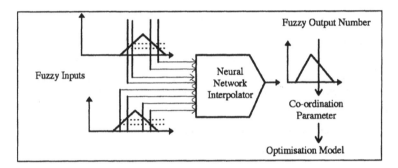

Fig. 6 : Fuzzy Neural Interpolator : in-line Inference Phase

4 The Real-Time ATFM Model

All the previous identification and learning processes are performed during an off-line step that we call the acquisition and representation of knowledge. This preliminary stage is essential for the performance of the regulation actions in real-time. The number of data transfers between the control and co-ordination levels necessary to reach the co-ordination, is directly dependent on the accuracy of the interaction prediction provided by the fuzzy-neural module. The more accurate the prediction the smaller the number of co-ordination iterations. Each co-ordination iteration has to improve, in real-time, the interaction prediction on the basis of the regulation actions provided by the control level. Having the neural network interpolator as a prediction tool, if the co-ordination is not reached, we choose to tune, in real-time, the interpolator parameters using classical back-propagation algorithm with the target output data provided by the control level.

4.1 The A.T.F.M Model Procedures

The different steps of the A.T.F.M model followed during each decision step are described below :

Let C be the number of data transfer needed before reaching the co-ordination (initially C=1).

Step 1 : System Analysis

Apply sequentially the System Analysis modules presented in section 3.1 so as to provide :

- a prediction of the sector overloads.
- a decomposition of the large air-traffic network into smaller subnetworks.
- an identification of interaction relations between the subnetworks.
- an evaluation of the interaction indicators.

Let denote respectively by $a1(i,j,s)$ and $a2(i)$ the inter-dependence indicator and the sector overload provided by the system analysis step.

Let denote by DT, the computation time of the System Analysis Procedure.

Step 2 : Fuzzy Interaction Prediction

For each inter-dependent subnetwork pairs (i,j)
For all common regulation sector s of the subnetworks i and j

- Affect a fuzzy-neural interpolator denoted by $FNI(i,j,s)$.
- Transform the crisp input data provided by step1 into triangular fuzzy normalised number $A1(i,j,s)$ and $A2(i)$ with $a1(i,j,s)$ and $a2(i)$ as the respective modal values. An error variation on this values is used to determine the supports.
- Introduce the fuzzy input data in the fuzzy-neural interpolator $FNI(i,j,s)$ and deduce a fuzzy number output $C(i,j,s)$ corresponding to the interaction prediction.
- Determine the interaction prediction vector P_j composed of the integer value of $C(i,j,s)$ with the highest membership function degree, for the subnetwork j.

Let denote by IT, the computation time of one interpolation procedure.

Step 3 : Co-ordination

Step 3.1 : Artificial Capacity Allocation

For all inter-dependent subnetworks j.
For all index i of a subnetwork inter-dependent of j .
For all common sector s.

- Subtract the core of $C(i,j,s)$ from the capacity of the common sector s in the subnetwork j .

Step 3.2 : Parallel optimisation

For all the subnetworks j.

- Compute the regulation actions using the 0-1 programming model, developed in Bertsimas et al [94].
- Deduce from the regulation actions of all the inter-dependent subnetwork i, the vector $U_j(P_j)$ composed of the action effect $U_j(P_j, i, s)$ of the subnetworks i on the subnetwork j in the common sector s.

Let denote by OT the computation time of one local optimisation procedure.

Step 3.3 : Co-ordination Evaluation

For all inter-dependent subnetwork j

- Verify if all the components of $U_j(P_j)$, which are the actual regulation effects on j, are included in the support of the predicted regulation effects C(i,j,s). If it is true, the co-ordination is reached, go to step 4, else go to step 3.4.

Step 3.4 : Tuning of the fuzzy-neural interpolator

For all interdependent subnetwork j
For all i of $U_j(P_j)$ such as the co-ordination is not satisfied

- Tune the fuzzy-neural interpolator FNI(i,j,s) using the classical back-propagation algorithm for the tuning input-output data ((a1(i,j,s), a2(i)), $U_j(P_j, i, s)$).
- C=C+1.
- Go to step 2.

Let denote by TT, the computation time of tuning procedure.

Step 4 : Regulation Action

- Apply the regulation action on each subnetwork.
- Go to step 5.

Step 5 : End.

4.2 Computation Time Constraint

Hence, a suitable A.T.F.M model should respect the following time cost constraint:

If C=1   DT+IT+OT<T
If C>1   DT+ C.(IT+OT+TT)< T

where T is the decision step duration.

The previous steps are summarised in the following figure :

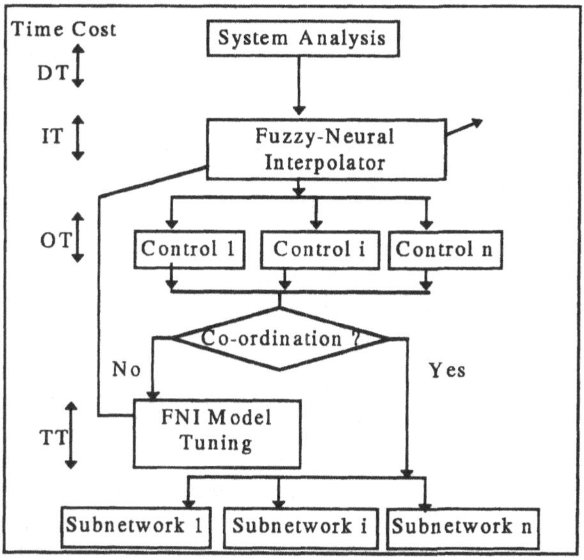

Fig. 7 : Real-Time ATFM Model Steps.

In order to reduce the number C of data transfers, it is necessary to build an accurate fuzzy prediction model. For this reason, the identification process is the most important step ensuring the success of this model. Nevertheless, comparing this approach with classical multi-level control models, which provide an arbitrary initial co-ordination vector to the control level, ignoring the available information about the system behaviour, it is reasonable to think that the classical approach needs a higher number of data transfers before reaching the co-ordination. So the essential advantage of the model proposed is the possibility of exploiting, in an off-line stage, all the available information about the system behaviour, in order to build up a fuzzy knowledge base that provides in real-time a first and accurate approximation of the regulation action. This should have as consequent to minimise the number C of data transfers.

5 Conclusion

This paper presents a real-time A.T.F.M model which copes with computation time problems by introducing the multi-level approach. The co-ordination level is detailed in order to show the different concepts used, such as interaction, fuzzy reasoning that leads to the best prediction of the co-ordination parameters. This prediction is used by the control units to perform a parallel and co-ordinated optimisation in order to reduce the multiple data transfers between the co-ordination and the control levels.

6 References

[Auger, 1993] Auger A., *Hiérarchie et niveaux de complexité*. In Systémique théorie et applications. Bouchon-Meunier B Le Gallou F. (eds) : 63-70. Lavoisier, 1993.

[Bertsimas and Stock 1994] Bertsimas D. and Stock S. *The Air Traffic Flow Management problem with Enroute Capacities*. Working paper Alerd p. Sloan School of management. WP #-3726-94 MSA.

[Bouchon-Meunier and Desprès, 1990] Bouchon-Meunier B. and Desprès S. *Acquisition numérique/symbolique de connaissance graduelles*. LAFORIA Technical report : 90/4, University of Paris-VI.

[Chin-Teng and Ya-Ching, 1995] Chin-Teng L.and Ya-Ching L., *A Neural Fuzzy System with Linguistic Teaching Signals*. IEEE Trans on Fuzzy Systems Vol 3, n°2 : 169-185, 1995.

[Dubois and Prade, 1992] Dubois D. and Prade H. *Gradual rules in approximate reasoning*. Info Sci. 6 :103-122, 1992.

[Ishibuschi et al. , 1993] Ishibuschi H. Fujioka R. Tanaka H. Neural network that learn from fuzzy if then rules. IEEE Trans on Fuzzy Systems Vol 1 : 85-97, 1993.

[Ishibushi et al., 1994] Ishibuschi H. Tanaka H. Okada H. *Interpolation of fuzzy If-Then rules by neural network*. Int J of Approximate Reasoning, 10 : 3-27, 1994.

[Koczy and Hirota 1993] Koczy L.T. and Hirota K. *Approximate Reasoning by linear rule interpolation and general approximation*. Int J of Approximate Reasoning, 9 : 197-225, 1994.

[Koczy and Zorat 1997] Koczy L.T. and Zorat A. *Fuzzy systems and approximation*. Fuzzy Sets and Systems, 85 : 203-222, 1997.

[Mesarovic M.D et al 1970] Mesarovic, M.D. Macko and Takanara Y. *Theory of multi-level hierarchical control systems*. Academic Press, New York, 1970.

[Odoni A. 1987] Odoni A. *The flow management problem in air traffic control*. In flow control of congested networks : 269-288, Springer Verlag, 1987.

[Tong R.M 1979] Tong R.M. *The construction and evaluation of fuzzy models*, in advances in Fuzzy Sets Theory and Application, Gupta M.M Ragade R.K. Yager R.R (eds). North Holland : 559-579, 1979

[Zerrouki et al. 1997] Zerrouki L. Fondacci R. Bouchon-Meunier B. Sellam S. *Artificial Intelligence Techniques for Coordination in Air Traffic Flow Management*. in 8th IFAC/IFIP/IFORS Symposium on Transportation Systems' 97. Chania, Greece. June 16-18 : 47-51, 1997.

From Numerical Interpolation to Constructing Intelligent Behaviours

Jianwei Zhang and Alois Knoll

Faculty of Technology, University of Bielefeld,
33501 Bielefeld, Germany

Abstract. In this paper we propose a general framework for describing and constructing sensor-based behaviours. We point out that a complex high-level task can be realised by a set of modular, cooperating behaviours. Each of these behaviours can be decomposed into local control actions which can be interpreted using linguistic "IF-THEN" rules. Several sample applications in real-world robotic systems are presented: a mobile gripper system equipped with proximity sensors and a two arm system with force/torque sensors. For controllers without sensor-action models, this framework can be universally applied after properly selecting the system inputs. Furthermore, "common sense" knowledge can be integrated and the control parameters can be rapidly adapted through incremental learning.

1 Introduction

To realise high-level robot tasks, the conventional robot control architecture employs the so-called SMPA (*Sensing-Modelling-Planning-Action*) strategy, which follows a strict sequential order of planning and execution of elementary operations. However, problems occur with such a control architecture: a). Algorithms for modelling and planning may be highly complex; b). The time delay from perception to action is usually long due to the computational burden; c). A system based on such an architecture is not fault tolerant. Therefore, a lot of recent work on robot control aims at finding efficient sensor-based solutions to reduce the temporal delay between perception and action.

Brooks' subsumption architecture [2, 11] essentially consisted of combining a set of parallel reactive behaviours without building complete world models. The main problems with this architecture are: a). Task-directed symbolic goals are difficult to be integrated in the behaviours (thus only insect-like "intelligence" can be emulated); b). The hard switch between different behaviours is unnatural.

We use the concept of behaviour in the context of realising tasks specified on a high-level. A behaviour is a control module which directly or indirectly uses the current perceptual information for achieving an explicit goal, i.e. the collective output of behaviours implements the task. Usually, each individual behaviour can be modularly developed and tested. If not only mobile robots but also robot arm systems are discussed, *sensor-based skills* instead of behaviours are employed to describe the basis control modules from the point of view of control engineers.

We give some examples of behaviours that are directly related to control:

Robot motion: *collision-avoidance, goal-direction, constant speed control, object-tracking, force control, following motion commands in natural language, etc.*
Robot vision: *visually guided location, active vision: track, saccade, camera coordination, etc*[1].

Like conventional process control, perception-action cycle can be implemented with either the model-based or the connectionist methodologies. Model-based approaches must specify explicit sensor-robot system models. Typical applications are calibrated methods for hand-eye coordination and the artificial potential-field for collision-avoidance. However, they suffer from the following problems: a). They are not adaptable to varying environments; b). They cannot be built incrementally or modularly; c). They cannot be interpreted symbolically. In one word, they are not really the way humans would do. Connectionist approaches use expert knowledge or learning to acquire the characteristics of the sensor-action system. Recently, such approaches are applied to the sensor-based control of robots as well as in classical process control as the so-called "computational intelligence" becomes a rapidly growing research area. Applications of artificial neural networks [1, 7, 4, 6] demonstrate the intelligent characteristics such as self-organising, adaptation and distributed processing, but the "block-box" structure stays as an obstacle for integrating symbolicist approaches which represent the other important part of human intelligence. Fuzzy control also finds applications in behaviour implementation [5, 8, 18], but these controllers are mainly realised with human desgin instead of self-adaptation.

In the following sections, we first discuss the important issues related to the implementation of sensor-based behaviours. Then we introduce the B-spline model and show how a behaviour and a local control rule can be specified and adapted based on this model. In this way, the advantages of neural networks and fuzzy systems can be combined. Two examples are given to further illustrate the construction process of a behaviour. The feasibility and advantages of the proposed method are demonstrated using two sample applications: a). motion for screwing with two robot arms; b). motion control of a mobile gripper system.

2 Issues in Realisation of Behaviours

2.1 Sensor Data for Control

In order to develop a robust on-line robot controller, external and internal sensor data should be applied directly in each control cycle instead of building and updating the world model. If sensor data is coupled with motion control in a simple form, the robot can decide its reaction in time. The idea of *"situatedness"*

---

[1] More behaviours for a eye-head system can be found in [3].

by Brooks [11] is comparable to this concept. By *"bounded rationality"* Simon [10] summarised the principle that humans often use only incomplete or imprecise knowledge for problem-solving.

Sensor data needed for direct integration in robot control possess the following properties:

- They are relative. These data are mainly derived from the external sensor measurements and their derivatives or the differences between the sensor values and the internal model. Such a variable value is not related to the robot or sensor alone, but to the interaction between the robot and its environment.
- They are local. Normally, only part of the environment, which is directly involved in the current robot motion, is perceived by the sensor system. Each sensor measurement represents one aspect of the object's features. No time-costly sensor fusion is performed (sensor data fusion is therefore transferred to task fusion).
- They are task-oriented. Modelling and interpretation of the sensor data depend on the control tasks. Only the control-relevant data are selected, preprocessed and represented.

2.2 Types of Controller Inputs

The complexity of the controller depends mainly on the dimension of the input space, i.e. the number of variables which influence the control action. Generally, these input variables can be classified into the following types:

- Direct sensor readings. These are normally one or multi-dimensional signals which can be processed relatively fast. The representation level of information is low. An example in Fig. 1(a) shown proximity sensors in the mobile robot. Another example is the six-Dimensional force/torque sensors mounted on the gripper of a robot arm, Fig. 1(b).

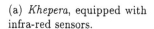

(a) *Khepera*, equipped with infra-red sensors.

(b) A 6D force/torque sensor mounted on the robot gripper.

Fig. 1. Two examples of sensors whose output is directly fed to controller.

– Feature description variables. They are extracted from signals and images and represent information of medium to high level. Fig. 2(a) shows the configuration of a hand-camera used for our experiment. Such a "self-viewing" configuration enables the camera to have two gripper fingers in its view. The extracted features can be the relative distance from the TCP (*Tool Centre Point*) to the centre of object to be grasped and the relative angle between the orientations of the gripper and the parallel grasping edges. As shown in [13], the projected *principal components* as features can be also grouped in this category.

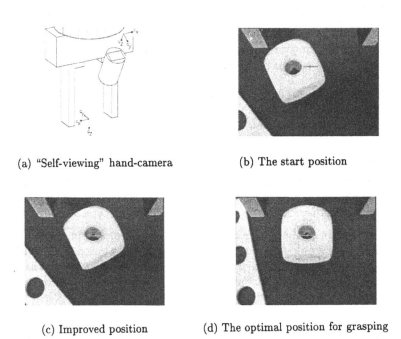

(a) "Self-viewing" hand-camera   (b) The start position

(c) Improved position   (d) The optimal position for grasping

Fig. 2. Visually guided grasping with a robot gripper.

– Combinations of planning and sensory information. Such a combination is particularly important when *purposive* instead of *reactive* behaviours are to be developed. The planning level assigns the symbolic information such as subgoals of tasks or geometric subgoals for collision-free paths. The sensory information is mainly the robot state estimation through the fusion of internal sensors. The difference between a subgoal and the current state may be taken as input variables. Fig. 3 depicts two variables applied to decide on the control action to keep a pre-planned path: d: the shortest distance between the robot and the pre-planned path segment, and α: the angular divergence between orientation of the path and the robot.

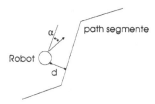

Fig. 3. Combination of planning and sensory information as inputs.

2.3 Hierarchical Decomposition of Behaviour Based on Rules

For many perception-action processes, no explicit mathematical models are available. One strategy of intelligent control is to partition the input space with into overlapping hyper-blocks (*lattice-based*) and to study the local control action for them. A control rule describes the relation between one typical configuration in the input space and the control action. There are good reasons for making such a perception-action mapping *Input_Space → Action* symbolically interpretable instead of a black-box:

- Linguistic modeling provides a way of transferring skill from human experts to robots;
- Analysis and validation of the controller development;
- Supervision of the learning process.

In order to make robot behaviours emerge and adapt to new environments, we suggest a modularisation of behaviours and using a coordinator to determine the interactions between them. The decomposability can be described with the following hierarchical conception:

A local control rule determines a correct control action for a subclass of the input space.

An elementary behaviour has an explicit goal and is implemented by a set of cooperating atomic rules.

The behaviour arbiter coordinates multiple simultanuously active behaviours to achieve a high-level task and is realised by a set of meta-rules.

The following section will demonstrate that B-spline basis functions can be used to partition the input space, which can then be interpreted with linguistic terms. The features of the B-spline model provide a suitable framework to describe local control rules, to aggregate multiple rules for constructing behaviours and to blend cooperating behaviours to carry out a predescribed task.

3 B-Spline Models for Constructing Behaviours

3.1 B-Splines Basis Functions

Although B-splines have been mainly used in off-line modelling, we have shown that they may constitute a suitable model for describing sensor-based behaviours.

B-spline basis functions are naturally defined convex function hulls which can be best interpreted as linguistic labels. The synthesis of a smooth curve with basis functions can easily be associated with the blending of local control actions. These points are the main motivation for our work on utilising B-splines to design behaviours.

In our previous work we compared the basis functions of periodical *Non-Uniform B-Splines* (NUBS) with a fuzzy controller. In this paper, we also follow the usage of this type of NUBS basis functions.

Assume x is a general input variable of a control system which is defined on the universe of discourse $[x_0, x_m]$. Given a sequence of ordered parameters (knots): $(x_0, x_1, x_2, \ldots, x_m)$, the i-th normalised B-spline basis function (B-function) $X_{i,k}$ of order k is defined recursively, see Fig. 4. More details are presented in [14].

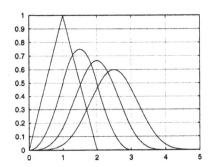

Fig. 4. Non-uniform B-functions of order 2, 3, 4, 5 defined for linguistic terms.

3.2 Local Rules and Their Aggregation

To determine the local control action of a MISO system with n inputs $x_1, x_2, \ldots, x_n$, which are viewed as *linguistic variables*, if we use

- periodical B-spline basis functions interpreted as linguistic terms like "small", "medium", "large" which do not possess crisp boundaries[2];
- singletons to specify local control values;

a local control action can be described in the following form:

IF $(x_1$ is $X^1_{i_1,k_1})$ and $(x_2$ is $X^2_{i_2,k_2})$ and $\ldots$ and $(x_n$ is $X^n_{i_n,k_n})$
THEN y is $Y_{i_1 i_2 \ldots i_n}$,

where

---

[2] In the CMAC network [4] they can be named as active units defined on the overlapping receptive fields of a sensor.

- x_j: the j-th input $(j = 1, \ldots, n)$,
- k_j: the order of the B-spline basis functions used for x_j,
- $X^j_{i_j,k_j}$: the i-th linguistic term of x_j defined by B-spline basis functions,
- $i_j = 0, \ldots, m_j$, representing how fine the j-th input is fuzzy partitioned,
- $Y_{i_1 i_2 \ldots i_n}$: the control vertex (deBoor points) of $Rule(i_1, i_2, \ldots, i_n)$.

The aggregation of all the local control rules can be represented as:

$$y = \frac{\sum_{i_1=0}^{m_1} \cdots \sum_{i_n=0}^{m_n} (Y_{i_1,\ldots,i_n} \prod_{j=1}^{n} X^j_{i_j,k_j}(x_j))}{\sum_{i_1=0}^{m_1} \cdots \sum_{i_n=0}^{m_n} \prod_{j=1}^{n} X^j_{i_j,k_j}(x_j)} \tag{1}$$

$$= \sum_{i_1=0}^{m_1} \cdots \sum_{i_n=0}^{m_n} (Y_{i_1,\ldots,i_n} \prod_{j=1}^{n} X^j_{i_j,k_j}(x_j)) \tag{2}$$

This is called a *general NUBS hypersurface*. Building a behaviour can be viewed as the process of shaping the control surface. In CAD applications, the criterion for defining the "ideal" surface can be the visual appearance or some measures like length, curvature, energy, etc. For control applications, they should optimise certain cost functions, e.g. the action-value in the Q-learning paradigm.

We tested a large amount of non-linear functions from low to rather high dimensions, [15]. It was shown that based on the B-spline model, any non-linear MISO functions can be approximated. This feature provides the basis of using this model for modelling general perception-action behaviours.

3.3 Steps for Constructing a Behaviour

The steps for developing a behaviour with B-spline models can be summarised as follows:

1. Select inputs.
2. Select the order of the B-functions for each input variable.
3. Determine the knots for partitioning each input variable.
4. Compute the virtual and real linguistic terms for all inputs.
5. Initialise the control vertices for the output.
6. Learn the control vertices.
7. If the results are satisfied, terminate.
8. Modify the knots for inputs, go to 4;
   or Refine the granularity and use more training data, go to 3;
   or Increase the order of B-functions, go to 3;
   or Delete certain inputs and/or add new ones, go to 2.

In step 3, it is very important to know how the knots should be distributed over the input space. An intuitive answer is to put the knots where the output has its extrema. If such information is available, e.g. by approximating an analytically representable function, we can apply this principle to select the knots.

If the output of a control system is unknown, the knots may first be equally distributed and then adapted with an approach similar to the optimisation of a self-organising neural network.

The control vertices can be initialised with the approximate *a priori* values, e.g. the experience data from experts if available. Otherwise they can be set to zero.

3.4 Adaptation of a Behaviour

Adaptation of a controller is usually transformed into an optimisation process, which often suffers from the problem of runnning into a local instead of a global minimum if numerous parameters affect the cost function in a non-linear, unpredictable manner. If the modification of a single parameter only results in a local change of the control surface the learning speed will increase significantly. We show that the B-spline model possesses this property.

Assume $\{(X, y_d)\}$ is a set of training data, where

- $X = (x_1, x_2, \ldots, x_n)$: is the input vector, and
- y_d : the desired output for X .

The Mean-Sqare-Error is defined as:

$$E = \frac{1}{2}(y_r - y_d)^2, \tag{3}$$

where y_r is the current output value during training.

The parameters to be found arethe local control actions $Y_{i_1,i_2,\ldots,i_n}$, which make the error in (3) as small as possible, i.e.

$$E = \frac{1}{2}(y_r - y_d)^2 \equiv \text{MIN}. \tag{4}$$

Each control vertex $y_{i_1,\ldots,i_n}$ can be modified by using the gradient descent method:

$$\Delta Y_{i_1,\ldots,i_n} = -\epsilon \frac{\partial E}{\partial Y_{i_1,\ldots,i_n}} = -\epsilon(y_r - y_d)\prod_{j=1}^{n} X_{i_j,k_j}^j(x^j), \qquad 0 < \epsilon \le 1 \tag{5}$$

This learning function can be classified as a back-propagation method. The only special feature of using B-spline basis function is that the gradient descent method can guarantee that the learning algorithm converges to the global minimum of the error function since the second partial differentiation with respect to $Y_{i_1,i_2,\ldots,i_n}$ is constant:

$$\frac{\partial^2 E}{\partial^2 Y_{i_1,\ldots,i_n}} = -\epsilon(\prod_{j=1}^{n} N_{i_j,k_j}^j(x_j))^2 \ge 0 \tag{6}$$

This means that the error function (3) is convex in the space $Y_{i_1,i_2,\ldots,i_m}$ and therefore possesses only one (global) minimum.

In the following, we show how to build elementary behaviours using the adapttion method through a one-deimensional example. Consider a control system with one sensor input and one output of action. Assume that the output should react to the sensor data like a $\sin(2\pi x^2)$ function. The process of adaptation is shown in Fig. 5. The set of symbolic rules interpreting the controller behaviour can be extracted as follows:

IF S_Reading IS zero THEN Action IS zero

IF S_Reading IS small THEN Action IS positive_middle

IF S_Reading IS medium THEN Action IS positive_big

IF S_Reading IS large THEN Action IS negative_big

IF S_Reading IS maximum THEN Action IS zero

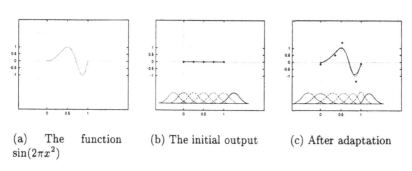

(a) The function (b) The initial output (c) After adaptation
$\sin(2\pi x^2)$

Fig. 5. Mapping the sensor readings into the action values emulating the function $y = \sin(2\pi x^2)$. The B-spline basis functions in (b) and (c) defined on the interval $[0, 1]$ represent the linguistic terms "zero", "small", "medium", "large", "maximum" (from left to right). The values of the diamond-points represent the linguistic terms of the control action, "zero", "positive_medium", "positive_large", "negative_large", "zero".

3.5 Rapid Reinforcement Learning

In unsupervised learning, it is usually possible to define an "evaluation function" if the desired data of the output are unknown. Such an evaluation function should describe how "good" the current system state $((x_1, x_2, \ldots, x_n), y)$ is. For each input vector, an output is generated. With this output, the system transits to another state. The new state is compared with the old one; an adaptation is performed if necessary.

Assume the evaluation function, denoted by $F(\cdot)$, results in a bigger value for a better state, i.e. for two states A and B, if A is better than B, then $F(A) \geq F(B)$. The adaptation of the control vertices can be performed with a similar representation as in supervised learning. Assume that the desired state is A_d. The change of control vertices can be written as:

$$\Delta Y_{i_1,\ldots,i_n} = S \cdot \epsilon \cdot |F(B) - F(A_d)| \cdot \prod_{j=1}^{n} X_{i_j,k_j}(x_j). \tag{7}$$

where $S = sign(F(A) - F(B)) * sign(F(B) - F(A_d)) * sign(y)$ represents the correct direction to modify the control vertex. For more details see [16].

3.6 Situations

Even for the same task, there may exist different evaluation functions in different situations. We use the following example of mobile robots to discuss the situations which the robot can possibly face, Fig. 6.

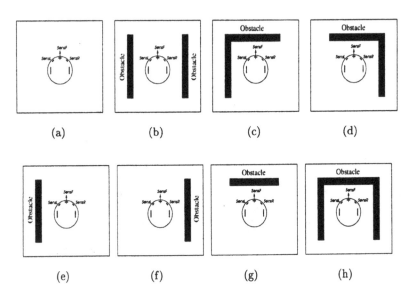

Fig. 6. Possible situations and actions (a): free space, straightforward; (b): in a corridor, straightforward; (c): turn right; (d): turn left; (e): turn right; (f): turn left; (g): turn left; (h): turn left.

In the situations of Fig. 6(b), 6(e), 6(f), the robot should try to keep the difference of *SensL* and *SensR* as small as possible. For the cases shown in Fig. 6(c), 6(d), the robot should try to minimise the sum of all three sensors *SensL*, *SensV* and *SensR*. Fig. 6(g) and 6(h) illustrate two cases, for which no reasonable evaluation function can be found, the robot can simply turn left. The evaluation function F can be summarised as follows:

– $F(SensL, SensF, SensR) = -(SensL + SensF + SensR)$, if $SensF$ is big (Fig. 6(c) and 6(d)).
– $F(SensL, SensF, SensR) = -|SensL - SensR|$, if $SensF$ is small, $SensL$ or $SensR$ is not zero (Fig. 6(b), 6(e) and 6(f)).
– $F(SensL, SensF, SensR) = 0$, otherwise (Fig. 6(a)).
– in cases of Fig. 6(g) and 6(h): simply turn left.

4 Sensor-Based Screwing Operation

4.1 Screwing Control Problem

Among assembly operations, insertion and screwing are important for investigating sensor-based control methods, [9]. In order to enhance the flexibility of a robotic system, approaches are necessary which make it possible to control a general-purpose hand/gripper based on sensor inputs. Only with sensors can the diverse uncertainties occurring during different screwing operations be detected and correctly handled.

The problem of the screwing of a bolt into a nut originates from our collaborative project which aims at the assembly of aggregates built from the wooden elements of a toy construction set. The "elevator control" of a toy aircraft was selected as one aggregate to be built, Fig. 7.

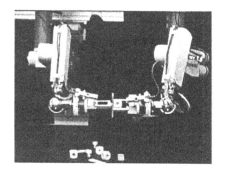
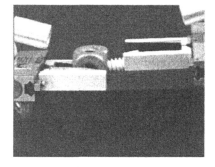

(a) Two cooperating manipulators   (b) Screwing operation

Fig. 7. The experimental set-up for fixtureless assembly.

For a general purpose arm/gripper system, uncertainties like imprecise grasping, slippage of the part in the hand and vibration must be taken into account. Without using sensors, such an operation can fail under each of these uncertainties. Therefore, sensor-based compensation motions become necessary. The resulting forces in the normal and orientation directions should be minimised and stable. Additionally, to guarantee a successful *screwing-in* phase, a constant force in the approach direction should be exerted.

4.2 Behaviours for a Successful Screwing Operation

The whole screwing skill needs the following behaviours:

> Compensation in the approach-direction

> Compensation in the normal- and orientation-directions

> Screwing

The input information is provided by the force feedback during the motion. In the screwing operation, instead of absolute forces, the deviations of the real forces from the desired ones are used as the input variables, which can be restricted to $\pm 2N$ in our application. The linguistic terms and their definition intervals are specified. At each of both ends of the input range $[-2N, +2N]$, two *virtual linguistic terms* are added to maintain the smooth controllability at the end of the interval [12]. If B-spline basis functions of order three are used, the generated linguistic terms can be seen in Fig. 8, where A_0 and A_9 are virtual linguistic terms, A_1 to A_8 are e.g. *HighNegForceError*, *LowNegForceError*, etc.

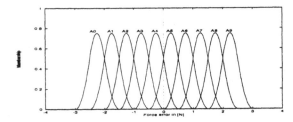

Fig. 8. The basis function for the inputs within the effective range $\pm 2N$.

Linguistic terms of the output variables are defined by control vertices. They can be specified approximately if data for the control process are available, or initialised as zero if there is no *a priori* knowledge. A sample rule is:

> IF   the deviation from the desired force is very high
> THEN the arm should move back in a big stretch

More details of the learning approach can be found in [17].

4.3 Experimental Results

We give an example of screwing with large positioning deviation of the bolt. Fig. 9 illustrates the control curves to compensate the force in the Y-axis i) by approximate initialisation using expert knowledge; ii) after some intermediate learning steps; and iii) after sufficient learning steps, which enables optimal force control for this task.

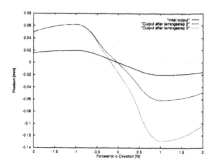

Fig. 9. The control curves during learning.

5 Purposive and Reactive Behaviours of Mobile Robots

B-Spline experiments were also carried out with the mobile robot system shown in Fig. 1(a). Controllers were tested for behaviours like keeping the pre-planned path, avoiding collisions with unknown obstacles, following human instructions and the coordination of them. In the following, we briefly describe three basic modules.

5.1 Approach of Subgoals (SA)

First, we introduce the the behaviour "Subgoal Approaching", which generates the appropriate speed and steering angle to be able to follow the current path segment to the next subgoal. Subgoals can be planned under the given representation of the environment. This module requires the pre-calculation of two variables *shortest distance to path d* and *angle of divergence* α (Fig. 3). The output variables are the robot's forward speed (*Speed*) and steering angle (*Steer*).

By discriminating the relations between the robot's current position and the path segment into the following classes:

- Completely off the path on the left side;
- Far away on the left side;
- Slightly left of the path;
- Almost on the path;
- Slightly right of the path;
- Far away on the right side;
- Completely off the path on the right side,

Rules for path tracking to the next subgoal can be either developed based on heuristic experiments or learned through real practice.

A typical rule of this module looks like this:

> IF   The robot is located slightly to the left of the path,
> but its orientation is almost on the path
> THEN It will steer slightly to the right by applying a high speed

Fig. 10 shows an example of tracking a sequence of pre-planned path segments.

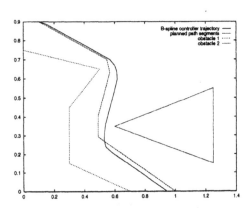

Fig. 10. Trajectory of the controller using the rule base "Subgoal Approaching"

5.2 Local Collision Avoidance (LCA)

The behaviour LCA is assigned to the task to avoid collisions with unknown or moving obstacles. By observing the current values of the proximity sensors, LCA calculates the speed and steering angle, which is required to avoid obstacles. Control rules can be extracted by

- either by modelling the human experiences coping with the following situations: "dead end", "obstacle from right", "obstacle from left", "obstacle ahead", "obstacle from half-left/right", "no obstacle nearby", or
- "learning by doing" with the unsupervised adaptation method.

5.3 Situation Evaluation (SE)

The behaviour "Situation Evaluation" uses the current sensors as input and generates the importance priority K as output. The rule base calculates K for all possible situations.

The output variable K is defined for the importance priority of the LCA rule base. Each specific situation is assigned its importance priority.

K	Situations
Very_Low:	no obstacle avoidance, subgoal approach only
Low:	slightly doing obstacle avoidance, mainly subgoal approach
High:	mainly obstacle avoidance, slightly trying to approach subgoal
Very_High:	obstacle avoidance has priority, subgoal approach is irrelevant

A typical control rule of this module looks like this:

> IF   The leftmost proximity sensor detects an obstacle which is close,
> and the other sensors detect no obstacle at all,
> THEN Steer halfway to the right at low speed.
>   Mainly perform obstacle avoidance.

5.4 Blending Behaviours

Behaviours can be blended analogously to the blending of single control rules. A *arbiter* with a meta-rule can be described as:

> IF situation_evaluation IS for_B_i THEN apply Behaviour B_i

As an example, the coordination of the rule bases LCA and SA is based on the importance priority K. By denoting the *Speed* and *Steer* parameters of both rule bases as $Speed_{SA}$, $Steer_{SA}$ for subgoal approach and $Speed_{LCA}$ and $Steer_{LCA}$ for local collision avoidance, the effective *Speed* and *Steer* becomes:

$$Speed = Speed_{LCA} \cdot K + Speed_{SA} \cdot (1 - K),$$

$$Steer = Steer_{LCA} \cdot K + Steer_{SA} \cdot (1 - K).$$

If more than two rule bases work together, the principle can be further applied. In general, for s rule bases to coordinate, s importance priorities, e.g. $K_1, K2, \ldots, K_s$ should be set. By classifying different situations, the dynamic decision for these parameters can be formulated with control rules and then integrated into the situation evaluation.

Fig. 11 shows two examples of the on-line collision-avoidance as well as the goal approaching behaviour. The starting condition of this scenario is that the robot is originally moving along a straight line towards a goal from bottom to top. In the left figure, the trajectories 1, 2, 3, 4 correspond to the cases of an unanticipated object moving at 10, 25, 50 and 90% of the robot's maximal velocity. Trajectory 4 is a straight course since the robot detects that its path is again free of objects. The right figure shows the object moving towards the robot. Curves 1, 2, 3, 4, 5 correspond to the robot trajectory when the moving object moves head on to the robot or with a deviation of 20, 40, 60 and 80 degrees.

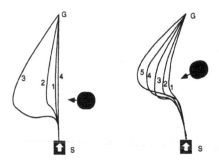

Fig. 11. Approaching a goal while avoiding an unanticipated object.

6 Discussion

We showed that sensor-based behaviours can be incrementally constructed based on a B-spline model. One level up, multiple behaviours can be also coordinated and blended just as multiple single rules. The approach possesses good interpretability, adaptability and generality if the dimension of the input space is limited.

Several advantages resulting from the approach are:

- Knowledge encoding by transforming numerical data to symbolic representation. As a result, huge amount of data is compressed with the "IF-THEN" structure. If the model of the input/output relation is not available, this compression is quite compact. The proposed model can serve as a bridge between numeric input/output data and symbolic control rules.
- Incremental methodology results in the transparency of the behaviour building process. The modular partition of a behaviour in local control rules is actually the reason for rapid convergence of learning. This property benefits from the appropriately selected cost or error function as well as the local influence of control vertices on the whole control surface.
- The combined design/learning methodology. What must be done in the design phase is quite simple: select input variables, determine the granularity of partitioning the input space and some approximate output values if they are available. This ability to integrate human knowledge can be viewed as one distinctive feature of the approach.
- Smooth output. If a B-spline basis function of order k is used, the output is $(k-2)$-times continuously differentiable.

With our approach, the perception-action cycle is finally represented in form of "IF-THEN" rules with optimised parameters. No complex programming and control expertise are needed. Fine-tuning of the main controller parameters can be done on-line and automatically. The method of combining design and learning can be applied to robot systems for acquiring a wide range of sensor-based skills.

References

1. J. S. Albus. A new approach to manipulator control: The Cerebellar Model Articulation Contorller (CMACS). *Transactions of ASME, Journal of Dynamic Systems Measurement and Control*, 97:220–227, 1975.

2. R. A. Brooks. A robust layered control system for a mobile robot. *IEEE Journal on Robotics and Automation*, RA-2:14–23, April 1986.

3. M. J. Daily and D. W. Payton. Behaviour-based control for an eye-head system. *SPIE Vol. 1825 - Intelligent Robots and Computer Vision XI*, pages 722–732, 1992.

4. W. T. Miller. Real-time application of neural networks for sensor-based control of robots with vision. *IEEE Transactions on System, Man and Cybernetics*, 19:825–831, 1989.

5. F. G. Pin, H. Watanabe, J. Symon, and R. Pattay. Autonomous navigation of a mobile robot using custom-designed VLSI chips and boards. *Proceedings of the IEEE International Conference on Robotics and Automation*, pages 123–128, 1992.

6. H. Ritter. Parametrized self-organising maps for vision learning tasks. In *ICANN Proceedings*, 1994.

7. H. Ritter and K. Schulten. Topology conserving mappings for learning motor tasks. In *AIP Conf. Proc. 151, Neural Networks for Computing*, pages 376–380, 1986.

8. A. Saffiotti, E. H. Ruspini, and K. Konolige. Blending reactivity and goal-directness in a fuzzy controller. *IEEE International Conference on Fuzzy Systems*, pages 134–139, 1993.

9. K. Selke and P. Pugh. Sensor-guided generic assembly. In *Proceedings of the 6th International Conference on Robot Vision and Sensory Controls, Paris*, pages 11–19, 1986.

10. H. A. Simon. *The Sciences of the Artificial*. MIT Press, Cambridge, MA, 1969.

11. L. Steels and R. Brooks (editors). *The Artificial Life Route to Artificial Intelligence: building Embodied, Situated Agents*. Lawrance Erlbaum Associates Publishers, 1995.

12. J. Zhang and A. Knoll. Constructing fuzzy controllers with B-spline models. In *IEEE International Conference on Fuzzy Systems*, 1996.

13. J. Zhang and A. Knoll. Constructing fuzzy controllers for multivariate problems using statistical indices. In *International Conference on Fuzzy Systems, Alaska*, 1998.

14. J. Zhang and A. Knoll. Constructing fuzzy controllers with B-spline models - principles and applications. *International Journal of Intelligent Systems (forthcoming)*, 13(2/3):257–286, February/March 1998.

15. J. Zhang and K. V. Le. Naturally defined membership functions for fuzzy logic systems and a comparison with conventional set functions. In *European Congress on Intelligent Techniques and Soft Computing, Aachen*, 1997.

16. J. Zhang, K. V. Le, and A. Knoll. Unsupervised learning of control spaces based on B-spline models. *Proceedings of IEEE International Conference on Fuzzy Systems, Barcelona*, 1997.

17. J. Zhang, Y. v. Collani, and A. Knoll. On-line learning of sensor-based control for acquiring assembly skills. In *Proceedings of the IEEE International Conference on Robotics and Automation*, 1997.

18. J. Zhang, F. Wille, and A. Knoll. Modular design of fuzzy controller integrating deliberative and reactive strategies. In *Proceedings of the IEEE International Conference on Robotics and Automation, Minneapolis*, 1996.

A Brief Logopedics for the Data Used in a Neuro-fuzzy Milieu

Vesa A. Niskanen

University of Helsinki, Dept. of Economics & Management
PO Box 27, FIN-00014 Helsinki, Finland
Fax: +358 9 708 5096, E-mail: vesa.a.niskanen@helsinki.fi
www.helsinki.fi/~niskanen/

Abstract
A Neuro-fuzzy reasoning algorithm, *Fmta*, which was constructed by the author, was applied to empiric data. This data comprised the ages, heights and weights of 126 schoolboys, and the aim was to explain and/or predict the weights of the system according to their ages and heights. *Fmta* yielded satisfactory results when compared with linear regression analysis, generalized mean and the Takagi-Sugeno algorithm.

1. Background

The author has examined Lotfi Zadeh's idea for *computing with words* both from the logico-methodological and empiric point of view [5, 6, 7, 8, 9]. Zadeh's idea maintains that we can apply computers when we mimic human linguistic reasoning, *i.e.*, when we use linguistic variables and linguistic logic. Although fuzzy systems, particularly within control, decision making and pattern recognition, deal with linguistic constituents, according to Zadeh, these systems usually apply *fuzzy set theory* whereas the utilization of *fuzzy logic*, in its narrow sense, is neglected. This has led to the situation that many fuzzy systems are actually black or grey boxes as is the case with neural networks.

The author has aimed to compute, *de facto*, with words. This approach, which is referred to as the *Fuzzy Metric-Truth Approach* (*Fmta*), has three main constituents: First, the linguistic constituent, the *Quasi-Natural Language* (*Qnl*), which aims to correspond with natural language. In this context the *Semantic Differential Technique* (*Sdt*), which is widely used within the behavioural sciences, is applied.

Second, within the truth qualification, the *Theory of Truthlikeness* (*Tt*) is utilized.

Third, fuzzy set theory and fuzzy logic has been used . The author has also fuzzified both the *Sdt* and *Tt*.

This approach thus takes into consideration linguistic, logical, semantic and psychological aspects. In the long run, we aim to construct a satisfactory logico-linguistic user interface between the user and the numeric neuro-fuzzy systems. In practice, we construct numeric neuro-fuzzy systems which correspond with systems utilizing fuzzy logic. Below the *Fmta* is briefly described and its applicability is assessed in the light of empiric data. For the sake of comparison, we also apply alternative algorithms. In addition, we aim to show that by virtue of the *Fmta* our data can speak, *i.e.*, we can attain the goal of computing with words.

2. Correspondence Between Fuzzy Set Theory and Fuzzy Logic

Within the prevailing application areas of neuro-fuzzy and fuzzy systems, such as control and decision making, the reasonings of these systems are usually based on *Fuzzy Associative Memories*. Below we will also focus on this subject matter. As was mentioned above, these systems are usually numeric by nature, and hence we are not fully able to utilize linguistic reasoning. On the other hand, conventional artificial intelligence usually applies formal languages and classical bivalent logic, but, mainly because of its bivalency, this approach is clearly less satisfactory than neuro-fuzzy systems in actual applications. As regards the *Fmta*, we aim to integrate these approaches intelligibly. In practice, we link the *Generalized Modus Ponendo Ponens* (*Gmpp*) syllogisms to fuzzy associative memories, *inter alia*.

From the logical standpoint, we use the *Gmpp*:

x is A

<u>If x is A', then y is B</u>

y is B'

in which the fuzzy set A resembles fuzzy set A' and fuzzy set B' resembles fuzzy set B. If A=A', we obtain the classic *Modus Ponendo Ponens*, and then we conclude that B'=B.

As regards fuzzy associative memories, they comprise true if-then rules similar to the second premiss of the *Gmpp*. If we establish that the input of an fuzzy associative memory is a true first premiss of the *Gmpp*, we can use a logical structure, when performing reasonings within these memories:

x is A (input)

<u>If x is A', then y is B (rule)</u>

y is B' (output)

Hence, we can provide a logical basis for fuzzy associative memories.

In practice, the *Fmta* applies the *Gmpp* as follows [6, 7]: We have two true premisses and the conclusion. The second premiss is a true R-type implication. The truth value of the antecedent of the if-then clause is derived from the fuzzified relative distance,

$$0 \leq Dist(A,A') \leq 1,$$

between the first premiss and this antecedent. The smaller the distance, the higher the degree of truth of the antecedent. For example,

Truth(x is A', provided that x is A)=$1-Dist(A,A')$).

Then, by applying fuzzy logic, we can derive the truth value of the consequent from the truth values of the antecedent and implication. Hence, we obtain the truth value

Truth(y is B)=T.

Finally, we apply the inverse function of *Truth*, and draw the conclusion

B'=$\{C \mid 1-Dist(C,B)=T\}$.

These conclusions are usually normalized fuzzy sets (often intervals). If A=A', then *Gmpp* yields B'=B.

The truth value T above, which is in a sense the degree of similarity between A and A', can simultaneously be regarded as being the firing strength of the rule in a fuzzy associative memory. Then, given an input, if we have m rules, we perform m *Gmpp* reasonings, one for each rule. The final output is based on the aggregation of the conclusions of the *Gmpp*.

The *Fmta* actually applies fuzzy logic and linguistic entities. By virtue of its horizontal nature, it also yields normalized fuzzy sets as outputs, and normalized outputs are important, particularly within decision making.

In practice, we often aim at constructing a system which, given the inputs, yields outputs similar to experimentally observed output values. Several operators and reasoning methods have been suggested in the literature, but below we only apply the generalized mean , *Gmean*, to the *Fmta* because it seems simple and appropriate to the metric approach. This operator is based on the formula [2]

$$Gmean(X_1,...,X_m;p;W_1,...,W_m)=(\Sigma_{i=1,...,m}W_iX_i^p)^{1/p}$$

in which X is a variable, W is a weight, $\Sigma_i W_i=1$ and p is a real number. The role of parameter p can be characterized as follows:

p approches $-\infty$, minimum of X_i.

p=-1, harmonic mean.

p approches 0, geometric mean.

p=1, arithmetic mean.

p=2, quadratic mean (root mean square).

p approcahes $+\infty$, maximum of X_i.

One simple method for applying the *Fmta* and *Gmean* is based on the following algorithm: Given m rules of the type

If $X_{i1}=A_{i1}$, ..., $X_{in}=A_{in}$, then $Y_i=C_i$ (i=1,...,m)

and the input $IN=(I_1,..,I_n)$,

1. Calculate the relative distances $D_{ij}=Dist_{ij}(I_j,A_{ij})$ in the constituents of the inputs and antecedents (i=1,...,m; j=1,...,n). $0 \leq D_{ij} \leq 1$.

2. Distance aggregations:
    $D_i=Gmean(D_{i1},...,D_{in};p_{dist};W_{dist1},...,W_{distn})$ $(p_{dist} \geq 1)$. Hence, we obtain relative distances based on metrics such as the City-Block ($p_{dist}=1$) and Euclidean metrics ($p_{dist}=2$). These are special cases of relative Minkowski metrics. $0 \leq D_i \leq 1$.

3. Specify transformed relative distances, TD_i, in order to exclude the firing of the irrelevant rules. For example, $TD_i=min\{1,t \cdot D_i\}$, $t>1$. $0 \leq TD_i \leq 1$.

4. Truth values of the antecedents are, for example,
    $T_i=1-TD_i$. $0 \leq T_i \leq 1$. These are the firing strengths of the rules.

5. Calculate $Gmean_{out}=G(C_1,...,C_m;p_{out};W_1,...,W_m)$ in which $W_i=T_i/\Sigma_{i=1,...,m}T_i$. This is the final normalized output.

6. Defuzzify, if necessary. Standard routines, such as center of gravity, can be used.

We can apply a neuro-fuzzy approach to these operations in order to obtain more satisfactory results. Particularly, by utilizing the correspondence with the operator *Gmean*, we can tune the systems fluently with the parameters p, C and W. We can also use the distance coefficient, t, for tuning.

3. Example Based on Empiric Data

3.1. Data Description

For example, consider the data presented in [9, p. 869]. This data comprises the ages in months, the heights in inches and the weights in pounds of 126 schoolboys. Our aim is to explain/predict their weights according to their ages and heights. Hence, we provide an example of human decision making, and the respective reasoning system has two inputs and one output.

From the standpoint of system construction, we aim to obtain a system whose outputs, the *predicted* values, are similar to the experimentally obtained, *desired* values. We will assess the goodness of a system in the light of the following widely-used criteria: The root mean square error of the residuals (*Rmse*), certain basic statistics of the residuals and the normality of the residuals.

The data was divided into two parts. The *training data* comprised 95 randomly selected observations, and the rest of the observations (31) were used as *control data* (Fig. 1, Table 1). According to a two-sample t-test performed on these data, when the variances of the respective populations were assumed to be equal, the null hypothesis was accepted at the 0.05 level of significance (*i.e.*, no difference between the means).

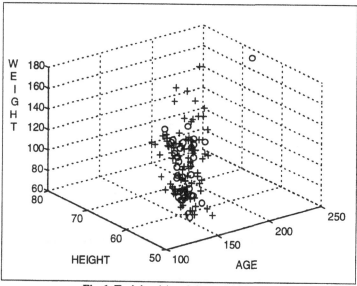

Fig. 1. Training (+) and Control (o) Data.

The system construction was based on the training data, whereas the assessments of the systems were performed using the control data. As usual, these systems were assumed to be applicable to interpolation, but extrapolation was the user's responsibility. As Figure 1 shows, one input vector of control data is clearly an outlier, and hence in this case the problem of extrapolation will arise.

Four reasoning algorithms were used: linear regression analysis, non-linear neural network, the Tagaki-Sugeno algorithm and the *Fmta*. As our aim is not knowledge engineering but rather to illustrate these approaches, the results are only tentative in nature.

	TRAINING			CONTROL		
	AGE	HEIGHT	WEIGHT	AGE	HEIGHT	WEIGHT
Mean	164.41	62.22	103.95	164.58	61.75	101.92
Standard Error	1.84	0.45	2.05	3.84	0.70	3.65
Median	163.00	62.00	105.00	160.00	61.80	100.00
Mode	144.00	60.00	112.00	140.00	56.80	112.00
Standard Deviation	17.94	4.40	19.93	21.38	3.91	20.32
Variance	321.97	19.38	397.39	457.05	15.31	412.98
Kurtosis	-0.75	-0.40	0.43	7.58	-0.88	3.46
Skewness	0.48	-0.15	0.65	2.17	0.15	1.30
Range	67.00	21.50	100.00	110.00	14.80	101.50
Minimum	139.00	50.50	71.50	140.00	55.00	70.00
Maximum	206.00	72.00	171.50	250.00	69.80	171.50
Sum	15619.00	5910.60	9875.00	5102.00	1914.40	3159.50
Count	95	95	95	31	31	31

Table 1. Descriptive Statistics of Training and Control Data.

3.2. Linear Regression Analysis

Linear regression analysis was performed by using the training data (Table 3). This algorithm was an appropriate benchmark because clear linear (Pearson) correlations prevailed between the input and the output variables (Table 2). Even though there was also a positive correlation between the independent variables, both of these variables were included in the system in the manner of [9].

	AGE	HEIGHT	WEIGHT
AGE	1		
HEIGHT	0.76	1	
WEIGHT	0.69	0.80	1

Table 2. Linear Pearson Correlations Between Variables.

Multiple R	0.814				
R Square	0.662				
Adjusted R Square	0.655				
Standard Error	11.708				
Observations	95				
Rmse	11.52				
Analysis of Variance					
	df	Sum of Squares	Mean Squares	F	Signif. F
Regression	2	24743.4	12371.7	90.3	0.000
Residual	92	12611.4	137.1		
Total	94	37354.7			
	Coeffs	Std Error	t- Statistic	P-value	
Intercept	-116.6	17.371	-6.712	0.000	
Age	0.211	0.104	2.030	0.045	
Height	2.987	0.424	7.044	0.000	

Table 3. Linear Regression Analysis Statistics, Training Data.

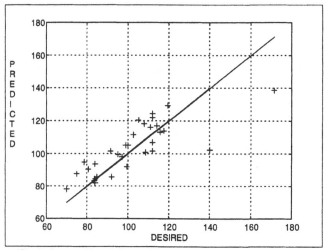

Fig. 2. Scatter Plot of Control Data, Desired *vs*. Predicted Weights, Linear Regression Analysis.

Then, these regression coefficients were used in the control data, *i.e.*,

$$weight = 0.21age + 2.99height - 116.60.$$

Figure 2 shows systematic error only when the weights were high, and this was expected because then extrapolation was performed. Statistics of the residuals are presented in Table 8.

3.3. Non-Linear System: Towards Neuro-Fuzzy Approach

Our data seems more or less linear by nature. However, in the actual world we usually deal with non-linear systems. The conventional approach usually describes these systems by using mathematical formulae, and hence we obtain mathematical systems. Then, it is possible that we would not be able to find an appropriate solution or the constructed mathematical system would be very complicated from the standpoint of comprensibility and calculation. In practice, supercomputer may cope with complicated calculations, but this procedure presupposes the availability of supercomputers and appropriate number crunching methods. We may also apply simplified, usually linear, systems, but then we often obtain oversimplified systems. An example of this problem area is weather forecasting.

As a mathematical approach, we apply the *Gmean*, because it is a good example of both a non-linear system and a neural network. In addition, in a sense, it is a numeric neuro-fuzzy system.

We will apply the *Gmean* in the form

$$Gmean(age, height, p, w_1, w_2) = (w_1 age^p + w_2 height^p)^{1/p},$$

in which $w_1 + w_2 = 1$. Our goal is to assign appropriate values to parameters w_1, w_2 and p in the light of the given criteria.

When tuning the parameters, we may apply conventional optimization algorithms, such as the Gauss-Newton method. In this context, we use a neural network which has one hidden layer, and this layer only contains one neuron, *viz.* the *Gmean* (*cf.* [4]). By using supervised learning in the training data, a backpropagation network and gradient descent optimization, the parameters were tuned. After 600 learning epochs, the initial values $w_1 = w_2 = 0.5$ and p=1 yielded the values 0.84, 0.16 and 3.09, respectively. We must bear in mind that this approach only yields local optimizations. Prior to the preceding procedure, the data was transformed to the closed interval [0,1] in order to apply the *Gmean*.

Figure 3 shows small systematic errors, but in general, this system seems slightly more satisfactory than the one constructed with linear regression analysis. The statistics of residuals is presented in Table 8.

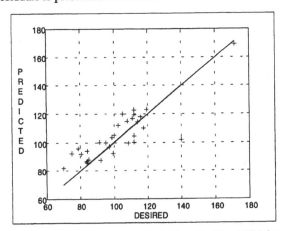

Fig. 3. Scatter Plot of Control Data, Desired *vs.* Predicted Weights, *Gmean*.

In addition to the non-linear approach, the preceding algorithm provides an example of how to use a fuzzy operator with numeric degrees of membership.

3.4. The Takagi-Sugeno Algorithm

The initial rules of our fuzzy system were based on scatter partition of the training data. In practice, Matlab's Fuzzy Logic Toolbox algorithm *Subclust* (based on the methods of [1, 11]) was applied, and the rules of Table 4 were obtained. A system with four rules seemed satisfactory in this context.

RULE	IF	THEN	
	Age	Height	Weight
1	151	58.3	86
2	172	65	112
3	193	67.8	127.5
4	150	61.8	118

Table 4. Initial Rules of Fuzzy System.

The Takagi-Sugeno algorithm [10] used the antecedents of the rules of Table 4 in the training data, but the consequents were linear functions (Table 5). These rules, which established a fuzzy associative memory, and the outputs of this memory were obtained by using the Matlab[TM] Fuzzy Logic Toolbox algorithm *Genfis2*. Once again, the goodness of this system was assessed in the control data.

RULE	IF		THEN
	Age	Height	Weight
1	151	58.3	-0.178age - 1.910height + 201.100
2	172	65	1.047age + 3.596height - 306.300
3	193	67.8	0.849age + 5.263height - 391.400
4	150	61.8	1.155age - 0.718height + 5.429

Table 5. Rules Used by *Genfis2*.

Figure 4 shows that this system yields values which are slightly too large, but it nevertheless is more satisfactory than the previous ones. The statistics of residuals are presented in Table 8.

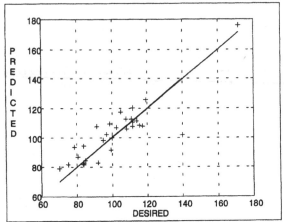

Fig. 4. Scatter Plot of Control Data, Desired *vs*. Predicted Weights, *Genfis2*.

In order to improve the results of *Genfis2*, the neuro-fuzzy Matlab Fuzzy Logic Toolbox algorithm *Anfis* [3] was also applied by using the rules of *Genfis2* (Table 4) as the initial values, but no better results were obtained. This outcome was probably due to the linear nature of the data, and hence it seems that only *Anfis* systems with greater number of rules would have yielded more satisfactory outputs .

3.5. *Fmta* Algorithm, a Neuro-Fuzzy Approach

The *Fmta* used in the training data the initial rules of Table 6, and these rules were obtained by using Matlab Fuzzy Logic Toolbox algorithm *Subclust* (two rules seemed sufficient).Then, the *Fmta* reasoning algorithm of Section 2 was applied with the parameters $p_{dist}=1$, $t=1.8$ and $p_{out}=1$. These values were heuristically established. The initial rules and the parameter t were tuned by applying a one-layer backpropagation neural network and gradient descent optimization. After 600 learning epochs we obtained $t=1.86$ and the rules of Table 7. The obtained fuzzy associative memory was assessed by using the control data.

RULE	IF		THEN
	Age	Height	Weight
1	164	63.5	108
2	142	55	76

Table 6. Cores of Initial Rules, *Fmta*.

RULE	IF		THEN
	Age	Height	Weight
1	152.0	65.3	156.1
2	156.8	55.7	36.5

Table 7. Cores of Tuned Rules, *Fmta*.

Figure 5 shows that the system yielded too small outputs when the desired values were very large. In the light of the given criteria, however, satisfactory results were obtained. The statistics of the residuals are presented in Table 8. More empiric justifications for the *Fmta* can be found in [5, 8, 9].

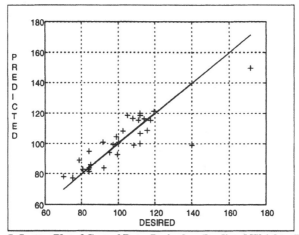

Fig. 5. Scatter Plot of Control Data, Desired *vs*. Predicted Weights, *Fmta*.

The great advantage of the *Fmta* over the other algorithms is that it is actually computing with words. We can use linguistic logic, *i.e.*, linguistic inputs and rules within reasoning, and we obtain normalized outputs which can be appropriately labeled. We can also operate both with truth values and with the principles of logic. In addition to the preceding data, which was precise and numeric by nature, we can cope with imprecise values, *i.e.*, fuzzy sets. Then, the values presented in Tables 6 and 7 can be regarded as being the cores of fuzzy sets and the supports are obtained by using similar algorithms (*cf.* [8]). For example, we can reason (Table 7, rule 1):

if age is about 152 months and height is about 65 inches, then weight is about 156 pounds.

or

if age is fairly young and height is fairly tall, then weight is fairly heavy.

This procedure, particularly if we aim to obtain outputs which can be labeled intelligibly, is unusual within the prevailing fuzzy associative memories.

3.6. Conclusions

The statistics and tests of the residuals of Table 8 show that, in the light of this data, the *Fmta* seems plausible and justified although these results were only assumed to be tentative in nature. This conclusion is also confirmed by Figures 2 to 5 which show the possible systematic errors of the algorithms.

Statistic	Linear regression	Gmean	Genfis2	Fmta
Mean	-0.679	-2.450	-1.551	1.551
Standard Error	2.182	1.912	1.802	1.802
Median	-3.728	-3.669	-3.402	3.402
Standard Dev.	12.148	10.646	10.034	10.034
Variance	147.582	113.335	100.673	100.673
Kurtosis	3.969	5.960	7.151	7.151
Skewness	1.796	1.829	1.981	-1.981
Range	54.085	55.508	54.317	54.317
Minimum	-15.799	-17.455	-16.321	-37.996
Maximum	38.286	38.053	37.996	16.321
Sum	-21.045	-75.957	-48.093	48.093
Count	31	31	31	31
Rmse	11.970	10.756	9.990	10.640
Test of normality (H0: normally distributed, Shapiro-Wilk test)	H1	H1	H1	H1
H0: mean=0 (t-test, sign test)	H0	H0 (t-test) H1 (sign test)	H0	H0
Outliers (Studentized residuals > 2)	2	1	1	2

Table 8. Statistics and Tests of Residuals.

The advantage of the *Fmta* over the prevailing algorithms is that we now have an applicable logico-linguistic user interface between the neuro-fuzzy systems and the user. This means that we can include both linguistic and more comprehensible entities in these systems. Hence, after a brief logopedics based on the *Fmta*, our data can speak, and we may compute with words.

References

[1]   S. Chiu, Fuzzy model identification based on cluster estimation, Journal of Intelligent and Fuzzy Systems, 2 (1994) 267-278.

[2]   H. Dyckhoff and W. Pedrycz, Generalized means as model of compensative connectives, Fuzzy Sets and Systems, 14 (1984) 143-154.

[3]   R. Jang, ANFIS: Adaptive-network-based fuzzy inference system, IEEE Transactions on Systems, Man and Cybernetics, 23/3 (1993) 665-685.

[4]   R. Krishnapuram & J. Lee, Fuzzy-connective-based hierarchial aggregation networks for decision making, Fuzzy Sets and Systems, 46/1 (1992) 11-28.

[5]   V. A. Niskanen, Empiric considerations on the fuzzy metric-truth approach. To appear, Fuzzy Sets and Systems.

[6]   V. A. Niskanen, The fuzzy metric-truth reasoning approach to decision making in soft computing milieux. To appear, Int. Journal of General Systems.

[7]   V. A. Niskanen, Metric truth as a basis for fuzzy linguistic reasoning. Fuzzy Sets and Systems, 57(1) (1993) 1-25.

[8]   V. A. Niskanen, Neuro-fuzzy systems within linguistic statistical decision making: Approximate reasoning without tears, submitted for consideration to L. Koczy, Ed., Soft Computing: Business and engineering applications (Physica Verlag).

[9]   V. A. Niskanen, The unbearable lightness of neuro-fuzzy multi-criteria decision making, in: P. Walden & al., Eds., The art and science of decision making (Painosalama, Turku, 1996), 168-178.

[9]   *SAS/STAT* User's guide, version 6.03 (SAS Institute Inc., Cary, 1988).

[10]   T. Takagi and M. Sugeno, Fuzzy identification of systems and its applications to modeling and control, IEEE Transactions on Systems, Man and Cybernetics, SMC-15(1) (1985) 116-132.

[11]   R. Yager and D. Filev, Generation of fuzzy rules by mountain clustering, Journal of Intelligent and Fuzzy Systems, 2 (1994) 209-219.

Evaluation of Fuzzy Quantified Expressions

Anca L. Ralescu[1]
ECE&CS Department, University of Cincinnati, USA
Anca.Ralescu@uc.edu

Dan A. Ralescu
Mathematical Sciences Department, University of Cincinnati, USA
Dan.Ralescu@math.uc.edu

Kaoru Hirota
Computational Intelligence and Systems Science Department
Tokyo Institute of Technology, Japan

Abstract

We present a fuzzy logic based quantitative treatment for expressions containing quantifiers. For this we develop an evaluation procedure for the truth value of expressions of the form $Qx \in X, p(x)$ where $Qx \in X$ is a quantifier and p is a predicate defined on X. This procedure is consistent, in the sense that it can be applied uniformly regardless of the type (exact or imprecise) of the quantifier and/or predicate used.

Key words: Fuzzy quantifiers, truth value, fuzzy cardinality

1 Introduction

Quantifiers, exact or imprecise, play an important role in achieving high expressive and descriptive power of natural language statements. In particular, imprecise/inexact quantifiers appear both directly and indirectly in dispositional statements often used to express heuristics. Quantifiers such as *most, slightly more than 50%, a few or less,* are often used. Yet a formal satisfactory quantitative treatment has, to a large extent eluded us. Current intelligent information processing requires among other the ability to handle statements with such quantifiers in a precise yet flexible way. For example, a

---

[1] Work partially supported by the JSPS short term fellowship at the Tokyo Institute of Technology, March - May 1997.

statement such as (i) *"Students who work hard have good results"*, is a disposition, that is, qualified by an imprecise quantifier (such as *"most"*). Restoring the quantifier the statement becomes *"Most students who work hard have good results"*. Such statements are often produced when we describe results of a summarization process, in order to capture and convey a more general meaning of a quantitative analysis. The importance of being able to manipulate such statements becomes obvious when we try to actually use them in a scheme of commonsense reasoning. We might be interested, given a database of records about students and their work performance to know to what extent that statement is true. Or, if in addition to (i) we have the statement (ii) *"About 85% if the students with good results will get high paying jobs"* we may be interested to use these statements and answer questions such as *"How many students in the class will get high paying jobs?"*. Regardless of the type of processing needed, a quantitative treatment of such statements calls for an apparatus capable of expressing imprecise quantifiers, and expressions such as *"work hard"*, *"good results"*, *"high pay"*. In addition, capability to perform computations on such expressions, and to re-express results in statements of similar format is necessary. It has been shown in [8] that fuzzy logic provides both the language and the computational mechanism necessary for expressing and computing with imprecise quantifiers, imprecise expressions, such as *"high paying jobs"*. A large body of research, including [2], [3], [4], [5], [7] has addressed various aspects of this treatment. Most recently, in [4] and [5] we proposed an alternative approach to expressing quantifiers and computing with these expressions.

Here we turn to the truth-value-problem, that is, we aim at developing a quantitative treatment for expressions containing quantifiers. For this we develop an evaluation procedure for the truth value of expressions of the form $Qx \in X, p(x)$ where $Qx \in X$ is a quantifier and P is a predicate defined on X. This procedure is consistent, in the sense that it can be applied uniformly regardless of the type (exact or imprecise) of the quantifier and/or predicate used.

Examples of quantifiers we are interested in include *for all* ($\forall$), and those formed by using determiners such as *some, most , a few*, such that statements of the following type are possible:
(a) $\forall x \in X, p(x)$;
(b) *Some* $x \in X$, $p(x)$;
(c) *Most* $x \in X$, $p(x)$

Suppose that in these examples we consider that $p()$ a crisp predicate, that is, $p()$ takes only the truth values true(1) and false(0). Then it is obvious that while (a) is either true or false, for (b) and (c) the truth depends on the meaning of *Some* , and *Most* . If in addition, we assume that $p()$ is a fuzzy predicate, then evaluating the truth values of the above statements becomes even more complex.

2. Notations, terminology and preliminary results

Throughout this paper X denotes the universe of discourse and we assume here that X is finite. For a set A, $CardA$ represents its cardinality, that is, the number of its elements. If A is a classical set then its cardinality is denoted by $|A|$. If A is a fuzzy set then $CardA$ denotes its (fuzzy) cardinality, while $|A|$ denotes the cardinality of its support. By definition the indicator function of a set A is

$$I_A(x) = \begin{cases} 1 & x \in A \\ 0 & otherwise \end{cases} \text{ and if } A = \{a\} \text{ we write } I_{\{a\}}(x) = I_a(x).$$

A fuzzy subset A of X is identified by its membership function $\mu_A : X \to [0,1]$. By $L_\alpha(A)$ we denote the α-level set of A, $L_a(A) = \{x \in X \mid m_A(x) \ge a\}$ for $0 \le a \le 1$.
$Qx \in X$ denotes a quantifier on X, where Q takes on various expressions such as *for all* ($\forall$), *there exists*($\exists$), *exactly k, most, a few*, etc. A quantifier on X is defined as a subset (crisp or fuzzy) of $CardX$.

A predicate p on X is defined as a subset X_p of X. The truth value of $p(x)$ is given by the value $I_{X_p}(x)$, if the predicate is crisp (that is, if X_p is a subset of X in the classic sense). p is an imprecise predicate if X_p is a fuzzy subset of X, and in this case p is represented by a membership function, $\mu_p : X \to [0,1]$. In this case $\mu_p(x)$ is the truth value with which p holds at $x \in X$. When p is an imprecise predicate we denote by X_p the support of the membership function, that is $X_p \equiv \text{support } \mu_p = \{x \in X; \mu_p(x) > 0\}$. Let $t_{\forall, X, p}$ denote the degree of truth for the expression $Qx \in X, p(x)$.

We adopt here a cardinality based approach to quantifiers. Our treatment of cardinality follows that proposed in [3] and further discussed in [6]. We briefly review the results to be used here.

Let $X = \{x_1, ..., x_n\}$ be a finite set and let A be a *fuzzy subset* of X represented by its membership function $\mu_A : X \to [0,1]$. Let $\overline{A}$ denote the complement of A with the membership function $\mu_{\overline{A}}(x) = 1 - \mu_A(x)$.

Let $\mu_A^{(1)} \ge \mu_A^{(2)} \ge ... \ge \mu_A^{(n)}$ be the values $\mu_A(x_i), i = 1, ..., n$ arranged in non-increasing order of their magnitudes. By convention, if $|A|$ denotes the crisp cardinality of support μ_A we define $\mu_A^{(0)} = 1$ and $\mu_A^{(|A|+1)} = 0$.

Definition 1[6]. The cardinality of a fuzzy set A, denoted $CardA$ is a fuzzy subset of $\{0,1,...,n\}$ with $CardA(k)$ being the possibility to which A has exactly k elements, $0 \le k \le n$.

Theorem 1([3],[6]).*The fuzzy cardinality of A is given by*
$$Card\, A(k) = \mu_A^{(k)} \wedge (1 - \mu_A^{(k+1)}),\ k = 0,1,...,n$$
Proof: We omit the proof as it is given in [3] and also sketched in [6].

Proposition 1 ([6]). $CardA(k) = 1$ if and only if A is a non fuzzy sets with k elements.

proof: See [6] proposition 1.

Proposition 2([6]). Let A be a fuzzy subset of X. Then
(i) $CardA$ is a fuzzy convex set.
(ii) $CardA(k) = Card\overline{A}(n-k)$, for $k = 0,1,...,n$

(iii) $Truth(Card\, A \geq k) = \begin{cases} \mu_A^{(k)} & if\, k \geq j \\ (1 - \mu_A^{(j)}) \vee \mu_A^{(j)} & if\, k < j \end{cases}$

where $j = \begin{cases} \max\{1 \leq s \leq n \,|\, \mu_A^{(s-1)} + \mu_A^{(s)} > 1\} & if\, A \neq \varnothing \\ 0 & if\, A = \varnothing \end{cases}$

proof: See [6] Propositions 2-4.

Remark 1 From proposition 2 (iii) it follows that if $support\,\mu_A$ has exactly $|A|$ elements then $Poss(Card\, A = |A|) = \mu_A^{(|A|)}$.

A non fuzzy version of the cardinality of a fuzzy set can be defined as follows.

Definition 2 ([6], Definition 1). The nonfuzzy cardinality of a fuzzy subset A of X, denoted by $ncard\, A$ is the integer
$$ncardA = \begin{cases} 0 & if\, A = \varnothing \\ j & if\, A \neq \varnothing\ and\ \mu_A^{(j)} \geq 0.5 \\ j-1 & if\, A \neq \varnothing\ and\ \mu_A^{(j)} < 0.5 \end{cases}$$
where $j = \max\{1 \leq s \leq n \,|\, \mu^{(s-1)} + \mu^{(s)} > 1\}$

Remark 2 $ncard\, A$ has the following property $card\, A(ncard\, A) = \max\limits_{0 \leq k \leq n} card\, A(k)$

Moreover the following proposition summarizes other important properties of $ncard\, A$.

Proposition 3 ([6]).
(i) If $A \leq B$ (i.e. A is a fuzzy subset of B) then $ncard\, A \leq ncard\, B$.
(ii) Let A be a fuzzy subset of X and let $L_{0.5}$ denote its 0.5 level set (a crisp set). If $L_{0.5}$ has exactly k elements then $ncard\, A = k$.

proof: The proof can be found in [6], proposition 5 for part (i) and proposition 9 for part (ii).

Remark 3 A statement similar to (i) in proposition 3 does not hold in general for the non fuzzy cardinality as the following example shows.

Let $A = \begin{pmatrix} x_1 & x_2 & x_3 & x_4 \\ 0.8 & 0.7 & 0.3 & 0.2 \end{pmatrix}$ and $B = \begin{pmatrix} x_1 & x_2 & x_3 & x_4 \\ 0.9 & 0.8 & 0.4 & 0.2 \end{pmatrix}$ be two fuzzy sets such that

$A \leq B$, that is, $\mu_A(x_i) \leq \mu_B(x_i)$, $i = 1,..., 4$.

Yet, $Card A = \begin{pmatrix} 0 & 1 & 2 & 3 & 4 \\ 0.2 & 0.3 & 0.7 & 0.3 & 0.2 \end{pmatrix}$ and $Card B = \begin{pmatrix} 0 & 1 & 2 & 3 & 4 \\ 0.1 & 0.2 & 0.6 & 0.4 & 0.2 \end{pmatrix}$ and therefore

it is not true that $Card A(k) \leq Card B(k)$ for all $k = 0,..., 4$.

3 Expressions with crisp quantifiers and crisp predicates

We start our discussion from the classical situation in which both the quantifier and the predicate used are crisp. More precisely, recall that we assume X finite, i.e. $X = \{x_1,..., x_n\}$ and let us denote by $X_p = \{x \in X \mid p(x) \text{ holds}\}$.

Definition 3. The degree of truth for the expression $\forall x \in X, p(x)$ is by definition
$$t_{\forall, X, p} = I_{|X_p|}(|X|) \tag{1}$$

Example 1. Let $X = \{0, 1, ...,10\}$ and let the predicate p be defined as $p = \{x / x \geq 0\}$. Obviously, $X_p = X$ and hence $t_{\forall, X, p} = I_{|X_p|}(|X|) = 1$.

Proposition 4. If p is a crisp predicate defined on X then the expression $\forall x \in X, p(x)$ is true if and only if $t_{\forall, X, p} = 1$.

proof: First we note that from the definition of the indicator function it follows that $t_{\forall, X, p} = 1$ or $t_{\forall, X, p} = 0$. To say that $\forall x \in X, p(x)$ is true it means that $X_p = X$, and hence $|X_p| = |X|$. In terms of the indicator function we can write $I_{|X|}(|X_p|) = I_{|Xp|}(|X|) = 1$. Therefore $t_{\forall, X, p} = 1$. Now suppose by contradiction that $\forall x \in X, p(x)$ is true and that $t_{\forall, X, p} \neq 1$, that is, $t_{\forall, X, p} = 0$. From the definition it follows that $|X| > |X_p|$ (in general $|X_p| \leq |X|$) and therefore that $X_p \subset X$ (since by definition $X_p \subseteq X$). Hence $X_{\neg p} = \{x \in X | \neg p(x) \text{holds}\} \neq \emptyset$ which means that the expression $\exists x \in X, \neg p(x)$ is true. This in turn means that the expression $\forall x \in X, p(x)$ is not true.

Proposition 5. If $\forall x \in X, p(x)$ is true in the sense of (1), and X_k is a subset of $k = 1, 2,..., |X|$ elements of X, then the statement $\forall x \in X_k, p(x)$ is true in the sense of (1).

proof: For fixed k we consider $X_k = \{x_{i1},..., x_{ik}\}$. Since $\forall x \in X, p(x)$ is true it follows that $p(x_{i_l})$, $l = 1, 2,..k$ is true. Therefore $X_{k,p} = \{x | x \in X_k, p(x) \text{holds}\} = X_k$, and hence $|X_{k,p}| = |X_k|$ from which it follows that $t_{\forall, X_k, p} = I_{|X_{k,p}|}(|X_k|) = 1$.

Corollary 1. If the expression $\forall x \in X, p(x)$ is true in the sense of (1) then the statement $Qx \in X, p(x)$ is true in the sense of (1) for any crisp quantifier Q.

Proof: The proof follows from proposition 2 and the fact that any crisp quantifier specifies the cardinality of a subset of X.

Corollary 2. If p' is a crisp predicate such that p implies p' (in the sense that whenever p is true p' is also true) and the statement $\forall x \in X, p(x)$ holds true in the sense of (1) then the statement $\forall x \in X, p'(x)$ holds true in the sense of (1) as well.

proof: The proof follows from the fact that if p implies p' then $X_p \subseteq X_{p'}$ and hence since $|X_p| = |X|$ it follows that $|X_{p'}| = |X|$.

Example 2. For $X = \{0, 1, ..., 10\}$ and p as in example 1 let p' be defined as $p' = \{x / x \geq -10\}$. Obviously, $X_{p'} = X_p = X$ and therefore $t_{\forall, X, p'} = I_{|X_{p'}|}(|X|) = 1$.

4 Expressions with crisp quantifiers and fuzzy predicates

We consider next the case when the crisp quantifier $\forall$ is and the predicate p is fuzzy. That is, p is defined in terms of a membership function $\mu_p(x)$ which indicates the degree to which $x \in X$ satisfies p. In this case $|X_p|$ is the cardinality of the support of the membership function, support μ_p. The cardinality, *Card* p, of the fuzzy set defined by $\mu_p(x)$, is the fuzzy set with membership function

$$Card\ p(k) = \mu_p^{(k)} \wedge (1 - \mu_p^{(k+1)}) \tag{2}$$

where $k = 0, 1, ..., |X_p|$, $\mu_p^{(k)}$ denotes the *kth* largest value of $\mu_p(x)$, with $\mu_p^{(0)} = 1$, and $\mu_p^{(|X_p|+1)} = 0$. By analogy with definition 3 we have the following definition.

Definition 4. The degree of truth for the expression $\forall x \in X, p(x)$ when p is a fuzzy predicate is by definition

$$t_{\forall, X, \mu_p} = Card\ p(|X|) \tag{3}$$

where for simplicity *Card* p denotes both the fuzzy cardinality of p and its membership function.

Using the definition for the membership function of *Card* p we obtain a formula for $t_{\forall, X, \mu_p}$ in terms membership function $\mu_p(x)$:

$$Card\ p(|X|) = \mu_p(|X|) \tag{4}$$

Remark 4 It can be seen that (3) reduces to (1) if p is crisp. Indeed, in this case *Card* $p = |X_p|$ is also crisp, and *Card* $p(|X|) = I_{|X_p|}(|X|)$.

Remark 5 It can be seen from (2) that the cardinality of a fuzzy set is not a normal fuzzy set, that is its height is never equal to 1. Therefore, $0 \leq t_{\forall, X, \mu_p} < 1$. This seems counterintuitive at first. However, a more careful inspection indicates that indeed, we cannot really say that $p(x)$ holds for *all* x as long as there are elements x for which it holds with degree strictly less than 1. More over, we can prove the following proposition:

Proposition 6. Let p be a fuzzy predicate on X.
(i) The degree to which $\forall x \in X, p(x)$ holds true is 0 if and only if $X_p \subset X$.
(ii) The degree to which $\forall x \in X, p(x)$ holds true is 1 if and only if p is a crisp predicate and $X = X_p$.

proof: (i) If $X_p \subset X$ then $|X_p| \triangleleft |X|$ and since $Card\ p(|X_p|+1) = 0$ it follows from the properties of fuzzy cardinality that $Card\ p(|X|) = 0$. Next, assume that $Card\ p(|X|) = 0$. Since $X_p \subseteq X$ it follows that $X_p \subset X$.
(ii) From (3) it follows that $Card\ p(|X|) = 1$. According to proposition 1 it follows p specifies a crisp set with exactly $|X| = |X_p|$ elements. Since $X_p \subseteq X$ it follows that $X_p = X$.

Example 3. Let $X = \{0, 1, ..., 10\}$ be as in the previous examples and let p be defined as $p \equiv \tilde{3} \equiv approximately\ 3$ with the membership function

$$\mu_p = \begin{pmatrix} 1 & 2 & 3 & 4 & 5....10 \\ 0.1 & 0.5 & 1 & 0.5 & 0....0 \end{pmatrix}. \text{ Then } X_p = \{1, 2, 3, 4\}, |X_p| = 4 \text{ and}$$

$$Card\ p = \begin{pmatrix} 0 & 1 & 2 & 3 & 4 \\ 0 & 0.5 & 0.5 & 0.5 & 0.1 \end{pmatrix}. \text{ Therefore } Card\ p(|X|) = Card\ p(10) = 0.$$

Corresponding to Proposition 4 we have the following proposition.

Proposition 7. Let $p(x)$ be a fuzzy predicate and assume that the statement $\forall x \in X, p(x)$ is true with degree $t_{\forall, X, \mu_p}$. Then the statement $\forall x \in X_k \subset X, p(x)$ is true with a degree $t_{\forall, X_k \mu_p} \geq t_{\forall, X, \mu_p}$.

proof: Let $X_k = \{x_{i1}, ... x_{ik}\}$ and let $\mu_{k,p}$ denote the restriction of μ_p to X_k. Then $t_{\forall, X_k \mu_{k,p}} = Card_k\ p(|X_k|) = \mu_{k,p}^{(|X_k|)}$ where $Card_k\ p$ is the fuzzy cardinality of $\mu_{k,p}$, and $\mu_{k,p}^{(|X_k|)}$ is the smallest value of $\mu_{k,p}$. From the definition of $\mu_{k,p}$ it follows that this value is greater than or equal to $\mu_p^{(|X|)}$ which is $t_{\forall, X, \mu_p}$.

Example 4. Let $X = \{0, 1, ..., 10\}$ and p be as in example 3.

Let $X_2 = \{2\} \subset X$. Then the restriction of μ_p to X_2 is $\mu_{2,p} = \begin{pmatrix} 2 \\ 0.5 \end{pmatrix}$, its cardinality is

$$Card_2 p = \begin{pmatrix} 1 \\ 0.5 \end{pmatrix} \text{ and } |X_2| = 1. \text{ Therefore}$$

$$t_{\forall, X_2 \mu_{2,p}} = Card_2\ p(|X_2|) = 0.5 \geq 0 = t_{\forall, X \mu_p}.$$

5 Expressions with fuzzy quantifiers and crisp predicates

We consider the case when $p(x)$ is a crisp predicate and Q is a fuzzy quantifier. Actually, following [1] we will call Q a determiner and call a quantifier an expression of the form Q of X. In the approach taken here we view quantifiers from a cardinality view point and consequently either X is a subset of the positive integers, or is the cardinality of a set. Thus Q is defined by a membership function $\mu_{Q\,of\,X}(k), k = 0, 1, ... |X|$. Since $p(x)$ is a crisp predicate its cardinality coincides with $|X_p|$ and it is a crisp quantity.

To define the truth value for the expression $Q\,x \in X\ p(x)$ in this case we notice first that in the case when both the quantifier and predicate are crisp the formula for computing the truth value can be rewritten as $t_{\forall,X,p} = I_{|X|}(|X_p|)$. By analogy with this we have the following definition:

Definition 5. The degree of truth for the expression $Q\,x \in X\ p(x)$ when p is a crisp predicate and Q is a fuzzy quantifier is given by

$$t_{Q,X,\mu_p} = \mu_{Q\,of\,|X|}(|X_p|) \tag{5}$$

In (5) $\mu_{Q\,of\,X}(k)$ plays the role of $I_{|X|}(k)$ in (1), that is, Q determines the cardinality of the set of elements in X for which the statement $p(x)$ is made.

Example 5. Let X be as in example 1, $p(x) = \{x | 2 \le x \le 4\}$ and let the determiner $Q \equiv most$ used to form the quantifier $most$ of X be defined by the membership function

$$\mu_{most\,of\,N}(k) = \begin{cases} 0 & if \quad k \le \dfrac{N}{2} \\ \dfrac{2(2k-N)}{N} & if \quad \dfrac{N}{2} < k \le \dfrac{3N}{4} \\ 1 & if \quad \dfrac{3N}{4} < k \le N \end{cases}$$

Then, for $X = \{0, 1, ..., 10\}$, since its cardinality is 10 we have

$$\mu_{most\,of\,X}(k) = \mu_{most\,of\,10}(k) = \begin{cases} 0 & if \quad k \le 5 \\ \dfrac{2(k-5)}{5} & if \quad 5 < k \le 7.5 \\ 1 & if \quad 7.5 < k \le 10 \end{cases}$$

and we have that the truth value for the expression
$Most\ values\ in\{0, 1, ..., 10\} are\ in\{2, 3, 4\}$ is equal to $\mu_{most\,of\,10}(3) = 0$.

Remark 6 For the particular case when $Q \equiv \forall$ by defining $\mu_{\forall of\,X} \equiv I_{|X|}$ (5) reduces to $I_{|X|}(|X_p|)$ which is equivalent to (1).

Remark 7 If the quantifier Q is normal it is possible that $t_{Q,X,p} = 1$ (when p is such that $\mu_{Q\,of\,X}(|X_p|) = 1$).

Proposition 8. (i) If Q is monotone non decreasing fuzzy quantifier (with non decreasing membership function $\mu_{Q of\ x}$) and p, p' are two predicates such that p implies p', in the sense that $X_p \subset X_{p'}$ then $t_{Q,x\,p'} \geq t_{Q,x\,p}$.

(ii) If $Q_i, i = 1,2$ are two fuzzy quantifiers such that $Q_1 \subseteq Q_2$ (fuzzy set inclusion), then $t_{Q_2,x\,p} \geq t_{Q_1,x\,p}$.

proof: The proof is straightforward and follows from the assumptions and the definition 5.

Example 6. Let X, p and the determiner $Q \equiv most$ be as in example 5. Let p' be defined as $p'(x) = \{x \mid 2 \leq x \leq 7\}$. p implies p' in the sense that $X_p \subset X_{p'}$ and hence $|X_p| = 3 < 6 = |X_{p'}|$. Therefore

$$t_{most,X\,p'} = \mu_{most of\ 10}(6) = 0.4 > 0 = \mu_{most of 10}(3) \geq t_{most,X\,p}$$

Example 7. Let X, p' and the determiner $Q \equiv most$ be as in example 6. Let the determiner $Q' \equiv approximately\ 80\%$ be given by the membership function

$$\mu_{approximately\ 80\% of\ N}(k) = \begin{cases} 0 & if & k \leq \dfrac{3N}{4} \\[2mm] \dfrac{5(4k-3N)}{N} & if & \dfrac{3N}{4} < k \leq \dfrac{4N}{5} \\[2mm] \dfrac{17N-20k}{N} & if & \dfrac{4N}{5} < k \leq \dfrac{17N}{20} \\[2mm] 0 & if & \dfrac{17N}{20} < k \leq N \end{cases}$$

Hence

$$\mu_{approximately\ 80\% of 10}(k) = \begin{cases} 0 & if & k \leq 7.5 \\ 2k-15 & if & 7.5 < k \leq 8 \\ 17-2k & if & 8 < k \leq 8.5 \\ 0 & if & 8.5 < k \leq 10 \end{cases}$$

Obviously $\mu_{approximately\ 80\% of\ N}(k) \leq \mu_{most of\ N}(k)$.

Also, $t_{Most,X\,p'} = \mu_{most of\ 10}(6) = 0.4 > 0 = \mu_{approximately 80\%}(6) \geq t_{approximately\ 80\%,X\,p'}$

6 Expressions with fuzzy quantifiers and fuzzy predicates

For the most general case we need to define the truth value such that it is consistent with each of the previous three cases. More precisely the definition of must be such that

$$t_{Q,X,\mu_p} = \begin{cases} I_{|x_p|}(|X|) & if & Q \equiv \forall, p\ is\ crisp \\ \mu_{|x_p|}(|X|) & if & Q \equiv \forall, p\ is\ fuzzy \\ \mu_{Q of\ |X|}(|X_p|) & if & Q\ is\ fuzzy, p\ is\ crisp \end{cases}$$

To achieve this effect we use the following definition.

Definition 6. The truth value for the expression $Q\, x \in X\, p(x)$ when both Q and p are fuzzy is given by

$$t_{Q,X,p} = \bigvee_{k=0}^{|X|} Card\, p(k) \wedge \mu_{Q\,of\,|X|}(k) \tag{6}$$

Remark 8 By substituting the definition for the fuzzy cardinality we obtain

$$t_{Q,X,p} = \bigvee_{k=0}^{|X|} \mu_p^{(k)} \wedge (1 - \mu_p^{(k+1)}) \wedge \mu_{Q\,of\,|X|}(k) \quad \text{first introduced in [3] in connection with}$$

aggregation of fuzzy sets.

Remark 9 Under the conditions of the previous sections equation (6) reduces to the corresponding equations given in each section. More precisely, suppose that both Q and predicate p are crisp. In particular, suppose that $Q = \forall$. Then $\mu_Q \equiv I_{|X|}$ and $Card\, p \equiv I_{|X_p|}$ and since $|X_p| \leq |X|$ (6) reduces to $t_{\forall,X,p} = Card\, p(|X|) = I_{|X_p|}(|X|)$ which is the same as (1); If p is a fuzzy predicate (6) reduces to $t_{\forall,X,p} = \mu_p^{(|X|)}$ which is the same as (4); finally, if Q is fuzzy and p is crisp its cardinality $Card\, p \equiv I_{|X_p|}$ and hence (6) reduces to (5).

Since on one hand, the fuzzy inclusion between two sets does not translate into a consistent relation between their cardinalities (see Remark 3) while on the other hand, it does translate into a relation between their non fuzzy cardinalities (see proposition 3(i)) we approximate (6) by substituting the non fuzzy cardinality, $nCard\, p$, in place of $Card\, p$. This means that, in effect, we reduce (6) to a particular case of (5), that is,

$$\tilde{t}_{Q,X,p} = \bigvee_{k=0}^{|X|} nCard\, p(k) \wedge \mu_{Q\,of\,|X|}(k) = \mu_{Q\,of\,|X|}(nCard\, p) \tag{6'}$$

where $nCard\, p(k) = I_{nCard\, p}(k)$. Corresponding to proposition 8 we have now the following proposition.

Proposition 9.
(i) If Q is a monotone non decreasing fuzzy quantifier (with non decreasing membership function $\mu_{Q\,of\,X}$) and p, p' are two predicates such that p implies (that is, $p \leq p'$ in the sense of inclusion of fuzzy sets) then $\tilde{t}_{Q,X,p'} \geq \tilde{t}_{Q,X,p}$.

(ii) If Q is a monotone non decreasing fuzzy quantifier then $t_{Q,X,\mu_p} \leq Card\, p(nCard\, p) \wedge \mu_{Q\,of\,|X|}(|X|)$.

(iii) If $Q_i, i = 1, 2$ are two fuzzy quantifiers such that $Q_1 \subseteq Q_2$ (fuzzy set inclusion), then $t_{Q_2,X,p} \geq t_{Q_1,X,p}$.

proof: We omit the proof as it is straightforward using the previous results.

Example 8. Let $X = \{0, 1, ..., 10\}$, p be as in the previous examples.
Let $p' \equiv$ "*approximately between* 4 *and* 6" given by membership function

$$\mu_{p'} = \begin{pmatrix} 2 & 3 & 4 & 5 & 6 & 7 \\ 0 & 0.5 & 1 & 1 & 0.5 & 0 \end{pmatrix} \quad \text{and let and the determiner}$$

$Q \equiv$ "*approximately* 40% *or* l arg *er*" with membership function

$$\mu_{Q \, of \, 10} = \begin{pmatrix} 2 & 3 & 4 & 5 & 6....10 \\ 0 & 0.6 & 1 & 1 & 1..... 1 \end{pmatrix}. \text{ Obviously, } \mu_p(i) \leq \mu_{p'}(i) \text{ for } i = 1,..., 4$$

and therefore $nCard \, p = 3 < 4 = nCard \, p'$. Thus

$$\tilde{t}_{Q, x \, p'} \equiv \mu_{Q \, of \, 10}(4) = 1 > 0.6 = \mu_{Q \, of \, 10}(3) \equiv \tilde{t}_{Q, x \, p}.$$

Similar examples can be constructed to illustrate parts (ii) and (iii) of proposition 9.

7 Conclusion

We have presented a fuzzy logic based approach to evaluation of truth values of expressions of the form where is a predicate defined on and is a quantifier defined on. In this approach the evaluation is consistent with any combination of fuzzy/non fuzzy quantifiers and predicates, in the sense that the same type of results carry over all these cases. Moreover, it appears that some concepts defined in a logic based context find their equivalent in this treatment. For example, the notion of monotone non decreasing quantifiers as defined in [1] and that in which the quantifier is defined by a monotone non decreasing membership function coincide. Results of this type need to be further exploited.

Acknowledgment. Thanks are due to Riad Hartani who patiently listened to A. L. Ralescu's exposition of these issues during a somewhat long train journey in Tokyo amid crowds, and still managed to make some useful comments.

References

1. J. Bairwise and R. Cooper, Generalized quantifiers and natural language (1980), preprint.

2. D. Dubois and H. Prade, Fuzzy cardinality and the modeling of imprecise quantification, *Fuzzy Sets Systems* **16** (1985)199-230

3. A. L. Ralescu, A note on rule representation in expert systems, *Information Sciences* **38** (1986) 193-203.

4. A. L. Ralescu (with B. Bouchon-Meunier, D. A. Ralescu), Combining fuzzy quantifiers. *Proceedings of the International Joint Conference of CFSA/IFIS/SOFT'95 on Fuzzy Theory and Applications, Taipei, Taiwan*, Dec. 7-9 1995.

5. A. L. Ralescu (with B. Bouchon-Meunier), Rules with fuzzy quantifiers and applications, *Proceedings of the Third European Systems Science Congress*, Rome, October 1-4, 1996.

6. D. A. Ralescu, Cardinality, quantifiers, and the aggregation of fuzzy criteria, *Fuzzy sets and Systems,* **69** (1995) 355-365.

7. R.R. Yager, Connectives and quantifiers in fuzzy sets, *Fuzzy Sets and Systems* **40** (1991) 39-75.

8. L. A. Zadeh, A computational approach to fuzzy quantifiers in natural languages, *Computers and mathematics,* **9** (1983) 149-184.

Author Index

Baldwin, J. F. 22, 62, 91
Bloch, I. 149
Bouchon-Meunier, B. 190

Desachy , J. 180
Dubois, D. 9, 79

Esteva, F. 79

Fondacci, R. 190

Garcia, P. 79
Godo, L. 79
Guesgen, H. W. 133

Hirota, K. 234

Knoll, A. 205

López de Màntaras, R. 79

Martin, T. P. 62, 91

Narazaki, H. 45
Niskanen, V. A. 222

Prade, H. 9, 79

Ralescu, A. L. 234
Ralescu, D. A. 234
Roux , L. 166

Shanahan, J. G. 91
Shigaki, I. 45

Tano, S. 117

Vargas-Vera, M. 62

Wendling , L. 180

Zadeh, L. A. 1
Zerrouki, L. 190
Zhang , J. 205

Springer
and the
environment

At Springer we firmly believe that an international science publisher has a special obligation to the environment, and our corporate policies consistently reflect this conviction.

We also expect our business partners – paper mills, printers, packaging manufacturers, etc. – to commit themselves to using materials and production processes that do not harm the environment. The paper in this book is made from low- or no-chlorine pulp and is acid free, in conformance with international standards for paper permanency.

Springer

Lecture Notes in Artificial Intelligence (LNAI)

Vol. 1504: O. Herzog, A. Günter (Eds.), KI-98: Advances in Artificial Intelligence. Proceedings, 1998. XI, 355 pages. 1998.

Vol. 1510: J.M. Zytkow, M. Quafafou (Eds.), Principles of Data Mining and Knowledge Discovery. Proceedings, 1998. XI, 482 pages. 1998.

Vol. 1515: F. Moreira de Oliveira (Ed.), Advances in Artificial Intelligence. Proceedings, 1998. X, 259 pages. 1998.

Vol. 1527: P. Baumgartner, Theory Reasoning in Connection Calculi. IX, 283 pages. 1999.

Vol. 1529: D. Farwell, L. Gerber, E. Hovy (Eds.), Machine Translation and the Information Soup. Proceedings, 1998. XIX, 532 pages. 1998.

Vol. 1531: H.-Y. Lee, H. Motoda (Eds.), PRICAI'98: Topics in Artificial Intelligence. XIX, 646 pages. 1998.

Vol. 1532: S. Arikawa, H. Motoda (Eds.), Discovery Science. Proceedings, 1998. XI, 456 pages. 1998.

Vol. 1534: J.S. Sichman, R. Conte, N. Gilbert (Eds.), Multi-Agent Systems and Agent-Based Simulation. Proceedings, 1998. VIII, 237 pages. 1998.

Vol. 1535: S. Ossowski, Co-ordination in Artificial Agent Societies. XVI, 221 pages. 1999.

Vol. 1537: N. Magnenat-Thalmann, D. Thalmann (Eds.), Modelling and Motion Capture Techniques for Virtual Environments. Proceedings, 1998. IX, 273 pages. 1998.

Vol. 1544: C. Zhang, D. Lukose (Eds.), Multi-Agent Systems. Proceedings, 1998. VII, 195 pages. 1998.

Vol. 1545: A. Birk, J. Demiris (Eds.), Learning Robots. Proceedings, 1996. IX, 188 pages. 1998.

Vol. 1555: J.P. Müller, M.P. Singh, A.S. Rao (Eds.), Intelligent Agents V. Proceedings, 1998. XXIV, 455 pages. 1999.

Vol. 1562: C.L. Nehaniv (Ed.), Computation for Metaphors, Analogy, and Agents. X, 389 pages. 1999.

Vol. 1566: A.L. Ralescu, J.G. Shanahan (Eds.), Fuzzy Logic in Artificial Intelliegence. Proceedings, 1997. X, 245 pages. 1999.

Vol. 1570: F. Puppe (Ed.), XPS-99: Knowledge-Based Systems. VIII, 227 pages. 1999.

Vol. 1571: P. Noriega, C. Sierra (Eds.), Agent Mediated Electronic Commerce. Proceedings, 1998. IX, 207 pages. 1999.

Vol. 1572: P. Fischer, H.U. Simon (Eds.), Computational Learning Theory. Proceedings, 1999. X, 301 pages. 1999.

Vol. 1574: N. Zhong, L. Zhou (Eds.), Methodologies for Knowledge Discovery and Data Mining. Proceedings, 1999. XV, 533 pages. 1999.

Vol. 1582: A. Lecomte, F. Lamarche, G. Perrier (Eds.), Logical Aspects of Computational Linguistics. Proceedings, 1997. XI, 251 pages. 1999.

Vol. 1585: B. McKay, X. Yao, C.S. Newton, J.-H. Kim, T. Furuhashi (Eds.), Simulated Evolution and Learning. Proceedings, 1998. XIII, 472 pages. 1999.

Vol. 1599: T. Ishida (Ed.), Multiagent Platforms. Proceedings, 1998. VIII, 187 pages. 1999.

Vol. 1604: M. Asada, H. Kitano (Eds.), RoboCup-98: Robot Soccer World Cup II. XI, 509 pages. 1999.

Vol. 1609: Z. W. Raś, A. Skowron (Eds.), Foundations of Intelligent Systems. Proceedings, 1999. XII, 676 pages. 1999.

Vol. 1611: I. Imam, Y. Kodratoff, A. El-Dessouki, M. Ali (Eds.), Multiple Approaches to Intelligent Systems. Proceedings, 1999. XIX, 899 pages. 1999.

Vol. 1612: R. Bergmann, S. Breen, M. Göker, M. Manago, S. Wess, Developing Industrial Case-Based Reasoning Applications. XX, 188 pages. 1999.

Vol. 1617: N.V. Murray (Ed.), Automated Reasoning with Analytic Tableaux and Related Methods. Proceedings, 1999. X, 325 pages. 1999.

Vol. 1620: W. Horn, Y. Shahar, G. Lindberg, S. Andreassen, J. Wyatt (Eds.), Artificial Intelligence in Medicine. Proceedings, 1999. XIII, 454 pages. 1999.

Vol. 1621: D. Fensel, R. Studer (Eds.), Knowledge Acquisition Modeling and Management. Proceedings, 1999. XI, 404 pages. 1999.

Vol. 1632: H. Ganzinger (Ed.), Automated Deduction – CADE-16. Proceedings, 1999. XIV, 429 pages. 1999.

Vol. 1634: S. Džeroski, P. Flach (Eds.), Inductive Logic Programming. Proceedings, 1999. VIII, 303 pages. 1999.

Vol. 1637: J.P. Walser, Integer Optimization by Local Search. XIX, 137 pages. 1999.

Vol. 1638: A. Hunter, S. Parsons (Eds.), Symbolic and Quantitative Approaches to Reasoning and Uncertainty. Proceedings, 1999. IX, 397 pages. 1999.

Vol. 1640: W. Tepfenhart, W. Cyre (Eds.), Conceptual Structures: Standards and Practices. Proceedings, 1999. XII, 515 pages. 1999.

Vol. 1647: F.J. Garijo, M. Boman (Eds.), Multi-Agent System Engineering. Proceedings, 1999. X, 233 pages. 1999.

Vol. 1650: K.-D. Althoff, R. Bergmann, L.K. Branting (Eds.), Case-Based Reasoning Research and Development. Proceedings, 1999. XII, 598 pages. 1999.

Vol. 1652: M. Klusch, O.M. Shehory, G. Weiss (Eds.), Cooperative Information Agents III. Proceedings, 1999. XI, 404 pages. 1999.

Lecture Notes in Computer Science

Vol. 1619: M.T. Goodrich, C.C. McGeoch (Eds.), Algorithm Engineering and Experimentation. Proceedings, 1999. VIII, 349 pages. 1999.

Vol. 1620: W. Horn, Y. Shahar, G. Lindberg, S. Andreassen, J. Wyatt (Eds.), Artificial Intelligence in Medicine. Proceedings, 1999. XIII, 454 pages. 1999. (Subseries LNAI).

Vol. 1621: D. Fensel, R. Studer (Eds.), Knowledge Acquisition Modeling and Management. Proceedings, 1999. XI, 404 pages. 1999. (Subseries LNAI).

Vol. 1622: M. González Harbour, J.A. de la Puente (Eds.), Reliable Software Technologies – Ada-Europe'99. Proceedings, 1999. XIII, 451 pages. 1999.

Vol. 1625: B. Reusch (Ed.), Computational Intelligence. Proceedings, 1999. XIV, 710 pages. 1999.

Vol. 1626: M. Jarke, A. Oberweis (Eds.), Advanced Information Systems Engineering. Proceedings, 1999. XIV, 478 pages. 1999.

Vol. 1627: T. Asano, H. Imai, D.T. Lee, S.-i. Nakano, T. Tokuyama (Eds.), Computing and Combinatorics. Proceedings, 1999. XIV, 494 pages. 1999.

Col. 1628: R. Guerraoui (Ed.), ECOOP'99 - Object-Oriented Programming. Proceedings, 1999. XIII, 529 pages. 1999.

Vol. 1629: H. Leopold, N. García (Eds.), Multimedia Applications, Services and Techniques - ECMAST'99. Proceedings, 1999. XV, 574 pages. 1999.

Vol. 1631: P. Narendran, M. Rusinowitch (Eds.), Rewriting Techniques and Applications. Proceedings, 1999. XI, 397 pages. 1999.

Vol. 1632: H. Ganzinger (Ed.), Automated Deduction – Cade-16. Proceedings, 1999. XIV, 429 pages. 1999. (Subseries LNAI).

Vol. 1633: N. Halbwachs, D. Peled (Eds.), Computer Aided Verification. Proceedings, 1999. XII, 506 pages. 1999.

Vol. 1634: S. Džeroski, P. Flach (Eds.), Inductive Logic Programming. Proceedings, 1999. VIII, 303 pages. 1999. (Subseries LNAI).

Vol. 1636: L. Knudsen (Ed.), Fast Software Encryption. Proceedings, 1999. VIII, 317 pages. 1999.

Vol. 1637: J.P. Walser, Integer Optimization by Local Search. XIX, 137 pages. 1999. (Subseries LNAI).

Vol. 1638: A. Hunter, S. Parsons (Eds.), Symbolic and Quantitative Approaches to Reasoning and Uncertainty. Proceedings, 1999. IX, 397 pages. 1999. (Subseries LNAI).

Vol. 1639: S. Donatelli, J. Kleijn (Eds.), Application and Theory of Petri Nets 1999. Proceedings, 1999. VIII, 425 pages. 1999.

Vol. 1640: W. Tepfenhart, W. Cyre (Eds.), Conceptual Structures: Standards and Practices. Proceedings, 1999. XII, 515 pages. 1999. (Subseries LNAI).

Vol. 1642: D.J. Hand, J.N. Kok, M.R. Berthold (Eds.), Advances in Intelligent Data Analysis. Proceedings, 1999. XII, 538 pages. 1999.

Vol. 1643: J. Nešetřil (Ed.), Algorithms – ESA '99. Proceedings, 1999. XII, 552 pages. 1999.

Vol. 1644: J. Wiedermann, P. van Emde Boas, M. Nielsen (Eds.), Automata, Languages, and Programming. Proceedings, 1999. XIV, 720 pages. 1999.

Vol. 1645: M. Crochemore, M. Paterson (Eds.), Combinatorial Pattern Matching. Proceedings, 1999. VIII, 295 pages. 1999.

Vol. 1647: F.J. Garijo, M. Boman (Eds.), Multi-Agent System Engineering. Proceedings, 1999. X, 233 pages. 1999. (Subseries LNAI).

Vol. 1648: M. Franklin (Ed.), Financial Cryptography. Proceedings, 1999. VIII, 269 pages. 1999.

Vol. 1649: R.Y. Pinter, S. Tsur (Eds.), Next Generation Information Technologies and Systems. Proceedings, 1999. IX, 327 pages. 1999.

Vol. 1650: K.-D. Althoff, R. Bergmann, L.K. Branting (Eds.), Case-Based Reasoning Research and Development. Proceedings, 1999. XII, 598 pages. 1999. (Subseries LNAI).

Vol. 1651: R.H. Güting, D. Papadias, F. Lochovsky (Eds.), Advances in Spatial Databases. Proceedings, 1999. XI, 371 pages. 1999.

Vol. 1652: M. Klusch, O.M. Shehory, G. Weiss (Eds.), Cooperative Information Agents III. Proceedings, 1999. XI, 404 pages. 1999. (Subseries LNAI).

Vol. 1653: S. Covaci (Ed.), Active Networks. Proceedings, 1999. XIII, 346 pages. 1999.

Vol. 1654: E.R. Hancock, M. Pelillo (Eds.), Energy Minimization Methods in Computer Vision and Pattern Recognition. Proceedings, 1999. IX, 331 pages. 1999.

Vol. 1661: C. Freksa, D.M. Mark (Eds.), Spatial Information Theory. Proceedings, 1999. XIII, 477 pages. 1999.

Vol. 1662: V. Malyshkin (Ed.), Parallel Computing Technologies. Proceedings, 1999. XIX, 510 pages. 1999.

Vol. 1663: F. Dehne, A. Gupta. J.-R. Sack, R. Tamassia (Eds.), Algorithms and Data Structures. Proceedings, 1999. IX, 366 pages. 1999.

Vol. 1666: M. Wiener (Ed.), Advances in Cryptology – CRYPTO '99. Proceedings, 1999. XII, 639 pages. 1999.

Vol. 1671: D. Hochbaum, K. Jansen, J.D.P. Rolim, A. Sinclair (Eds.), Randomization, Approximation, and Combinatorial Optimization. Proceedings, 1999. IX, 289 pages. 1999.